Battleground

GALLIPOLI

Other guides in the Battleground Europe Series:

Walking the Salient *by* Paul Reed
Ypres - Sanctuary Wood and Hooge *by* Nigel Cave
Ypres - Hill 60 *by* Nigel Cave
Ypres - Messines Ridge *by* Peter Oldham

Walking the Somme *by* Paul Reed
Somme - Gommecourt *by* Nigel Cave
Somme - Serre *by* Jack Horsfall & Nigel Cave
Somme - Beaumont Hamel *by* Nigel Cave
Somme - Thiepval *by* Michael Stedman
Somme - La Boisselle *by* Michael Stedman
Somme - Fricourt *by* Michael Stedman
Somme - Carnoy-Montauban *by* Graham Maddocks
Somme - Pozieres *by* Graham Keech
Somme - Courcelette *by* Paul Reed
Somme - Boom Ravine *by* Trevor Pidgeon
Somme - Delville Wood *by* Nigel Cave

Arras - Vimy Ridge *by* Nigel Cave
Arras - Bullecourt *by* Graham Keech

Hindenburg Line *by* Peter Oldham
Epehy *by* Bill Mitchenson
Riqueval *by* Bill Mitchenson

Boer War - The Relief of Ladysmith, Colenso, Spion Kop *by* Lewis Childs

Accrington Pals Trail *by* WilliamTurner

Poets at War: Wilfred Owen *by* Helen McPhail and Philip Guest

Battleground Europe Series guides in preparation:
Ypres - Polygon Wood *by* Nigel Cave
La Basseé - Givenchy *by* Michael Orr
La Basseé - Neuve Chapelle 1915 *by* Geoff Bridger
Walking Arras *by* Paul Reed
Arras - Monchy le Preux *by* Colin Fox
Somme - Following the Ancre *by* Michael Stedman
Somme - High Wood *by* Terry Carter
Somme - Advance to Victory 1918 *by* Michael Stedman
Somme - Ginchy *by* Michael Stedman
Somme - Combles *by* Paul Reed
Somme - Beaucourt *by* Michael Renshaw

Walking Verdun *by* Paul Reed

Poets at War: Edmund Blunden *by* Helen McPhail and Philip Guest

Boer War - The Siege of Ladysmith *by* Lewis Childs
Isandhlwana *by* Ian Knight and Ian Castle
Rorkes Drift *by* Ian Knight and Ian Castle

With the continued expansion of the Battleground series a Battleground Europe Club has been formed to benefit the reader. The purpose of the Club is to keep members informed of new titles and key developments by way of a quarterly newsletter, and to offer many other reader-benefits. Membership is free and by registering an interest you can help us predict print runs and thus maintain prices at their present levels. Please call the office 01226 734555, or send your name and address along with a request for more information to:

Battleground Europe Club
Pen & Sword Books Ltd, 47 Church Street, Barnsley, South Yorkshire S70 2AS

Battleground Europe

GALLIPOLI

Nigel Steel

Series editor
Nigel Cave

LEO COOPER

This book is dedicated with respect and admiration to
three late friends who told me how it felt to be at
Gallipoli over eighty years ago.

To

Lieutenant-Colonel Malcolm Hancock MC

Ivor Powell

and

William Wright

First published in 1999 by
LEO COOPER
an imprint of
Pen Sword Books Limited
47 Church Street, Barnsley, South Yorkshire S70 2AS

ISBN 0 85052 669 8

A CIP catalogue of this book is available
from the British Library

Printed by Redwood Books Limited
Trowbridge, Wiltshire

*For up-to-date information on other titles produced under the Leo Cooper imprint,
please telephone or write to:*
Pen & Sword Books Ltd, FREEPOST, 47 Church Street
Barnsley, South Yorkshire S70 2AS
Telephone 01226 734222

CONTENTS

INTRODUCTION BY
SERIES EDITOR

It has been a long time coming, but it is a real pleasure to be able to write an introduction to this book, a completely revised and updated version of Nigel Steel's earlier book, *The Battlefields of Gallipoli – Then and Now*. It is anticipated that this will be the first of a number of guides on that ill-fated expedition's battlefield; it sets the scene for the heroism and stoic endurance that stretched through the spring, summer, autumn and early days of winter 1915.

The writing shows a profound knowledge of the campaign, of the battles and of the ground today, accompanied with a love of the landscape and a considerable empathy with those who were there. Alas, it is soon coming to the time when there will be no veterans of the campaign alive; books like this are all the more important as they attempt to explain what happened on the ground. And it is best if those who were there are allowed to speak for themselves, and Nigel Steel here makes good use of the various oral and documentary records that survive. History can become a plaything of societies and propagandists, so that we have come to a situation in which most

people think this was an Australian campaign. Most certainly it was vitally important to that nation's development and it helped to bring it out onto the world stage. But this has overshadowed the contribution of others, notably the Newfoundlanders, the New Zealanders and the British (and, indeed, the Irish) – and, perhaps, above all, the French.

Nigel Steel's route through Gallipoli is in many ways a highly personal one – his descriptions of what can be seen come quite definitely from his heart. The narrative of events is cogent and well explained, put carefully into the context of the ground and of that most redoubtable and tenacious of foes, the Turk. By the time that the reader has finished the book – even if he or she has not been to this sad but beautiful place – the impact of the tragedy of Gallipoli will be that much clearer. I do not think that a military historian can be asked to achieve more.

Nigel Cave,
Ely Place, London

Turkish prisoners of war being led down from the line by British troops in Gully Ravine. (Q15337)

ACKNOWLEDGEMENTS

Since *The Battlefields of Gallipoli - Then and Now* was first published by Leo Cooper in 1990 I have been helped by a great many people and I am concerned that I have forgotten to include some of them here. I hope they will forgive me. As my debt to those who assisted me in the years between 1985 and 1990 remains undiminished, I felt it best to incorporate these new names into my original list and so with these additions it is reproduced again here.

Beginning with the formal acknowledgements, most of the contemporary material has been taken from the archive collections held in the Imperial War Museum. Principally the old photographs in this book have been taken from the Photograph Archive and much of the unpublished written material from the Department of Documents and I am grateful to the Keepers of those Departments, the Assistant Director, Collections and to the Trustees of the Museum for their help and permission to reproduce them here. The negative numbers of each IWM photograph is included after the appropriate caption. I would also like to thank the copyright holders of the collections of private papers listed in the bibliography for their permission to include quotations in the text. In addition, I consulted the Papers of General Sir Ian Hamilton at the Liddell Hart Centre for Military Archives, King's College London and I am grateful to the Trustees of the Liddell Hart Centre for allowing me access to the papers and for their permission to include quotations in the book. I would also like to thank Sir Ian's literary executors. Finally I am grateful to the following for allowing me to use material I have recorded with them: the late Joe Guthrie; the late Lieutenant Colonel M E Hancock; the late Ivor Powell; and the late William Wright. I would also like to thank the Keeper of the Sound Archive for her permission to use extracts from the IWM interviews with Colonel Hancock and Major G B Horridge. All books from which quotations have been taken are listed in the bibliography at the end and I would like to acknowledge the permission of their publishers to include extracts from them here. The maps drawn for the book have all been based on official maps printed at the time of the campaign or as part of the Official Histories published after the end of the war and I am grateful to HMSO for permission to reproduce adapted versions of these maps.

On a more personal note, I would like to thank again the three Gallipoli veterans to whom the book is dedicated: Malcolm Hancock, Ivor Powell and William Wright, and also the following who have helped at various times during the writing of this book: the President and Fellows of Corpus Christi College, Oxford; also from Oxford University the boards of the English and History Faculties; my grandfather, parents and wife's parents; all of my colleagues with whom I have worked in the Department of Documents over the past ten years but particularly Rod, Phil, Simon, Stephen, Penny, Tony, Dave, Wendy, and in various other departments at the IWM: Greg Smith, Richard Bayford, Colin Bruce, Mike Hibberd, Paul Cornish, Neil Young, Bryn Hammond, Rosaleen King, Judy Newland, the ever obedient Peter Hart and my para-colleague Malcolm Brown; Professor Sir Michael Howard; Dr Mike Weaver; Dr Rhodri Williams; David Richardson, Volkan Susluoglu and Philip Noakes of the CWGC; Dr Mete Tunçoku; Tolga Ornek, Kemal Gokakin, Oktay Gokakin, all the members of their film crew, Ekrem Boz and Izzet Yilderim without all of whose help and kindness in April 1998 the revisions would not have been possible; Stewart Gamble; Leo Cooper, Tom Hartman, Charles Hewitt, and Roni Wilkinson; Tom Bader; Harry Musselwhite who, probably without realizing it, set me off on the path to Gallipoli; David Evans; our two good friends who roamed with us over the Peninsula in July, 1987, Bob and Jacqui Ridge-Stearn; and my wife Marion. I consider myself fortunate indeed as, without her companionship, critical judgement and unstinting support, I would never have done any of this, and it was for her that I began it in order to discover how and why her great-uncle, Corporal Harry Allen, was killed above Gully Ravine on 28 June, 1915.

The author – then and now! (1988/1998)

INTRODUCTION

For seventy years after the end of the fierce fighting that took place there, Gallipoli remained an exquisitely beautiful place. Enveloped by an air of tragic loneliness, the battlefields seemed overwhelmingly sad. Writing in 1956 Alan Moorehead, the first modern historian of the campaign, observed that,

> The cemeteries at Gallipoli are unlike those of any other battlefield in Europe.... In winter moss and grass cover the ground, and in summer a thick carpet of pine needles deadens the footfall. There is no sound except for the wind in the trees and the calls of the migrating birds who have found these places the safest sanctuary on the peninsula.... Often for months at a time nothing of any consequence happens, lizards scuttle about the tombstones in the sunshine and time goes by in an endless dream.[1]

Yet beneath this pervasive aura of pathos the striking magnificence of the countryside continued to shine through like sunshine piercing a cloud after a summer storm. Communication was difficult and security tight. The Dardanelles, both its shorelines and the whole of the surrounding area, remained firmly within the grip of the Turkish military authorities. There were few visitors and little to disturb the tranquil isolation of the landscape.

Beginning in around 1985 things began to change. New metalled roads started to appear. At first they linked the villages that were spread across the south-western half of the peninsula. But gradually the network was extended further into the hinterland, reaching out to formerly inaccessible points that no-one had been able to visit regularly since 1915. Houses were also built, particularly across the open bowl above V Beach at Cape Helles and the attractive strip of coastline running south from Suvla Bay. Retrospective memorials, bigger and more bombastic than the original, modest, obelisks that they often replaced, were thrust up. The character of the battlefield changed.

Although this in itself at first seemed disappointing, on calmer reflection the changes do appear to have been beneficial. Combined they have made Gallipoli a more open place; one that is much easier to visit. Large numbers of people now come, most conspicuously a trail of young Australians and New Zealanders passing briefly through the place where their countries first made their own independent entrances onto the world's stage. The Turks also visit, particularly in sizeable groups on days associated with their great victories such as 18 March and 10 August. It is right that they should do so. For, after all is said and done by the frustrated descendants of the Allied troops, Gallipoli was a Turkish triumph. Soon after the war the remains of the Ottoman empire underwent a huge upheaval. Under the charismatic leadership of Mustafa Kemal, who had first established his reputation during the campaign, the central Anatolian territory eventually emerged as the democratic republic that exists today. Many of the Turkish statues and memorials now focus on Kemal, or Atatürk as he became known, as much as the forces that, in part, he commanded.

The best time to visit Gallipoli is in the early summer. Although by then the magnificent wild flowers which spread across the old battlefields in the late spring have all but disappeared and the lush rich tones of green have dissolved into a harsher wash of yellow, the bleaker perspectives seem more characteristic of the landscape as it appeared during the war. Movement is also easier, with fewer crops to disturb and a hard, dry soil underfoot that makes the going easier. It is important to remember at Helles and Suvla that the fields surrounding the cemeteries are not just part of a historical landscape but an integral part of the local economy. The wheat, sunflowers and melons that grow across them must be treated with respect and care taken to avoid causing any damage. Likewise the more marginal parts of the peninsula such as inside Gully Ravine or along the Kiretch Tepe Sirt are isolated and a long way from the nearest houses. Common-sense must be applied when visiting them and sensible precautions taken to minimize risks. Çanakkale, the region's largest town and centre of government, can be reached with relative ease from Istanbul, Ankara and Izmir. Although the main roads are in poor condition and often crowded, there are regular bus services, the commonest means of public transport in Turkey. Once at Çanakkale tours of the battlefields are run by a number of travel agencies in the town or individual visits can be arranged either by taxi or minibus. For those planning on spending more time on the peninsula cars can be hired and driven from the three main cities. But accommodation on the peninsula itself is limited and needs to be investigated in advance.

The aim of this book is not to give another detailed account of the complete Gallipoli campaign, for this I would, naturally, refer visitors to *Defeat at Gallipoli*.[2] It is intended instead to relate the battlefields, beaches and cemeteries to the central parts of the fighting that took place on and around them; to describe them as they appeared during the fighting and contrast this with how they can be found today. On all three stages of the campaign a curtain has since fallen of peace and serenity. Beneath its heavy velvet the great and bloody energy of the campaign lies smothered, while along the sorrowful course of the cemeteries' trees dark shadows move upon the stage like ghosts abroad determined to keep alive the spirits of the dead. For Gallipoli has not yet been able to overcome its sense of haunted unrest.

At Helles, and to a large extent at Suvla, where the ground is generally flat, farms have re-established themselves as they have in France and Flanders. To find evidence of the battle one needs a helpful map and the mental ability to suppress the crops and see only the underlying fall of the land. Time and the farmers have swept away all traces of the intensely desperate life that once clung so tenaciously onto these same fields. At Ari Burnu, where the Australian and New Zealand Army Corps bit out their tiny fortress, all is different. Nothing has been done. The British Army cleared up in 1919 when the peninsula was re-occupied after the armistice. The dead were buried and most of the remaining debris removed. Later, in 1923 when the Turks regained their European territories, the cemeteries that had been created there were guaranteed under the terms of the Treaty of Lausanne. But whereas at Suvla and Helles this then allowed the farmers to resume their natural role, at Anzac the terrain made this impossible; as no-one had been there before the war no-one tried to return.

Today the Anzac area is a national park dedicated to the memory of those who died on both sides. From halfway along Brighton Beach to the Chailak Dere the ground is tightly controlled. There are restrictions on activities such as camping which is forbidden and also the construction of permanent buildings, the one exception being the very civilized flushing toilets now found immediately beyond Ari Burnu Cemetery! The reasons why it is so important to respect these rules were made dramatically clear in July 1994 when a devastating fire swept through the whole of the park. It was started accidentally by a shepherd cooking corn on the slopes of Chunuk Bair and from there it spread north to the edges of the Suvla Plain and south halfway to Helles. The long term effect of the fire on the landscape appears to have been slight and in many ways it has ironically restored a more historically recognisable appearance to the battlefields, particularly along the seaward slopes of Sari Bair which had become heavily wooded.

Battleground Europe: Gallipoli is a revised and updated edition of *The Battlefields of Gallipoli - Then and Now* which was published by

Leo Cooper in 1990. This new version of the book follows very closely the general format of the previous and in many places is identical to it, moving through the battlefield areas in an overall sweep, from Helles up to Suvla, describing each significant feature in turn and relating them to both maps and photographs. By moving in this way the text hopefully provides first a basic guide to the landscape but also through this a reminder of the major events of the campaign so that the significance of each place can be fully appreciated by the visitor on the spot. It also compares the contemporary wartime battlefields with their situation today, over eighty years later, by combining photographs with literary descriptions. By the end of the journey, on the peaceful summit of Hill 60, the traveller will have been presented with an overall picture of the whole environment of Gallipoli, as it was then and as it remains today.

The geography of the battlefields is very complicated, particularly at Anzac. It is hoped finally that this book will help to dispel the inevitable confusion of names and places and eventually allow this new clarity to increase the understanding of the historical events themselves.

As to why one should be interested in Gallipoli at all after so many years have passed, perhaps the best explanation has been given by the Official British Historian of the campaign, Brigadier General C F Aspinall-Oglander, who wrote at the start of his 'Epilogue':

The drama of the Dardanelles campaign by reason of the beauty of its setting, the grandeur of its theme and the unhappiness of its ending, will always rank amongst the world's classic tragedies. The story is a record of lost opportunities and eventual failure; yet it is a story which men of British race may ponder if not without pain yet certainly not without pride; for amidst circumstances of unsurpassed difficulty and strain the bravery, fortitude and stoical endurance of the invading troops upheld most worthily the high traditions of the fighting services of the Crown.[3] (Official History)

Chapter One

THE LANDINGS, 25 APRIL

The inexorable train of events that led to the campaign at Gallipoli had its roots in the British government's response to a request from Russia for help in their struggle against the Turks in the Caucasus. On 2 January 1915 the Secretary of State for War, Field Marshal Lord Kitchener, informed the Russians that 'a demonstration' would be made against the Turks.[1] However, as no troops were available Kitchener felt that it would have to be a naval action and the most appropriate place for this would be against the Dardanelles, the narrow length of water leading from the Mediterranean into the Sea of Marmara. Over the ensuing weeks, in a series of clearly defined steps and mainly at the instigation of the First Lord of the Admiralty, Winston Churchill, this simple act of drawing Turkish resources away from the Caucasus was transformed into an elaborate scheme for the Navy to attack and seize the Dardanelles with the aim of affording even greater aid to Russia than had originally been anticipated. The naval commander in the Mediterranean, Vice-Admiral Sackville Carden, prepared a plan involving four stages that was finally approved by the War Council on 28 January.

The first two stages of Carden's plan, the reduction of the defences around the entrance to the Dardanelles, were completed by the middle of March. The third stage, the reduction of the defences around the Narrows, the narrowest length of the Dardanelles, was set for 18 March. But by this time Carden had been replaced in command by Vice-Admiral John de Robeck. Initially the navy did well, subduing the fire from the shore as had been expected. But as the second division of ships began to withdraw in the early afternoon the first in a series of mysterious losses

Vice-Admiral Carden

Vice-Admiral De Robe

14

The Aegean, 1915

occurred. By the end of the day three ships had been lost and another three severely damaged. The extent of these casualties, together with their apparent lack of explanation, disconcerted de Robeck and the renewal of the attack on the following day was cancelled. Instead, at a meeting on 22 March, it was decided that a military force would first have to land on the peninsula to free the area around the Narrows before the Navy could clear a passage through them.

The initial decision to send the 29th Division, the last regular division of the British army not yet engaged on the Western Front, to support the Navy had been taken by Kitchener on 16 February but overturned by him four days later on the basis that it could not after all be spared. However, on 10 March this decision was again reversed and the 29th Division was despatched to the Mediterranean on 16 March. In the area since February had been the Royal Naval Division (RND), comprised of Royal Marines, supernumerary Royal Naval reservists and wartime volunteers who had been formed into an infantry division by Churchill, and the first two divisions of Australian and New Zealand troops, formed into the Australian and New Zealand Army Corps (ANZAC), who had arrived in Egypt in December 1914 to complete their training en route for the Western Front. These disparate units were formed into the Mediterranean Expeditionary Force (MEF) and General Sir Ian Hamilton, having been appointed Commander-in-Chief by Kitchener on 12 March, arrived at Mudros Harbour, the main naval base, on the day before the naval battle and saw the peninsula for the first time whilst it was underway. Neither he nor his troops were ready to launch an immediate invasion of the peninsula, this contingency not having been anticipated prior to the meeting on 22 March, and before it could be done he would have to remove the whole force to Egypt to reorganise.

Hamilton's plan for the landings, drawn up over the following month, was based on the premise that his task was still to assist the Navy in the capture of the Dardanelles. To do this the land around the Narrows and along the shores between there and the Mediterranean would have to be taken. He decided to facilitate this and the landing of the greatest number of troops in one day by splitting his force into two serious landings and two further feints intended to confuse the Turkish defenders about where the real thrust of the landings was actually going to fall. The 29th Division would be landed on the tip of the peninsula around Cape Helles with the aim of pushing north-east up towards the central Kilid Bahr plateau. Simultaneously the northern slopes of the plateau would be threatened by a second landing made by the Anzacs at Gaba Tepe. The RND would pretend to land at the neck of the peninsula near Bulair and part of the division of French troops, designated the Corps Expéditionnaire d'Orient (CEO), would land on the Asiatic coast at Kum Kale. Their role would be to prevent the Turkish artillery there from firing into the backs of the 29th Division landing at Helles, while the remainder of the CEO appeared in their transports further south off the coast near Besika Bay. The first projected date for the landings was 23 April but bad weather forced its postponement for 48 hours and it was not until Sunday 25 April, over a month after the Naval attempt on the Narrows had failed, that the operation could begin.

Around, above, behind each strip of open sand the Turks, under German supervision, had been meticulously laying out their defences with scientific precision for over thirty five days since the failed naval attack. At Helles in particular wire, mines, machine-guns, pom-poms, trenches, all focused sharply on the slender beaches. For the British troops the experience of the landings there and the wholesale devastation that resulted stand as a symbol of the tragedy of Gallipoli. In his subsequent despatch about the landings Hamilton wrote:

> It is my firm conviction that no finer feat of arms has ever been achieved by the British soldier - or any other soldier - than the storming of these trenches from open boats on the morning of April 25.[2] (General Sir Ian Hamilton)

One subaltern, Lieutenant Guy Nightingale, writing barely a week later, confirmed this view in a letter home.

*The German officers whom we have taken prisoners say it is
absolutely beyond them how we ever effected a landing at all. If
there was one place in the whole world that was impregnable it
was this Peninsula and they say no army in the world except ours
could have seen half its numbers mown down and still come on
and make good a landing. It has certainly been a tough job.*[3]

(Lieutenant Guy Nightingale)

Nowhere else in the British story is the acquiescent headlong dash into
invisible, almost impregnable, defences illustrated more clearly than
here. In overcoming these defences the 29th Division exhausted itself.
Unable to continue the fight they could not seize the opportunity that
lay before them and, by the time they were ready, so too were the Turks.
The opportunity had passed and, despite their dubious moral success,
the landings remained a failure.

The landing of the Anzacs ten miles to the north near Gaba Tepe
was also an impressive feat, but there the defences along the shore
were neither as extensive nor permanent. The opposition that the
Anzacs encountered came later on the hills and plateaux above the
beach. Yet for them the experience was perhaps of even greater
significance. They were not professional soldiers, they were wartime
volunteers and they were fighting for the first time in their own right
as Australians and New Zealanders. In both countries, the story of the
Anzac landing and the eight months that followed it have become a
legend and an integral part of the national character. However,
regrettably, like many other legends, this one too is based on a distorted
record of the past.[4] It deceives by omission. In it there is no place for
the 29th Division, or any other British unit who fought hard to the
south at Helles. No one talks of Lancashire Landing or the Vineyard,
just the Nek and Lone Pine. The British feature only as the troops who
threw away the great opportunity of Suvla Bay in the later stages of the
campaign.

The extent of the Anzac achievement, from the landing to the
evacuation, is undeniable. Conditions of life within their lines, even at
Gallipoli, were almost unique, comparable only to a siege, and the
original men of the Australian and New Zealand units were indeed
impressive. Inspecting them at Mena before the campaign began
Hamilton enthused in his diary about their 'superb physique ... There
is a bravery in their air - a keenness upon their clean cut features - They
are spoiling for a scrap!'[5] But, whilst no one would seriously wish to
detract from what the Anzacs did, the implication that they alone did it
introduces such a deep and fundamental flaw that it threatens to

destroy the credibility of the whole legend. It is sad, because it is unnecessary, to see the feats of the Anzac soldiers undermined by the political perceptions of later years; for their unembellished story would be sufficiently strong to stand alone without the aid of this perfidious crutch of deceit.

Anyone approaching Gallipoli today would do well to remember not only their deeds, but also those of the ordinary British soldiers, as well as the Indian, Newfoundland, French, and African troops who stood beside them. They all fought together, even though sometimes many miles apart. They lived similar lives in similar holes in the ground. They had the same diseases and were part of the same strategic plan. In the end when standing in the shadows of the main Allied memorials it can only be to the disparagement of all to suggest that any one of them suffered more than or fought in exclusion of the other. The modern story would be stronger and to the greater credit of all if it suggested neither.

Frost bitten soldiers lying on straw in shelters constructed from biscuit boxes at Sulva following the great storm at the end of November. (Q13644)

Chapter Two

HELLES

Just after first light on 25 April, under the command of Major-General Aylmer Hunter-Weston, the 29th Division landed on the southern end of the Gallipoli Peninsula on five beaches lettered S, V, W, X, and Y.

A simple way of picturing the juxtaposition of the five southern beaches in relation to each other and to the Achi Baba ridge is to place the right hand flat on the table, palm downwards, fingers together, thumb extended, and elbow slightly raised. The top of the elbow is the Achi Baba peak. The wristbone marks the village of Krithia, with Y Beach below it on the right. The tip of the little finger is X Beach; W Beach is between the tips of the second and third fingers; V Beach between the tips of the first and second; while the curve between forefinger and thumb marks Morto Bay, with S Beach at the end of the thumb.[1]
(Official History)

The covering force for the landing, the 86th Brigade, was to land first on the three central beaches to clear the defences and establish a preliminary line from the village of Sedd el Bahr through to X Beach - the index finger to the little finger - which would then cover the later disembarkation of the main force. Simultaneously, two subsidiary groups were to land on both of the outer beaches to secure the flanks and it was confidently expected that these troops would join up with the main force as it advanced the six miles along the narrow width of the Peninsula towards the first day's objective: the Achi Baba ridge north of Krithia.

The timetable for the day was clear. In a retrospective report Lieutenant Colonel Henry Tizard, Commanding Officer of the 1st Battalion, Royal Munster Fusiliers, recorded that 'it was surmised that by 8 a.m. the ground above the beaches would have been won; by noon we should be in the vicinity of the village of Krithia, and have taken the Hill of Achi Baba that night'.[2] But throughout the campaign this objective was never taken, standing instead tantalisingly clear behind the Turkish lines and allowing free and complete observation of nearly all the Allied positions in the south.

The road from Achi Baba to Sedd el Bahr still follows the same

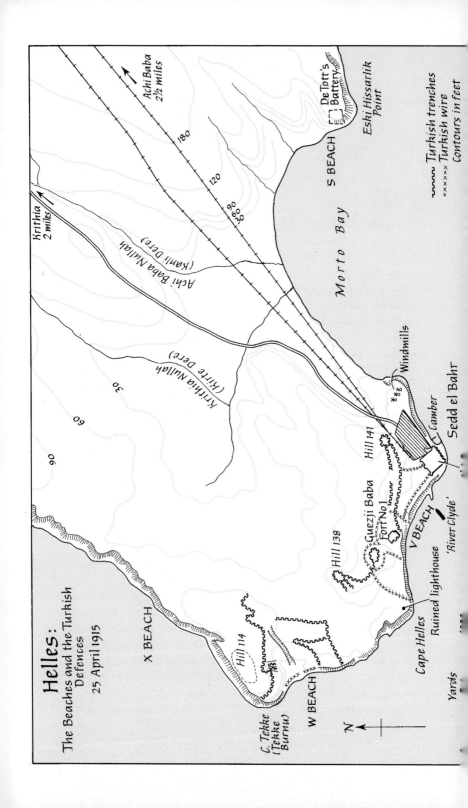

Helles:
The Beaches and the Turkish Defences
25 April 1915

N

Yards

C. Tekke
(Tekke Burnu)

X BEACH

Hill 114

W BEACH

Cape Helles

Ruined lighthouse

'River Clyde'

V BEACH

Hill 138

Guezji Baba
Fort No 1

Hill 141

Sedd el Bahr

Camber

Windmills

Krithia Nullah
(Kirte Dere)

Achi Baba Nullah
(Kanli Dere)

Krithia
2 miles

Achi Baba
2½ miles

Morto Bay

S BEACH

De Tott's
Battery

Eski Hissarlik
Point

⌐⌐⌐ Turkish trenches
xxxxx Turkish wire
——— Contours in feet

30

60

90

90

60

30 60
90
120
180

route it did before the landings, rolling gently down through the cracked, yellow fields from Krithia which is now called Alçitepe. In 1915 this was the correct name for the nearby peak of Achi Baba and the village itself was known as Kirte Köyü. Two miles beyond the last house the road bends sharply and drops down a hill before passing the gate of Skew Bridge Cemetery. A short distance beyond this another road cuts back sharply to the left, signposted to the Motel Abide and the Çanakkale Sehitler Abidesi, the imposing Turkish Memorial set on the shores of the Dardanelles. Unsignposted, it also leads to S Beach and the French cemetery above Morto Bay.

S Beach

The landing at S Beach was the smallest of all five attempted at Helles. It involved just three companies of the 2nd Battalion, South Wales Borderers together with a detachment of engineers, medical and artillery personnel and a few marines. They were landed in the north-east corner of Morto Bay and the attack, closely supported by HMS *Cornwallis*, was split into two sections with two companies attacking the cliff above S Beach from inside the Bay, and the third rowing out into the Dardanelles to attack this point from behind. The position was taken with relative ease and few casualties.

The bay itself is situated immediately inside the entrance to the Dardanelles and its placid waters are undisturbed by the constant traffic passing through the narrow channel into the Mediterranean. Its shoreline runs for about one and a half miles from the back of the Old Fort at Sedd el Bahr to the promontory of Eski Hissarlik Point near the

The Turkish Memorial to the Çanakkale War lodged above the north-eastern fringes of Morto Bay. (April 1998)

site of De Tott's Battery. Into the bay run the Krithia Nullah (or, in Turkish, Kirte Dere named after the village down from which it flows) and the Achi Baba Nullah (or Kanli Dere which translates as Bloody Stream). These two rivulets help to carve up the ground south of Krithia in a way that was unrealised by the staff at GHQ who believed the slope up to Achi Baba to be gentle and mildly curved. S Beach, beneath Eski Hissarlik Point, is now heavily overgrown. Where the boats landed the shallow strip of white sand, which circuits the length of the bay, ends abruptly in a cluster of sharp marram grass. Further round to the left the cliffs above the Dardanelles are more barren than those inside the Bay, with much of the stone exposed, and barely sprinkled by soil.

Given the success of the landing here it is ironic that on this site now stand the main Turkish Memorial and Cemetery that commemorate the place where their homeland was successfully defended in 1915. Started in 1954 but not completed until 1960, the Memorial stands more than 41 metres high and, while appearing initially to possess very little intrinsic beauty, its undeniable strength as it towers impressively over the Dardanelles, particularly when floodlit at night, soon overcomes its monotonous grey symmetry.[3] Moving inland from the ground above Morto Bay and running parallel to the shoreline of the Dardanelles, a broad, paved avenue reaches away from the base of the Memorial towards a statue showing Mustafa Kemal looking down on the slopes of Sari Bair shortly before he led his famous counter-attack

Panorama of Morto Bay seen from the cliffs above S Beach. Moving left to right along the opposite shoreline of the Bay the view encompasses the Camber (extreme left) beneath the houses of Sedd el Bahr, the two tall trees marking the grave of Lieutenant Colonel Charles Doughty-Wylie VC, the Helles Memorial, the scrub covered summit of Hill 141 running inland to the low ground, the mouth of the Krithia Nullah (Kirte Dere), the white buildings of the Motel Abide, the mouth of the Achi Baba Nullah (Kanli Dere), the white wall surrounding the French cemetery with the tip of its Memorial emerging from the trees at its innermost end and (in the extreme foreground) the terraces surrounding the Turkish Memorial. (April 1998)

across them on 10 August. Cradling the plinth like a pair of out-stretched arms is a wall along which has been inscribed a list of names, officers first, then NCOs and finally private soldiers, recording some of those Turkish 'immortals' who died in the campaign. Added to the main Memorial only in 1992, along with the symbolic cemetery of headstones which stands between the statue and the Dardanelles, it appears to be an attempt by the Turkish authorities to personalise an otherwise rather austere national monument. At the head of the wall is a plaque, summarising very briefly the events of the campaign, which is unfortunately inaccurate:

The Çanakkale War (Savaslari)

The Çanakkale War started on 19 February 1915 and ended on 17 December 1915 with Turkish victory. The Turkish army participated in her land defences with 425,000 soldiers, 253,000 of whom were lost as immortals. The allied force who attempted to cross to Çanakkale participated with 525,000 soldiers and they lost 284,000 soldiers died: 200,000 British, 48,000 French, 20,000 Australian, 10,000 New Zealanders and 6,000 Indian. The allied nations who understood that they could not cross to Çanakkale left these holy lands on 10 January 1916.

While the allied force did ultimately number around half a million men, it was the total number of casualties including killed, wounded and sick that was estimated by the British official history to be 252,000.[4] Of this number around 35,000 British and Commonwealth troops lost their lives, together with 15,000 French.[5]

The accuracy of the Turkish statement is disappointing, but in many ways immaterial. The Memorial, cemetery and statuary are all part of a larger concern than the simple recording of historical truth. Emerging like a phoenix from the surrounding battlefield, they epitomise instead the spirit of a people who resisted a force that believed itself to be superior and through their tenacious and costly defence preserved the integrity of their nation. Whenever the events of the campaign are commemorated on the peninsula, such as on 25 April, the Turks gather here and after the civic ceremonies are over, the ordinary people

ABA NULLAH

The French cemetery and Memorial at Helles. The five ossuaries are located beneath the central obelisk. (April 1998)

wander quietly between the box hedges and flowering shrubs remembering. There is much to think about. As the long list of names draws sadly away into the shadows behind the statue, the individual letters are lost in an anonymous, monochromatic wash that seems to drift in a disembodied haze across the pale face of the wall. In the small cemetery more soldiers' names are set in stone and beneath each one is shown the year of their birth and the name of their hometown. Moving slowly amongst them, visitors are quickly reminded that the Ottoman Empire of 1915 was much larger and more cosmopolitan than the Anatolian territory that today forms modern Turkey. The dead came from far afield, from Mesopotamia, the Hejaz and the Caucasus. Yet they fought together as one people to protect the thing that was central to them all: their homeland.

Beneath the terraces of the Memorial there is a small but effective museum of battlefield relics. The plain glass cases contain numerous rusting souvenirs of the conflict, some large like the mule saddle for carrying ammunition and others small such as the used and unused cartridge cases. Inevitably there is a plethora of brass badges and the variety of names that these record show that the allied force too came from countries spread across the world. There are many from Australia and New Zealand. But even from the British Isles all four nations of the Union are represented: the South Wales Borderers and Royal Welsh Fusiliers, the Kings Own Scottish Borderers and Royal Scots Fusiliers, the Royal Munster and Royal Dublin Fusiliers and a range of English county regiments. Like the Ottomans who faced them, these men too came from the wide and distant corners of an empire united by conflict.

From the ground beneath the Memorial, looking west to the distant Mediterranean, in the foreground one can see clearly across Morto Bay to Sedd el Bahr, which translates as the Barrier of the Sea. Beneath the village, near the very tip of the land, is the small dock called the Camber and above it stand the ruins of the Old Fort. Looking across to the right beyond the roofs of the houses are two tall trees that stand guard over the grave of Lieutenant Colonel Charles Doughty-Wylie VC on the summit of Hill 141 and beyond this in the distance is Guezji Baba on which now stands the British Memorial to the Missing. At sea level the shoreline curves back from the village along the edge of the bay, sweeping first past the Krithia and then the Achi Baba Nullahs with the Motel Abide lodged between them, until it reaches the foot of a hill that starts to climb steeply up towards the hinterland. On this slope, straining over the tops of the surrounding trees, stands the whitewashed French Memorial at the bottom of the trenches which led up to the French lines. Thus, within the breadth of this single bay, the memorials of three adversaries, now reconciled, stand silent and stare perpetually out to sea.

The road from the Turkish Memorial winds back down to the French Memorial through a thick belt of trees, passing the rusting remains of two French artillery pieces. As it flattens out alongside the sea, opposite the place where HMS *Goliath* was sunk in the early hours of 13 May by the Turkish torpedo boat *Muavenet-i Millet*, a small gravel driveway leads off towards the French compound. Set high on the side of the hill the Memorial is a clear landmark, but hidden within the surrounding forest the cemetery that flanks it remains largely unseen. From the drive a steep path climbs up to a pair of tall gates and, entering the protected enclosure of the grounds, leads crisply along an avenue of neatly cut hedges to the gate of the cemetery.

During the campaign the French used four burial grounds, one inside the Old Fort at Sedd el Bahr, another further inland and one each used by the two divisions of the CEO along the margins of Morto Bay. After the war in 1919 these were regrouped into two new plots, complemented in traditional French style by two ossuaries. Three years later a mission from the Army Ministry removed some of the remains back to France. But in 1923, following the ratification of the Treaty of Lausanne, the two French cemeteries were further reduced to one on the present site containing 2340 identified graves and five ossuaries holding the remains of a further 12,000 bodies. The engineer who supervised the building of the British cemeteries at Helles wryly observed in an account of his own work that this gradual process of refinement was carried out with a degree of logic and order starkly at odds with the more intimate and personal way in which the British and Commonwealth cemeteries were created.

> *The French War Cemetery was simplicity itself. Some 10 acres of land had been graded off and divided mathematically... Down the centre aisle - either side - the officers had been delegated a spot, then the sergeants, corporals etc down to the troops. Conveniently near, a bone-house had been built in which the skeletons had been placed. From here an allocation was made to each 'grave'.*[6] (A E Cooke)

The way in which it was constructed and its distancing over many years from any original wartime location perhaps accounts for the sense of lonely isolation that hangs over the cemetery. Somehow its grandeur and precision is unable to overcome an underlying sense of artificiality.

Passing the Motel Abide the road crosses over the Achi Baba Nullah and returns through the fields to the junction beyond Skew Bridge. There it rejoins the main Krithia Road and makes its way across the new bridge that spans the Krithia Nullah before climbing the final few yards to the first house of Sedd el Bahr, now correctly spelt Seddulbahir. In a small, enclosed square in the centre of the village the road divides. Straight on, dropping gently down a slight incline, it comes to an abrupt end at the dilapidated red and white barrier that used to protect the entrance to the Old Fort. The barracks which lay beyond it are now empty and, like the more historical sites of 1915, have been abandoned to the elements. The Dardanelles, from the Aegean tip at Helles to the Sea of Marmara 65 kilometres to the north beyond Gallipoli town, remain a militarily sensitive areas in Turkey. But since the collapse of the Soviet Union they are no longer as strategically important as they once were and many of the camps garrisoned by nervous conscripts that once protected the shoreline are now gone.

Beside the barrier is a small Turkish memorial to the first casualties

of the war. On 3 November 1914 Winston Churchill, as First Lord of the Admiralty, ordered the squadron of British ships blockading the Dardanelles to bombard the defences at the entrance even though Great Britain had not yet declared war against Turkey. In the Old Fort at Sedd el Bahr two shells succeeded in igniting the Turkish magazine and caused the deaths of 5 officers and 81 men who are now commemorated by this slender obelisk. It stands at the top of a cobbled pavement that

The memorial in Sedd el Bahr commemorating the Turkish soldiers who died during the bombardment of the Old Fort by the British squadron blockading the Dardanelles on 3 November 1914. (April 1998)

drops down to the harbour at the Camber where the medieval buttresses of the Old Fort stand firmly embedded in the narrow terrace of ground that cuts between them and the sea. It was along this shelf that the remnants of the half company of Royal Dublin Fusiliers who landed at the Camber on 25 April were forced to retreat to join up with the main party which had landed at V Beach. The site of this landing can today be reached either by following the bumpy dirt track which skirts the opposite side of the Old Fort past the last houses of the village, or by returning to the square. Leaving this instead by the alternative exit, past the new mosque, the continuation of the main road from Alçitepe runs on, parallel to the shore before reaching a left turn. Following this offshoot, it passes first the British Memorial on Guezji Baba and eventually leads down as far as Fort No.1 with its commanding view on to the sands of V Beach.

V Beach

Early on the morning of 25 April Private Denis Buxton of the 88th Field Ambulance looked out towards the Peninsula from his transport and tried to record what he could see in his diary.

> 6.30. I cannot attempt to describe the scene: 'it is a beauteous morning, calm & free', rather misty, with a few fleecy clouds & a hazy sun, some of the sky pink, & the sea a lovely blue.[7]

In this morning light two battalions of the 86th (Fusilier) Brigade were inexorably closing in on V Beach. The 1st Battalion, Royal Dublin Fusiliers had been divided into six tows of boats, five directed at the beach itself and the sixth set to land at the Camber. Set adrift by their steam pinnaces to row the last few hundred yards nothing at that moment appeared to move in the stillness except the muffled oars dipping in and out of the water. As they closed on the shore with the hope of complete surprise growing, the illusion was suddenly broken. The normally restrained Official History burst into life to describe this moment with a scintillating metaphor. 'A tornado of fire swept over the incoming boats, lashing the calm waters of the bay as with a thousand whips.'[8] More prosaic but no less powerful was the description sent home by a rating from HMS *Cornwallis* who was serving in one of the boats forming the tows.

> Our steam boats slipped us about two hundred yards from shore & we had to row the remainder. The Turks waited until we got close in & then opened a murderous fire. The troops which

Transports desembarking troops under cover of fire from warships.

was the Dublins started to fall like leaves in the autumn. Anyway we managed to get them ashore & went back for another boat load. It was then I got hit in the right shoulder & of course down I went. Anyway we got the boat ashore and the soldiers - those that could - got out. By this time all my boats crew were either killed or wounded so we had to stop there under a hail of bullets from maxims & rifle fire. This was 7 am and we remained there for about 9 hours.[9] (AB Dick Rickus)

From the *River Clyde*, alongside of which the Dublins' tows had grounded, Lieutenant Colonel Henry Tizard watched as the devastation of the Turkish fire tore through the boats.

I don't think that out of about 240 who were in the boats that more than 40 of them got ashore without being hit; most of them were killed outright. I saw many cases just then where men who had jumped out of the boats having to wade ashore got hit and fell face downwards in the water, a chum, who had got ashore, seeing this, would come back and pull him out of the water so that he should not be drowned. In nearly every case the men who did this were killed. Men in the boats who were hit tried to get away from the hail of lead by getting out of the boats on the far side in order to keep out of sight, thus getting the boat between them and the shore. There were four or five boats along the shore at intervals broadside to it, and behind each of them were four or five men who had been hit. Some were holding on to the

V Beach seen from the edge of the cliffs beneath Fort No.1. The beach runs for 300 yards between the base of the cliffs to the edge of the Old Fort in Sedd el Bahr (top left) and the vanished base of the *River Clyde's* main pier (top right). Above the centre of the beach stand the cemetery and the new Mocamp motel. (August 1988)

> *gunwales and others were hanging on with their arms through the ropes which are looped round the boats so as to prevent themselves sinking in the water which was up to their waists. After a time I noticed these men sunk from exhaustion and loss of blood and were drowned. The water by this time all along the shore and especially around the boats was red with blood.*[10]
> (Lieutenant Colonel Henry Tizard)

In ignorance of this devastation, the Royal Munster Fusiliers waited inside the *River Clyde* to undertake their part in the ordeal. As part of

The *River Clyde* looking back to Cape Helles and the seaward tip of the cliffs beneath Fort No.1 from V Beach near the base of the main pier. **(1915/1998)** (Q50468)

an attempt to land a second battalion on the same beach within minutes the *River Clyde,* an old collier, had been fitted out to be run aground with a hidden cargo of 2000 men ready to storm out onto V Beach through four large sallyports cut along each side of the ship. It was a modern Trojan horse conceived by Commander Edward Unwin RN who assumed the captaincy of the ship and won the VC for his actions during the landings. As the Fusiliers waited, with half of the 2nd Battalion, Hampshire Regiment, for the doors to be thrown back and the air to roll in, the sound of the 'thousand whips cracked continuously against the metal hull.'[11]

Five minutes after the ship grounded the precarious pontoon link with the shore was established and the assault could begin. These men, too, were burned up in the fire, filling the gangways with the dead until the wounded were suffocated by their weight and a path had to be cleared before the second wave could follow. Even after the pontoon had been displaced and it dropped the men into water so deep that they drowned helplessly, whenever ordered, throughout the day they continued to run for the shore to join the handful of exhausted men stranded vulnerably on the beach.

Once it was dark a further attempt was made to land the remaining troops by which time they were able to make their way ashore with relative ease, only the occasional sniper firing blind into the darkness. Throughout the night the disembarkation continued, with the situation so urgent that the fresh troops were obliged to land before the earlier casualties could be evacuated. 'Not a pleasant job with wounded men calling for help and groaning with agony. However we had to insist on it,' Captain George Stoney, one of the Military Landing Officers, later wrote to his brother.[12] Despite an interruption during the night when, at about 2.00 am, the Turks suddenly broke out into a concentrated burst of rifle and machine-gun fire, by dawn on 26 April, a full day late, the remnants of the V Beach battalions were finally ashore and ready to move off to clear the village.

Standing today on the top of the cliffs beside Fort No.1 as they reach out into the Dardanelles, it is impossible to look down to the

HILL 141

DOUGHTY-WYLIE'S TREES

DOUGHTY-WYLIE'S TREES

Panorama of V Beach from its north-western edge looking in the direction of Sedd el Bahr. On the right of the old picture, taken after the area had become the main French base, can be seen the *River Clyde* connected to the shore by a long, curving pier. Inland, on the centre of the horizon, is the outline of the Old Fort and on the left, beyond the ruins of the village, the crest of Hill 141. Today this hill is marked by the two trees that stand

OLD FORT

above the grave of Lieutenant Colonel Doughty-Wylie VC. Directly opposite, on the water's edge, the disappearing remains of the *River Clyde's* main pier can be seen in front of the Mocamp motel. Between these two points over the last decade the new houses of the village have filled the centre of the bowl, almost completely obscuring Doughty-Wylie's trees in the process. **(1915/1988/1998)** (Q25130)

water's edge without remembering the 'tornado of fire' that engulfed the invading Fusiliers and the subsequent day they spent burnt out on the shore.[13] From there the beach draws out beneath one's feet, shimmering gold against the dark blue of the sea. It is still exactly as it is described in the Official History:

> *Dominated on the west by Fort No.I and on the east by the old fort and the village of Sedd el Bahr, V Beach lies at the foot of a natural amphitheatre which rises by gentle slopes to a height of a hundred feet. The actual beach is a sandy strip some 10 yards wide and 300 yards long, bordered in most places by a low bank about 5 feet high.*[14]

The only difference from 1915 is the absence of the *River Clyde*, a permanent landmark throughout the campaign. Alan Moorehead remarked that, after the war, 'although she had been shelled a thousand times they towed her off the beach at Sedd-el-Bahr and at Malta engineers soon patched up her broken plates. In 1920 she was sold to a Spanish owner, and in the nineteen fifties she was still sailing in the Mediterranean under the name of *Muruja Y Aurora*.'[15] By the early 1960s the former *River Clyde* was under threat of bring scrapped. A desperate campaign was launched in Great Britain to save the ship and bring her back to act as a floating museum. But it was to no avail and in 1966 the *River Clyde* was finally broken up.

Behind the beach there have since been many changes. In the centre, the Mocamp motel stands squarely opposite the point the *River Clyde* ran aground. Behind it, wantonly cast across the arid slopes like petrified streams of volcanic lava, the new houses of Sedd el Bahr reach steadily down towards the shore. They have been built in a range of incongruous designs. Wealth and style ooze out of the windows of one, whilst beside it the pretty wooden porch of another looks out of place without the lush green pastures of the Alps around it.

A Commonwealth War Graves Commission (CWGC) maintenance team restoring the stone Cross of Sacrifice at the rear of V Beach Cemetery. (July 1987)

Today V Beach is used for leisure. On holiday weekends the beach is covered with visitors. Adults lie along the sand, whilst their children splash noisily in the thin white waves. In many ways it is reassuring to see life returning merrily to the place where so many soldiers died. Yet it is also sad, for these people have only recently appeared. For seventy years the beach and all the land around it remained the same. Down on the shore the earth bank still stood, a little shorter from the winter waves, but distinct and obvious. The spit of heavy rocks that ran out into the sea towards the site of the *River Clyde*, having stood its ground against the sea for years, has now all but disappeared. It may be that the stones have been buried beneath the Mocamp or that they have been conscripted into the regimented borders of the nearby gardens; it really does not matter. The simple fact is they have gone.

With them too has gone the peaceful beauty of the beach; the calm serenity and reassurance of the sea that used to hang like a mantle over the sand. It used to be quiet and dignified there. One could stand at the foot of the rocky spit, staring out to sea, trying to imagine against all odds what the landing must have been like. The tiny waves would tumble over and over against the stones, scraping at the silence with their melancholy guilt. But now the bathers do not understand what fascination is held within the sea and they do not care. There is no reason why they should, but their carefree indifference destroys all attempts at contemplation.

Above the nearest end of the beach, at the spot where half of the Dublin Fusiliers attempted to land, stands V Beach Cemetery. Many of the soldiers and sailors killed alongside them in the boats who were buried here were not interred until after the village had been cleared.

> *It was a gruesome business, and the stench was awful, as all the bodies had lain in the sun for two days, and some had been in water. In one grave two hundred and four men were buried, and in a smaller, quite close by, five officers. Shells began to fall, and the burial party retired to what cover they could find until comparative peace reigned again. The moon was up as the Chaplain quoted from the Prayer Book he could not see to read, and the 'last-post' rang out to an accompaniment of deep guns booming and the cracking of rifles in the distance.[16]* (Reverend C. J. E.Peshall RN)

A month later, on 23 May when visiting the French headquarters in Sedd el Bahr, Compton MacKenzie, who was serving at GHQ as an Intelligence Officer, journeyed slowly via the cemetery.

> *I wandered about by myself on V Beach for the rest of the*

morning, looked with awe at the rusted bulk of the River Clyde, *and knelt for a few moments by those two long graves, at the head of which a painted board commemorated: Gallant dead of the Dublins and Munsters and others.*[17] (Captain Compton MacKenzie)

The headstones of the five officers, including Father Finn the Roman Catholic Chaplain of the Munster Fusiliers who was killed with the regiment on the beach, still pinpoint the positions of these original graves. But of the individual men who were buried in the mass graves the exact locations are now unknown. Instead, following their standard practice, the Commonwealth War Graves Commission erected Special Memorials to them wherever possible. These memorials are exactly the same as the other headstones, but bear, along the base, the added explanation that these men are only somewhere 'Known to Be Buried in this Cemetery'. On each of the Commission's headstones and memorials there was a place where personal messages of up to 62 characters, chosen by the family, could be inscribed. Almost to a man the memorials in V Beach Cemetery read:

THEIR GLORY SHALL NOT BE
BLOTTED OUT

The statement is a common one on headstones throughout the Peninsula, but here it appears continually on one headstone after another. Walking amongst them is like inspecting a guard of honour. The spirit of these regular soldiers rises up from the ground to proclaim that it is not their individual glory that remains still, but that of their regiments through them.

As part of the final post-war settlement the beach itself and the earth bank that ran behind it were also included in the area granted to the Commonwealth War Graves Commission, along with the land of the cemetery. Together, but without the missing *River Clyde*, they formed a natural memorial to the men of the Dublin and Munster Fusiliers who died. Yet the changing use of the beach has severely disturbed the harmony of this memorial. Uniquely at Helles the surrounding development represents a threat to one of the Commission's sites. Yet there is little that can be done. One can only hope that the threat remains, as it currently is, a minor one caused by high spirits and ignorance. If not, if the steady growth of the village continues towards it, then like the fragile earth bank and the *River Clyde's* spit of rocks, the immediate impact of seeing V Beach from the top of the cliffs will eventually be lost and this would be a great shame. For at Gallipoli, the view down onto this beach ensures that the memory of the Dublin and Munster Fusiliers moving without hope towards it remains alive.

Sedd el Bahr

From the edge of the cemetery there used to be a clear view across to Sedd el Bahr. Yet it is down these intervening slopes that the new houses have since flowed. Further round to the left it is still possible to see clearly the natural bowl shape of the land as the gradual slope climbs up towards the stirring memorial to Sergeant Yahya, or Yahya Çavus in Turkish, the NCO who commanded this part of the beach's defences on 25 April. In a report on the landings his commanding officer acknowledged the importance of the role he played.

On account of the bravery and courage of Sgt Yahya of Ezine ... the shore of the cove was strewn with enemy bodies. Sgt Yahya, by his heroism and the resolution, tenacity and devotion to duty with which he imbued those with him, held his position with the men of his sections until evening against numerous and heavy bombardments, and was responsible for killing hundreds of enemy soldiers.... Sgt Yahya's example should have been honoured in the highest degree. However, owing to the death of the company officers and the evacuation of the battalion commander to hospital wounded, Sgt Yahya's heroism could not be reported.[18]
(Colonel Mahmut)

The new Turkish statue commemorating the tenacious defence of V Beach by Yahya Çavus on 25 April 1915. (April 1998)

Although for these reasons the actions of Yahya Çavus went unrecognised during the battle, this omission has since been rectified. A modest obelisk in a fenced enclosure stood for many years near the spot where he and his men held their position. But when that fell down it was replaced in 1992 by a powerful statue that shows him leading a bayonet charge against the advancing men of the 29th Division. Around the base of the new memorial a ring of reconstructed trenches have been sited and, although artificial, from them it is possible to see with chilling clarity the strength of the Turkish positions that faced the men of the Fusilier battalions as they assaulted the beach beside the *River Clyde*. In his first Despatch, General Sir Ian Hamilton gave a detailed description of the defences there.

> *On the very margin of the beach a strong barbed-wire entanglement, made of heavier metal and stronger barbs than I have ever seen elsewhere, ran right across from the old fort of Sedd-el-Bahr to the foot of the north-western headland. Two-thirds of the way up the ridge a second and even stronger entanglement crossed the amphitheatre, passing in front of the old barrack and ending in the outskirts of the village. A third transverse entanglement, joining these two, ran up the hill near the eastern end of the beach, and almost at right angles to it. Above the upper entanglement the ground was scored with the enemy's trenches, in one of which four pom-poms were emplaced; in others were dummy pom-poms to draw fire, while the debris of the shattered buildings on either flank afforded cover and concealment for a number of machine guns, which brought a cross-fire to bear on the ground already swept by rifle fire from the ridge.*[19] (General Sir Ian Hamilton)

The problem that faced those on the beach on the morning of 26 April was how this fire could be circumvented if they were going to advance. Nothing would be gained by attempting a frontal assault across the wire. The only route off the beach was through the battered remains of the Old Fort, positioned above the extreme right-hand edge of the beach beyond the *River Clyde*. Before dawn a party of troops was collected on this side of the beach by Major Arthur Beckwith whose intention was slowly to work his way through the Old Fort to reach the inland edge of the village.

On board the *River Clyde* the Staff Officers assigned to the landing watched as this new initiative began to encounter the same resistance seen on the previous day. Colonel Weir de Lancey Williams and Lieutenant Colonel Charles Doughty-Wylie soon realized that they would need to co-ordinate individual actions, such as Beckwith's, if they were eventually to succeed. So, together with Captain Garth Walford and Captain Stoney, they went ashore. They agreed that Williams would attempt to advance under the lee of the cliffs beneath Fort No.1, while Doughty-Wylie would lead the attempt to advance through Sedd el Bahr from the Old Fort with one party moving through the centre of the village and another along the edge of the bowl. Towards the middle of the morning this advance began.

The *River Clyde* run aground off V Beach looking from the base of the cliffs beneath Fort No.1 across the entrance of the Dardanelles to the distant Asiatic shore with the distinct outline of Kum Kale on the extreme right. Note in the old picture the remains of the thick barbed wire defences which had yet to be cleared and in the same area in the modern shot the walled enclosure of the cemetery. **(1915/1987)** (DOC600)

It was a rotten job. The place had been knocked all to pieces by the navy, all the streets were blocked with bricks etc. These snipers had got back & were hid in amongst the ruins about 200 in all. We were split up into parties & my party accounted for about 80 of them, but they averaged about two of our chaps each & nearly every one was hit through the head. I had some lucky escapes, I can tell you.[20] (Private Len Blunden)

Progress was very slow and casualties heavy. Within an hour momentum was slacking and Doughty-Wylie decided to recharge it, moving to the head of the party inside the village armed only with his cane. Outside the village he sent Stoney to link up with Beckwith whose party had begun to advance across the open ground between the buildings and the barbed wire. After a time, Corporal William Cosgrove, 6' 6' tall, of the Royal Munster Fusiliers took over at the head of the section working on the wire when his warrant officer,

The ruins of Sedd el Bahr showing the destruction of the village caused by the landings at Helles. The rising level of the street in the old photograph suggests that the view is away from the Old Fort in the direction of the distant front lines. In the rebuilt village, its modernised name now spelt Seddulbahir, the road leads in the opposite direction towards the southern tip of the peninsula with the Old Fort beyond the trees in the distance. The road to Fort No.1 and W Beach leads directly off to the right. (1915/1987) (Q61120)

Sergeant Major Bennett, was killed. Standing up, he ran to the wire and began to draw the metal stanchions from the ground. Hit by the crossfire from the bowl he fell but carried on, tearing the wire and its supports with his hands until a path was cleared.

Inside the village Doughty-Wylie made similar progress. Having reached its edge and with Walford dead, he combined the remnants of his party with that which Stoney had brought round through the bowl, and prepared to charge the final objective, a redoubt placed firmly on the top of Hill 141 which the men then called the Castle. By 2.30 pm it had been taken; but he had been killed at the foot of the hill, his place at the head of the charge having been taken by Stoney. Reaching the hill later in the afternoon, having been ordered in the morning back on to the *River Clyde*, Williams found Doughty-Wylie's body on the top of the redoubt.

> *The men round about were full of admiration & sorrow. They told me he was first the whole way up the slope & it was only in*

the last few yards that some 4 or 5 men had got up to and passed him actually over the Castle walls; personally I noticed him on two or three occasions always in front and cheering his men on. As soon as I came up and realized that he was dead I took his watch, money & a few things I could find & had him buried where he fell. I had this done at once having seen such disgusting sights of unburied dead in the village that I could not bear to leave him lying there. This was all done hurriedly as I had to reorganize the line & think of further advances or digging in; we just buried him as he lay & I said 'The Lord's Prayer' over his grave & bade him goodbye. That night when things had quieted down I asked Unwin to have a temporary cross put up to mark his grave. I left next day & was unable to go back to visit the place until about a week ago. I then found the cross had been put up; but the grave wants building up a little. I am firmly of the opinion that poor Doughty-Wylie realized he would be killed in this war; he was rather a fatalist: I am also convinced that he went singing cheerily to his end.[21] (Colonel Weir de Lancey Williams)

Corporal William Cosgrove VC.

Captain Garth Neville Walford VC.

Colonel Doughty-Wylie, Captain Walford and Corporal Cosgrove were all awarded the Victoria Cross.[22]

Nearly seven months after his burial, on 17 November, Doughty-Wylie's widow is held to have visited his grave. If this is so, she was certainly the only British woman to land on the Peninsula throughout the whole campaign. At the time Mrs Doughty-Wylie was working for the French Hospital Service and it was through them that she received permission to go ashore. Once the British troops at Helles had started their advance towards Krithia on 28 April V Beach became the main French base. From then until their evacuation in December the Headquarters of the CEO occupied the Old Fort and the ruins of the village, while the bowl was filled with piles of French stores and munitions. Visiting the area at the beginning of June Lieutenant Guy Nightingale of the Royal Munster Fusiliers described to his mother how, 'it is so different now. Not a blade of grass left, only rows and rows of tents and horses with a great round patch of cornfields and poppies in the middle surrounded by barbed wire', protecting the graves of the men who had landed there alongside him on 25 April.[23] Like these graves, that of Doughty-Wylie was now also within French jurisdiction.

The grave of Lieutenant Colonel Charles Doughty-Wylie VC CB CMG on Hill 141, with the wreath laid on the grave by his widow during the campaign being inspected by a French officer. The modern, rebuilt grave now bears a standard CWGC headstone. (1915/1988) (Q13709)

Landing via the *River Clyde*, which had become the centre of the beach's main pier, Mrs Doughty-Wylie walked up through the Old Fort and the village to Hill 141. There she laid a wreath at the head of the grave beside the cross made by the ship's carpenter from the *River Clyde*. It was a quiet and unique visit - a gesture of French respect and sympathy which it is hard to imagine the British military authorities would have allowed.

Today Hill 141 is still crowned by the grave. For, unlike any other isolated battlefield grave at Gallipoli, Doughty-Wylie's has been allowed to stay where first it was dug. The building of the solid concrete grave that exists today was not a simple matter. A E Cooke was the engineer sent out to Gallipoli by Sir John Payne Gallwey Ltd, the company responsible for supervising the construction of the cemeteries for the then Imperial War Graves Commission. In an account of the eighteen months he spent there from April 1923 he described the problems he encountered when he came to reinforce the grave.

> *The grave was located on a small knoll just outside of the village. I was requested by the I.W.G.C. to make the site more permanent as his widow had in view building a monument over it. We went to the spot & I instructed my men to make a trench down to solid ground around it, then to pour concrete in it and to cap the whole grave with a 6' slab of concrete. We got started first by removing the tangle of barbed wire over it and then*

carefully to remove the top-soil. Within a few inches his body became visible - enveloped in a ragged uniform with belt huddled in a crouched position. I marked off the location of the foundation I wanted. I then mounted 'Harry' to visit the other cemeteries on my morning round. I got back as soon as I could and looked. I did not know whether to laugh or to cry. What had obviously happened is that the trench in the soft soil had collapsed so that my men removed the body from the grave and finished the excavations. Then they had placed his skull at the top of the grave and made a geometric pattern of his bones - even to his finger bones! I hurried to get the foundations around the bones and waited to put the concrete slab over him. I hope he now rests in peace.[24] (A. E. Cooke)

Looking like a crusader's tomb the smooth concrete sarcophagus lies firmly on the top of the hill. At the head, instead of the wartime cross, is one of the flat headstones used in all the Gallipoli cemeteries and a narrow moat of gravel encircles the base, flanked by two tall upright trees that help to identify the summit of the hill from the sea and all directions on land.

The view from the foot of Doughty-Wylie's grave to V Beach in 1985 when the ruins of the Old Fort (left) and the cliffs beneath Fort No.1 (right) were still clearly visible and in 1998 with only the tip of the Helles Memorial (extreme right) now discernible above the rooftops.

The remains of the guns in Fort No.1. In the background of the old picture the ruins of the old barracks above V Beach stand to the left with opposite, on the far right, Hill 141 and on the horizon the outline of the Asiatic coast. **(1915/1988)** (Q13229)

Until the village erupted over the intervening slopes in the late 1980s there used to be a clear view from Doughty-Wylie's grave down to the beach that showed more clearly than ever the natural shape of the bowl. It was easy to see why the whole of that area was commonly described as an amphitheatre, with the hill appearing 'to command the open beach, as a stage is overlooked from the balconies of a theatre', even though the beach itself was just out of sight beneath the earth bank.[25] Yet, over the last ten years it is across the upper edge of the bowl in particular that the houses have now spread. The magnificent view of the beach from Hill 141 has been almost completely obscured, with just the seaward edge of the Old Fort visible on the extreme left through a gap in the buildings and the tip of the Helles Memorial visible above the trees on the right. In its place an ugly curtain of concrete has fallen across the stage.

The Helles Memorial

Across from the Yahya Çavus memorial, opposite the fruit trees planted on the site of the old Turkish barracks, stand the ruins of Fort No.1. Built in the classic style of Turkish tabya, defensive fortifications that have been covered by earth both to disguise them and provide protection from bombardment, they appear to have changed little since the Royal Navy first attempted to destroy them in February, 1915. Between the empty, lifeless doorways the guns still lie in the same places they did when the British soldiers, resting in the nearby base camp, clambered curiously over them, only the carriages have disappeared, causing the rifled barrels to sink further down into the earth.

Back up the slight hill that runs behind the fort the road returns to the small parking area beside the Helles Memorial to the Missing. From the terraces around its base there is a clear view across the fields to the coastline, with the tip of a new lighthouse positioned near that ruined in 1915 and the misty outline of the Plains of Troy beyond Kum Kale across the entrance to the Dardanelles. Following round the crestline of the Helles cliffs to the right, a small drop indicates the position of W Beach and beyond it lies the slight rise of Hill 114. Between these features and the Memorial, distinguished by its thick covering of green scrub, lies Hill 138, named after its height in feet. Called Beyaz Tepe in Turkish, after the landings it was known to the British as Hunter-Weston Hill after the Commander of the 29th Division and later the VIII Corps. The Memorial itself has been built on a second hill, known to the Turks as Guezji Baba, that in addition to being the closest hill to the sea is also the highest point in the coastal area, 159 feet high. From this dominating position it is possible to see clearly across to V Beach in the south-east and W Beach in the north-west. The tactical importance of the hill is obvious. Yet it was given no British name and did not even feature on the maps issued prior to the landing. On 25 April, although Hill 138 was given as one of the objectives to the troops landing at W and X Beaches, the higher peak of Guezji Baba was not included. Only the smaller hill had been noticed from the sea by the British planners, even though in fact the two hills are complementary peaks of the same mass. Instead, it was hoped that the successful advance of the troops from V Beach would make all the positions between the two beaches untenable. However, in the aftermath of the devastation there, it was the Turkish redoubt on Guezji Baba which ironically was responsible for holding up the south-easterly advance that might have been able to clear the defences of V Beach from behind.

The Helles Memorial on Guezji Baba between V and W Beaches bearing the names on engraved panels mounted on the outer faces of the surrounding wall of all the British, Indian and Newfoundland soldiers who died at both Helles and Suvla, the sailors of the Royal Navy who were lost during the campaign and those Australians who went missing at Helles in May. (August 1988)

The Memorial above Cape Helles commemorates the missing British soldiers of the Gallipoli campaign. Rather than have separate memorials in each of the theatres where operations took place, it was decided to place a single one on the coastline at Helles because this area was the first to be taken on 25 April 1915 and the last to be given up on 8 January 1916, thus remaining in British hands for longer than any other piece of the Peninsula. In his book, *The Unending Vigil*, about the work of the Commonwealth War Graves Commission, Philip Longworth explains that Guezji Baba was chosen by Sir John Burnet, the architect of the memorials and cemeteries at Gallipoli, because it stood directly above the bleak cliffs that lined the Dardanelles. It was his intention that the Memorial 'should "be simple and even austere ... and be easily seen from vessels passing through the Dardanelles".'[26] Yet around the base, invisible from this distance, it would 'be rich in decoration "illustrative of the campaign", besides bearing the names of the individual dead and memorials to the units that fought there.'[27] The resulting obelisk, placed squarely in the centre of a raised terrace and surrounded by a simple wall, is, as Burnet intended, quiet and subdued. It is built of warm, honey-coloured Hopton Wood stone and the final appearance is discreetly mournful and reserved, a characteristic further highlighted by contrast with the powerful, brooding columns of the Turkish Memorial in Morto Bay.

The Helles Memorial is principally concerned with the British and Indian soldiers and the men of the Royal Navy who died during the campaign but who have no known grave. Approximately 27,000 men of the British, Dominion and Indian armies are commemorated on the Gallipoli Memorials. 13,000 of them are buried as unknown soldiers in the various cemeteries, but 14,000 are completely unaccounted for. In the initial stages of planning the Australians and New Zealanders both insisted on having their own Memorials and today these are principally at Lone Pine and Chunuk Bair respectively. But it was agreed that all of the British troops from both the VIII Corps at Helles and the IX Corps at Suvla would be commemorated here. At the base of the obelisk the names of each of the divisions and brigades which served in them are listed on large plaques and the detailed composition of each is given on the inside of the wall. On the four outer faces of this are the names of the individual regiments with all their missing listed in alphabetical order of rank. In all the Memorial has 20,752 names inscribed upon it.

W Beach

Continuing round past the base of the Memorial the track winds its way back to rejoin the main road where it continues northwards in the direction of the Mediterranean coastline. Around 500 yards beyond the junction, a second, smaller road veers left off the larger one, skirting

The view from the Helles Memorial on Guezji Baba to W Beach, or Lancashire Landing, (the break in the cliff-top) with the old Turkish camp on Hill 114 beyond the gully which climbs up from the beach. (August 1988)

the inland edge of Hill 138 before meandering on towards W Beach and the distant Hill 114. Until the military presence along the shore of the Dardanelles was reduced in the mid 1990s, the summit of Hill 114 used to be marked by the presence of an anti-aircraft battery housed in a small military camp whose borders ran down to the edge of the beach. Access to the whole area was very strictly controlled and anyone approaching either directly along the road or over the top of the cliffs was firmly challenged and warned off. The situation was intensely frustrating, as W Beach was not only central to the landings on 25 April but also became the focal point of the main British camp at Helles. In retrospect, now that the soldiers have withdrawn, the tight security that they wielded over the beach ironically appears to have been beneficial. The landscape bounded by Hill 138, Hill 114 and the sea has altered little. With the exception of the camp itself, no buildings have been erected, no houses or motels built and even few crops sown in the surrounding fields.

After following the side road down to its lowest point, near a small isolated Ottoman cemetery, it leads to the rusting remains of the camp's old barrier. Beside the concrete foundations of the guard house a rough, unmade track heads off towards the sea, quickly disappearing into a thicket of trees that lines the way down to the beach. Before the garrison left this twisting gully was kept open and clear of obstacles. Observation was important and only waist high bushes were allowed to grow. But over the past five years a sprinkling of small pines, that now average around six to ten feet high, have come to dominate the scene. The breathtaking vista of the open beach that used to unfold soon after the track started to drop down sharply to sea level is consequently

48

denied until almost the last moment. But this suspense and the uncertainty of exactly how the beach is going to look until one is upon it add considerably to the dramatic impact of the view when it does finally open up. Rolling down to the water's edge in a magnificent perspective, around the beach nothing appears to have changed at all. The rough broken ground, rising and falling capriciously over the small hillocks of sand that lie hidden beneath the scrubby grass, still falls steadily down from the surrounding heights of the cliff tops to the sandy margin of the sea. Looking easy from a distance, the going across this empty wasteland is actually hard. The soft white sand melts easily away beneath each footstep and clumps of dwarf holly scratch angrily at passing legs. It takes longer than expected to reach the pure sand of the beach but once there, turning round to look back inland, the reward is one of the most enthralling views on the Peninsula.

Bigger than V Beach, 'W Beach consists of a strip of deep, powdery sand some 350 yards long and from 15 to 40 yards wide, situated immediately south of Tekke Burnu'.[28] There is no wide open bowl running evenly off the rear of W as there is at V. Instead, the sand on either side runs quickly up to the base of a pair of steep cliffs. Between them a broad gully, initially the width of the beach, climbs up the centre contracting sharply as it winds its way, like a twisted funnel, on to this higher ground which it reaches near the site of the entrance to the old camp. On 25 April the defences dug into this area were every bit as severe as those which faced the Dublin and Munster Fusiliers at V Beach; but at W, despite the wider beach, they were even more sharply focused by the claustrophobic shape of the funnel.

Much time and ingenuity had been employed by the Turks in turning the place into a death trap. Close to the water's edge a broad wire entanglement extended the whole length of the shore, and a supplementary barbed network lay concealed under the surface of the sea in the shallows. Land mines and sea mines had been laid. The high ground overlooking the beach was strongly fortified with trenches to which the gully afforded a natural covered approach. A number of machine guns also were cunningly tucked away into holes in the cliff so as to be immune from a naval bombardment whilst they were converging their fire on the wire entanglements.[29] (General Sir Ian Hamilton)

Among the troops landed on W Beach was Brigadier-General Steuart Hare, in command of both the 86th Brigade and the covering force. At the last moment, as his tow was approaching the shore Hare noticed a gap in the defences above the northern end of the beach. Immediately

W Beach looking east towards Cape Helles with the Asiatic shore and Kum Kale in the distance across the Dardanelles. In the modern photograph the Helles Memorial can be seen on the left beyond Hill 138, giving the reverse view of the shot on page 48. (1915/1998) (Q61099)

HELLES MEMORIAL

he directed his boat and those nearest to him to land beneath the cliffs on the left enabling them to attack the northern defences from the flank. The early seizure of the northern crestline was of vital importance in allowing the men from the centre tows to start moving

off the beach up the gully between the cliffs. The main body, the 1st Battalion, Lancashire Fusiliers, approached in the centre of the line.

We spent the night on HMS Euryalus *and landed in boats in tows early at daylight. I can tell you the sight of the peninsula being shelled by the fleet was grand with the sun rising above it all. We kicked off right outside the supporting ships and went in fairly fast until we were right under the canons mouth. The noise of the 10" etc: were deafening. We never got a shot fired at us till the oars were tossed and then they started in earnest. The first bullet that struck the water brought up loud jeers from our men, but poor devils then little thought what they were in for.*[30] (Lieutenant Douglas Talbot)

Flying over W Beach as the onslaught fell, Commander Charles Samson RN of the Royal Naval Air Service looked down as the intensity of the fire turned the sea to foam. As the boats grounded the Fusiliers leapt into the sea and immediately fell over the first barrier of wire hidden beneath the water.

There was tremendously strong barbed wire where my boat landed. Men were being hit in the boats and as they splashed ashore. I got up to my waist in water, tripped over a rock and went under, got up and made for the shore and lay down by the barbed wire. There was a man there before me shouting for wire-cutters. I got mine out, but could not make the slightest impression. The front of the wire was by now a thick mass of men, the majority of whom never moved again.[31] (Captain H. R. Clayton)

In order to pass over this barrier an almost instinctive determination was needed.

As soon as I felt the boat touch, I dashed over the side into three feet of water and rushed for the barbed wire entanglement on the beach; it must have been only three feet high or so, and three bays, because I got over it amidst a perfect storm of lead and made for cover, sand dunes on the other side, and got good cover. I then found Maunsell and only two men had followed me. On the right of me on the cliff was a line of Turks in a trench taking pot shots at us, ditto on the left. I looked back. There was one soldier between me and the wire, and a whole line in a row on the edge of the sands. The sea behind them was absolutely crimson, and you could hear the groans through the rattle of musketry. A few were firing. I signalled to them to advance. I shouted to the soldier behind to signal, but he shouted back 'I am shot through the chest.' I then perceived they were all hit.[32] (Major H. Shaw)

The scramble through the water's edge had also affected the Fusiliers' ability to return the fire of the Turks in the cliffs. Whilst dragging themselves through the water, many of the soldiers had dropped their rifles in the sand. Once over the wire they then found themselves pinned to the ground as the bolts jammed.

The only thing left to do was to fix bayonets and charge up the crests, which was done in a very gallant manner, though we suffered greatly in doing so. However, this had the effect of driving the enemy from his trenches, which we immediately occupied.[33] (Major George Adams)

Slowly the men began to work their way up the cliffs on the right and eventually succeeded in reaching the crestline. With both crests taken the men in the centre were then slowly able to advance up the gully to the flatter ground beyond.

A month later Talbot told his fiancée that he spent the night at 29th Division Headquarters where he dined with Major-General Hunter-Weston.

'They all drunk our health and the General said our landing was one of the finest deeds that had been performed, far, far finer than Quebec; in fact they treated us like heroes. He said that every man should have a VC if they had their rights.'[34]

In fact six men were initially recommended for the award of this decoration but, forgetting the example of Rorke's Drift, the War Office refused to sanction what they considered an unprecedented number of VCs to the men of one unit. Instead the recommendations were returned to the battalion with the instruction that the number was to be reduced to four.

Consequently the Lancashire Fusiliers had to choose who would be put forward again for the award. By this time it was midsummer and many of the original members of the battalion who had landed in April had been killed in the subsequent fighting. Lieutenant Guy Nightingale of the Royal Munster Fusiliers reported to his mother in August the rumour as to how the selection had been made. 'One officer, one N.C.O. and one man from the Lancs Fusiliers have all got the V.C. They all drew lots among the officers as to who was to get it and a fellow called Willis got it.'[35] Captain Richard Willis had been the commander of C Company at the landing and together with Sergeant Alfred Richards and Private William Keneally his award was gazetted on 24 August, 1915. The official citation explained that these three had 'been selected by their comrades as having performed the most signal acts of bravery and devotion to duty'.[36]

In fact the battalion returned four names as they had been ordered. But the fourth name, that of Corporal John Grimshaw, was rejected by the War Office as that of a second NCO instead of that of a second private as had been requested. Corporal Grimshaw was awarded the Distinguished Conduct Medal instead. However, a year later the matter was re-opened and this time the War Office agreed to allow his name, together with the other two names that had originally been submitted, to go forward for the award and on 17 March, 1917, Corporal Grimshaw was gazetted VC, this award cancelling that of the DCM. With his were published the names of Major Cuthbert Bromley and Sergeant Frank Stubbs. Both of these awards were made posthumously.

On the eve of the landing Hare published an order exhorting his troops to carry through their task 'in such a way that the men of Albuhera and Minden, of Delhi and Lucknow may hail us as their equals in valour and military achievement, and that future historians may say of us as Napier said of the Fusilier Brigade at Albuhera, "Nothing could stop this astonishing infantry".[37] In the end they exceeded even the achievements of their ancestors. For during the landings on 25 and 26 April the 86th Brigade won seven VCs, as well as numerous other awards for extraordinary gallantry, and the fact that six of these were won by this single battalion forms a fitting tribute to their achievement on that morning.

Looking inland today from the centre of the sand the tides of passion and anguish released by the landing on 25 April seem to rebound still within the contorted funnel formed by the steep cliffs on either side. The whole area is rich with vitality and sensual energy. Across the shallows which run along the water's edge frothing breakers turn and crash over the deep purple shadows of four buried piers. Scything through the translucent azure of the sea, as sinister as a school of sharks' fins, these ruins provide incontrovertible proof of the

British presence. Overhead the odd solitary bird dips and glides on the vigorous currents of the air. Facing directly out across the Mediterranean, beyond the deceptive security of the Dardanelles, the shape of the beach channels the full fury of the wind over the clumps of marram grass and dwarf holly, chafing them relentlessly with sudden showers of sand. Although these powerful forces are wholly natural and the antithesis of the death and devastation wrought by the war, somehow they imbue W Beach with an air of excitement and regenerating life that completely transcends that hopeless anguish of V Beach.

On either end of the strip of sand the two sets of cliffs have very distinctive shapes. To the south, curving round to Cape Helles, they are very steep, almost perpendicular, and appear to be built of a series of coloured strata. Only lightly covered with scrub, it is easy to see why the Lancashire Fusiliers who faced this way off the beach encountered such difficulties. Directly opposite, to the north, the ascent is slightly less intimidating. A relatively gradual slope falls down from the crestline to the sea, becoming easier as it moves further inland. It is no surprise that it was the men on this flank of the landing, led by Hare, who succeeded first in overcoming the Turkish defences. Climbing up the earth banks of this cliff today is not easy but possible with care. From the plateau above it, the beach draws away in a narrow yellow strip to the Cape Helles cliffs beyond. Underfoot a network of shallow trenches runs along the perimeter, eventually twisting its unsteady way back as far as the old Turkish camp. Rather than the beach defences that faced the Lancashire Fusiliers on the first day of the campaign, it appears to be the remains of the British fortifications as they stood on the eve of the evacuation in January 1916. The four piers that played such an integral part in the steady removal of the men can also be seen even more clearly from here, as can the sharply narrowing shape of the funnel as it leads off the beach to the high ground near the barrier to the Turkish camp. Across the gully, there is a fine, uninterrupted view across to Hill 138 with the Helles Memorial on top of Guezji Baba slightly further back and to the right. Beyond it, out of sight, lie Fort No.1 and V Beach.

It was across the intervening ground between W Beach and these hills that the main British camp at Helles evolved. Landing there on the morning of 26 April Buxton noted how within 24 hours the beach and had already become cluttered with stores and equipment.

> *The shore is covered with men asleep & awake, mules, horses,*
> *G. S. Wagons, limbers, Maltese carts, bykes, motor bykes (with*

despairing riders!) barrels & cans of water, boxes of beef, jam, bacon, cheese & potatoes, dixies, ammunition, rifles, and large coils of Turkish barbed wire, cut & piled in heaps. The rising ground is spattered with bits of equipment & a few dead.[38]
(Private Denis Buxton)

Having moved off the beach onto the surrounding cliff-tops on 28 April, he described ten days later how quickly a permanent Base Camp had started to develop.

We are still here, where we were when I last wrote home ... It was a lovely scrubby bit of land covered with cistus and scented shrubs and lizards ten days ago, but now almost every bit of vegetation is worn off, and it is baking hot and a bit dusty in the wind: and instead it's covered with hospital tents, dugouts, horselines, mulelines, camp kitchens, ammunition, stacks of bicycles and hundreds of wagons of different sorts and sizes. It's also got its roads and telegraph posts. So we're in quite a civilized part of the world, you see.[39] (Private Denis Buxton)

Over the next few months, with V Beach given over to the French, W Beach was to become the main entry point for all British troops and goods, with the whole of the gully filled with stores. Along the banks, spreading right beyond the cliff tops towards Hill 138, a vast tented city grew up. It was the establishment of a whole community to which the infantry soldiers of the front line would return as if to home.

The community took some time to evolve. For the first weeks most of the ground around the beach was considered safe, with the Turkish guns presenting little serious threat. At that time anyone who 'constructed for himself a bomb-proof shelter was laughed at for his trouble.'[40] But at the end of the second week in May this all changed when the Turks installed two big guns behind Achi Baba and regularly began to shell the area. Shrapnel began to penetrate the vulnerable bivouacs and it became imperative to build defences against the shells from inland. The changing priorities of the camp were ironically observed by the official press correspondent attached to the MEF, Ellis Ashmead-Bartlett.

The gradual development of W Beach was on much the same lines as that of any seaside resort at home. When the shells came from Achi Baba only, certain sites at once rose in price and were eagerly sought after by the settlers. These were the ones which commanded a sea view, and were constructed on terraces cut out of the cliff overlooking the blue waters of the Dardanelles. No

The landing of the 1st Battalion, Essex Regiment at W Beach on the morning of 25 April with the distinctive shape of the Cape Tekke headland in the background. **(1915/1998)** (Q37880)

shells, either direct or indirect, could reach them from the land side, and the happy aristocracy of the place looked with scorn on their neighbours, who were still obliged through lack of space or the nature of their duties to live in exposed dugouts in the open valley running up from the beach.[41] (Ellis Ashmead-Bartlett)

The restored status quo did not last long. At the end of the month the arrival of the German submarine *U21* altered the situation again. The ignominious removal of the British battleships, which had covered the Asiatic coast and prevented any serious Turkish threat from developing

there, suddenly allowed a battery of guns like those which had already
begun to fire from beyond Achi Baba to be established there as well.

*Prices along Sea View fell with a horrid and disastrous slump,
the hotels were almost empty, and every one was trying to take a
place in the country farther inland.... It was just as if you had
taken a house on the Lees at Folkestone, to wake up one fine
morning and find shells from Boulogne coming in your front
windows. The Sea View dwellers never foresaw this contingency.
They only built their homes to protect themselves against shells
from Achi Baba. Now they found themselves in an awkward
predicament, for their dwellings, being constructed on terraces
along the face of the cliff, could not be built up in front, and they
either had to face the risk or abandon them altogether. Some fled
to the top of the cliff; others had by this time become fatalists
and, smoking their pipes, thought of happier days in the past and
conjured up fresh hopes for the future. Others, again, sunk their
pride and descended into the valley once more to make terms
with those whom they had lately looked down upon. Many had a
working arrangement which answered very well. When the shells
were coming from Achi Baba, they invited those in the valley up
to Sea View, and when they were coming from Asia, they
themselves descended to the valley and lived with their friends.
But here again the unhappy inhabitants of Lancashire Landing
were often checkmated by the Huns firing both from Asia and
from Achi Baba at the same time.*[42] (Ellis Ashmead-Bartlett)

As the summer continued the threat to the environs of W Beach
became more constant; but the camp continued to spread. Eventually it
covered much of the small plateau of Hill 114 above Tekke Burnu and
in a mirror image the area opposite this on the other side of the beach.

Looking back across both of these areas from the terraces of the
Helles Memorial beyond the intervening slope of Hill 138 the distance
is filled with the area of the camp. The ground around the beach is
generally level but undulates slightly, stretching in a chequered pattern
of green and yellow over the edge of the cliff. In summer the rustling
sunflowers stir in the breeze that rolls off the water. Far out to sea the
distant tankers slowly steam like phantoms of the British fleet. The
base camp was at the heart of Helles, drawing in the fresh blood of
supplies from the trawlers plying the islands and pumping it up
relentlessly to the margins of the front line. Life flowed through it
towards Achi Baba and the casualties drained back again, empty and
exhausted. All this is gone. The camp has vanished into the rolling

Looking north-east across the narrow gully that climbs up from W Beach showing the horselines and wagon parks that quickly grew up there after the landing. The Helles Memorial can be seen on the extreme right of the modern photograph. **(1915/1998)** (Q13301)

HELLES MEMORIAL

winds. Yet something remains. There is still a strange suggestion of the momentous events that passed there. The presence of the camp, teeming with inhabitants each living keenly under the threat of distant guns, lies not too deeply beneath the crops that now grow along its avenues. A faint outline of the tented city still flickers in the chimeric shadows of the clouds.

X Beach

After passing the left fork to W Beach, the main road from Seddulbahir continues parallel to the sea for approximately 800 yards before it reaches the wall of Lancashire Landing Cemetery positioned on top of a small ridge above W Beach called Karaja Oghul Tepe. Inside the wooden gate the grass is green and flowers grow in profusion. By mid-summer the best displays are over. The colours have begun to fade and the leaves are beginning to pale. The luxuriant beauty of the Gallipoli cemeteries is best seen in the spring when the blooms are radiant and the perfume of the lavender hangs on the air, drifting through the branches of the shrubs that stand among the headstones and around the trunks of the trees.

The cemetery was begun, as its name suggests, immediately after the Lancashire Fusiliers landed on the nearby beach, taking its name from the title given to the whole area by Sir Ian Hamilton in honour of the Fusiliers' achievements there. These first graves, in their original position, now form Row I of the cemetery, with only 4 of the 86 graves identified, including that of Captain Thomas Maunsell who vaulted with his Company Commander, Major Shaw, over the wire on the beach. Further up the slight slope of the cemetery in Row E is the grave of Major George Adams, another of the Company Commanders at the forefront of the charge that day. Adams was killed 16 days later after the end of the Second Battle of Krithia as he stood talking to Captain Willis, one of the VC winners. His death was a shock to the battalion which was on the point of leaving the front line to return to the base and as soon as he heard the news the Reverend Oswin Creighton, the 86th Brigade chaplain, arranged for the body to be brought back to Lancashire Landing so that it could be buried alongside those others of the regiment who were already buried there. Hurrying back in the hope of conducting the funeral in person, he arrived too late and discovered that the body had already been buried.

'So I just said a few prayers over the grave, and went with the two majors to see about a piece of ground being railed off to

Lancashire Landing Cemetery, with row G moving left to right into the centre of the picture with the grave of Gunner F Joynson at the near end of the row, as it appeared during the campaign and in its present state with the unusual headstone blocks used by the CWGC at Gallipoli in place of the more common upright headstones. (1915/1998) (Q13769)

serve as a L[ancashire] F[usiliers] burying-place, where some day a memorial might be erected above the beach where they made their famous landing.'[43]

All the regiment were determined that this particular spot should be theirs and they went to great lengths to include even those men who were subsequently attached to other regiments. Two graves along from Adams is that of Lieutenant Talbot. At the end of May he had been attached to the 8th Battalion, Manchester Regiment, a battalion of the 42nd (East Lancashire) Division, for the imminent Third Battle of Krithia. During this battle he was killed near the front line and immediately buried nearby. When two of his friends from the Lancashire Fusiliers made enquiries about possibly recovering his body they discovered that the withdrawal of the British line to the point from which it had started on the morning of the battle meant that his grave was already by then 'in front of our lines'.[44] However, after the line was advanced again in July the grave was once more accessible and the regiment tried a second time. One of the officers later wrote to Talbot's mother announcing their success.

> *'I know that his body was afterwards laid in our own private Regimental Cemetery on the beach where the Regiment has made its name so famous. He lies as he always hoped he would - should death call him - with those he knew and loved - his brother Officers.'*[45]

Unlike the cemetery at V Beach which was used only up until the French troops took over the area, because it was near the British base the cemetery at Lancashire Landing could not long continue only for the use of this one regiment. For most of the campaign, from the early summer on, men of other units and regiments were also buried there. Consequently, today at Lancashire Landing the personal inscriptions at the bottom of the headstones show no sign of the regimental uniformity seen at V Beach. Instead, each grave has an individual character, making the cemetery much less austere. Moving among the headstones here the sadness and the grief gently bubble through like a clear spring from a hard rock face. For some, like Sapper G. A. Wild, killed on 17 June, the wistful message reads like a card pinned to a wreath at a funeral at home:

THE EVENING STAR
SHINES ON ONE WE LOVED
FROM ALL AT HOME

Nearby, the more robust pride of the family of Private G. F. Morgan, a Royal Marine killed on 14 July, celebrates his willingness to die for a cause in which he believed:

DIED AS HE LIVED
GAME TO THE LAST

A simple statement of loss, without fuss or pomp, affirms the belief of those who miss Private F. Wilkinson, also of the Royal Naval Division and killed on the same day as Private Morgan:

HEARTS THAT HAVE LOVED
CAN NEVER FORGET

It is a salutary experience strolling around the cemetery at Lancashire Landing. Here, at last, among the flowers and the trees that stretch across this large cemetery that is much the size it was when the campaign drew to an end, can be found the quiet solitude that has been worn away from V Beach by the creeping evolution of the village.

Yet despite the presence of so many not from their regiment the Lancashire Fusiliers and the feat of their landing are never far away. When searching through the headstones they appear frequently and in the corner of the cemetery nearest the gate, at the end of Row C, among the other graves, is that of William Keneally VC. He survived the vicious fight at the landing but was killed two months later on 29 June above Gully Ravine. Like Adams, Talbot and many others, he has been buried 'with those he knew and loved', his regiment.[46] The monument that Oswin Creighton said he hoped would be built never was. The memorial to the Lancashire Fusiliers lies instead in this their cemetery.

After the Lancashire Fusiliers had succeeded in gaining control of the beach and the cliffs, the majority of men moved off across the open ground in front of the present cemetery towards Hill 138. The remaining men pushed straight ahead from the top of the gully aiming to link up with the men of the 2nd Battalion, Royal Fusiliers who had landed at the same time as they had on X Beach, the final landing place selected on the tip at Helles. A mile to the north-east along the Aegean coast, X Beach was a narrow ribbon of sand at the foot of a steep cliff, very similar in appearance to S Beach. A landing there was not expected by the Turks and the garrison holding the cliff consequently much smaller than that positioned at either V or W Beaches. No extensive defences or gun positions had been dug and the major problem facing the landing troops was climbing the cliff-face. Yet, perhaps the most significant factor in the success of this landing was the close co-operation between the Navy and the Army; a practice that was not always followed elsewhere. The Commanding Officer of the Royal Fusiliers later recorded his debt to the Captain of the *Implacable*, the ship from which their tows had set off, and his description of the support afforded by the battleship stands as a salutary reminder of what might have been achieved at other beaches had conditions allowed.

> *At about 5.15 a.m. we started off in our tows, with our mother ship,* Implacable, *in the middle, like a most majestic eagle and her brood. The Captain of the* Implacable, *Lockyer, was splendid - they were all top-hole; he had his anchor over the bows with a bit of spar, and took his ship right in along with our boats, till the anchor dragged; we all thought it splendid, and it most*

HMS *Implacable* covering the landing of troops at X beach.

undoubtedly saved us many losses in the boats and landing.... As we got ashore the Implacable *raised her sights and fired further over our heads. We got off very lightly while getting ashore; I can only put it down largely to the way our mother-ship plastered the beach for us at close range; however, we had our bad time later on. About 100 yards from the shore the launches cast us off and we rowed in for all we were worth, till the boats grounded, then jumped into the water, up to our chests in some places, waded ashore and swarmed up the cliff, very straight but, fortunately, soft enough for a good foothold. We then came under fire from front and both flanks.*[47] (Lieutenant Colonel Henry Newenham)

Although the Royal Fusiliers landed more easily than the three other battalions of their brigade, the 'bad time', as Newenham said, came later.[48] Their main thrust was to be southwards, in the direction of W Beach. Yet they also had to form a line facing east that would cover this advance and it was not until after 11.00 am that the forward parties of the battalion reached the edge of Hill 114 where they linked up with the left of the Lancashire Fusiliers. Throughout the rest of the day this part of the line remained weak. Most of the troops who landed at W were immediately sent off to the right in an attempt to break through the heavy defences around the redoubts on Hill 138 and Guezji Baba. Shortly after 3.00 pm Hill 138 was taken and the successful troops immediately started to push on towards what they believed to be Hill 141 at the rear of V Beach. But it was here that the failure to distinguish between Hill 138 and Guezji Baba became significant. The hill that they had actually started to attack was Guezji Baba. Yet when it was eventually taken its capture was mistakenly reported back to Divisional Headquarters as that of Hill 141. Subsequently both of these confusing messages were relayed to Colonel Tizard in the *River Clyde*.

Soon after 4-0 p.m., I got a message saying that the Worcester Regiment had taken Hill 138, and a little later another one to say that they had taken Hill 141. This I knew was not correct as I could see that hill from the bridge of the vessel. I therefore thought it must mean Hill 114 which was on the other side of 'W' Beach.[49] (Lieutenant Colonel Henry Tizard)

By nightfall the troops from W Beach had reached the inland edge of the two hills but could go no further. During the night the Turks began a series of fierce counter-attacks along the length of the line from X Beach to Guezji Baba. In the centre these attacks forced the British back almost to the top of the cliffs above W Beach; but, precariously, the line was held. However, in defending themselves the troops had again become exhausted. At daybreak they were unable to resume the slow advance of the previous day and it was not until after 2.30 pm on 26 April that they were finally able to unite with the troops from V Beach to begin the task of moving on Achi Baba, almost a whole day after they had been expected to take it.

The road continues on past Lancashire Landing Cemetery for a short distance before it turns north-east like the coastline itself and begins to run towards the old front line. Beyond the bend there is a slight dip in the level of the cliffs above Bakery Beach where the ASC first produced bread on 21 May, one of the few sources of fresh food available on the Peninsula. The path which climbed up from the beach there also provided a short cut to the base camp from the road that ran along foot of the cliffs, cutting out the tedious trek round Tekke Burnu at the end of a long, hot journey from the line. About half a mile beyond the bend the track and the top of the cliffs converge. This is the site of X Beach. The exact location of the cliffs climbed by the Royal Fusiliers is difficult to find because of the nature of the beach. It is not a long strip of sand at the foot of a gully or stage of an amphitheatre; it is a broken, uneven shoreline with almost sheer cliffs towering above and it does not require much imagination to realise why a landing here was not expected.

From the fields in front of Lancashire Landing Cemetery the broken edge of the X Beach cliffs can just be seen in the middle distance. From there also, through the tops of the trees that fill the funnel between the cliffs, one can see the gully leading down to W Beach and, over to the left across the corn and sunflowers, Hill 138. Behind this, its base partially hidden, stands the Helles Memorial and out of sight beyond it is V Beach. The real distance between these three main beaches is very small and it is perhaps this realization, the intimate proximity of all three that can be seen from one spot with a single turn of the head, that is the greatest reward of a visit to Helles. It overcomes the historical convenience of dealing with the three landings as separate events and reasserts the fact that they were all part of the same movement. Across these few quiet fields the fighting raged for two whole days, until the line ran from X Beach on the left to Hill 141 on the right, now highlighted by Doughty-Wylie's trees. At the forefront of the fighting was the 86th Brigade. By 30 April, out of a nominal strength of 104 officers and approximately 4000 men, the Brigade had withered to 36 officers and 1850 men. From this bleak fact one can see that the price paid for the unparalleled achievement of the landing was the devastation of the Fusilier Brigade, that 'astonishing infantry'.[50]

Chapter Three

THE NORTHERN LIMITS

See Map
page 70

Immediately after the three main beaches at Helles had been finally secured attention turned to the problem of advancing along the Peninsula. Before Krithia and Achi Baba could be taken the 29th Division would first have to cross the intervening plain. During the afternoon of 27 April, while awaiting the transfer of the French troops from Kum Kale, the Division therefore moved forward to take up a line that ran from just north-east of S Beach directly across the peninsula to a point a few hundred yards south of the mouth of Gully Ravine, a deep ravine that entered the Aegean a mile and a quarter north of X Beach. An attack was ordered for 28 April which officially became known as the First Battle of Krithia. The ambitious plan was for the line to wheel right through approximately 45° from an anchor position in the Dardanelles beyond S Beach until it stretched up past the east side of Krithia to a point known as Yazy Tepe or Hill 472 (its height in feet). For the first hour, until about 9.15 am, events went well; but soon, as a result of a sharp bend that had existed in the original line, the early momentum began to wane and the troops began to dig in along their new line. On the left the line had been advanced a mile and now ran straight across to the opposite coast at a point 400 yards beyond the designated anchor point.

A week later, on 6 May, the British force at Helles made a second attack on the same objectives. This time, in addition to the 29th Division, the troops included brigades drawn from the Royal Naval and 42nd Divisions, the French CEO and two brigades of Anzacs who had been sent down once the line there had also finally been secured. Although the individual details differed the basic outline of this Second Battle of Krithia was similar to the First. By the end of 8 May the line had only been advanced another 600 yards. The battle's plan had been equally grand, involving a general advance, the same right wheel and then finally the lining up of the anchor point with these advanced positions. The communication of these complicated movements had been very poor. The Turkish front line was protected from assault by an outpost line of machine guns and, except on the right where the French troops had a lesser distance to cross before reaching them, these forward positions themselves were not even breached. For the troops it was a hard, frustrating struggle against a largely unseen enemy, and casualties were heavy.

The Third Battle of Krithia, often referred to by its date as the Battle of the Fourth of June, was a much better planned attack than either of the previous attempts. The objectives were strictly limited and for the first time neither Yazy Tepe nor Achi Baba featured as the aim of the attack. Details were carefully worked out and orders issued well in advance. The preceding artillery bombardment even included a ruse whereby at 11.20 am the allied guns would stop as if the assault was about to begin only to recommence firing ten minutes later when it was hoped the Turkish trenches would be fully manned. Yet it was all to no avail. Despite the initial success of the 127th (Manchester) Brigade in the centre of the line, a withdrawal from the right pulled back the whole line until only 250 - 500 yards of new gains remained. Commander Samson, who observed the battle from his aeroplane, drew a salutary conclusion in his memoirs.

> *If reinforcements had been at hand there is no doubt that we would have rolled the Turks back and taken Krithia and Achi Baba. The Turks, as history has proved, were greatly shaken, and were on the point of retirement. One final punch would have completely defeated them; but alas, we had no fresh troops to put into the line, and human nature has its limits. Great feats of arms were done that day; but the actual results were practically negligible.*[1]

After the failure of this third offensive it was obvious that Achi Baba could not be reached by this method. New tactics were needed and during the remainder of June and July, three concentrated attacks were launched against small sections of the line which were all relatively successful. On 21 June the French, using their superior artillery strength, captured the Haricot Redoubt in what was termed the Third Action of Kereves Dere. A week later, on 28 June, the British troops on the far left of the line launched the Action of Gully Ravine against all the Turkish trenches lodged between the sea and the Gully, eventually capturing most of them. The third, and least successful, was mounted two weeks later on 12-13 July when the 52nd Division on the left of the French attacked around another of the stream beds in the Action of Achi Baba Nullah.

This attack was the last independent attempt to gain ground at Helles. On 6 August, as part of the larger offensive aimed at the capture of the Sari Bair Ridge north of Anzac, units of the 29th and 42nd Divisions attempted to capture a Turkish position next to the Krithia Road known as the Vineyard. As had happened so many times before, little was gained by the attack except heavy casualties. From the end of that attack

> 'the British and French troops in the south were destined to make no further serious attacks ... and, except that the 52nd Division succeeded in straightening out its line to the west of the Vineyard in November, the opposing fronts at Helles remained virtually unchanged from the 8th August till the final evacuation exactly five months later.'[2] (Official History)

So ended the efforts of the allied troops at Helles. The fierce fighting of the landing had proved to be merely a foretaste of what they would have to endure again and again as they vainly staggered up towards elusive Achi Baba. Time after time the resolve of the Turkish front line commanders had wavered, only to be strengthened by those in higher command, and on each occasion the line had been held; although a little further on the same process then had to be repeated again. Samson's conclusion about the Third Battle of Krithia can be applied equally well as an epitaph to all of the fighting that took place at Helles between 28 April and 8 August. Throughout, 'great feats of arms were done ... but the actual results were practically negligible'.[3]

From the area around the beaches, as from the sea itself, the long climb up to Achi Baba over which all this fighting ranged 'appears to be open and undulating' with no natural obstacles to a successful advance across it.[4] In fact, hidden in the folds of the ground are four deep stream beds, or deres, complemented by a network of cross-cutting tributaries which make it difficult to move forward up the peninsula for even a short distance without having to cross at least one of them.

On the left, running down into the Aegean, is the Saghir Dere, renowned among the British troops as Gully Ravine or the Gully. On the first erroneous maps that were issued to the 29th Division Gully Ravine was shown as a meandering stream bed; but when the Division started to advance on 28 April it was found to be in fact a tortuous, jagged ravine in places over 100 feet deep that completely separated the coastline from the hinterland. Further across the peninsula two more deres run down from the Achi Baba foothills into Morto Bay. They are not so deep, only 15 to 20 feet at their deepest, but instead are complicated by numerous straggling offshoots which branch off the course of the main beds. The first, three quarters of a mile to the east of Gully Ravine, is called in Turkish the Kirte Dere, but better known to the British as the Krithia Nullah, both names referring to the village that stands at its head. The second, less than half a mile further over to the east just beyond the Krithia Road, is the Kanli Dere (or Bloody Stream) but referred to throughout the campaign as the Achi Baba Nullah as it runs in line with the peak of the hill. Finally, there is a fourth, the Kereves Dere, which is set at an angle of 45^0 to the other three and runs directly down into the Dardanelles. For most of the campaign it formed the furthest boundary of the French lines and was fiercely contested by the CEO in each of the summer battles.

Although a great tactical problem these deres were used in the British Official History to divide up the ground of this area into four convenient spurs. From the Aegean coast to Gully Ravine the ground was labelled GULLY SPUR, between Gully Ravine and the Krithia Nullah FIR TREE SPUR after the wood that was located just behind the front line there, between the Krithia and Achi Baba Nullahs KRITHIA SPUR, and in the area bound by the Achi Baba Nullah, the Kereves Dere and the Dardanelles KEREVES SPUR.

> *Gully Spur, the narrowest of the four, varies in breadth from a quarter of a mile to less than 100 yards. It was for the most part bare and open, and immediately south of Y Beach devoid of all cover. Fir Tree Spur is intersected by a succession of tiny traverse nullahs running into [the Krithia Nullah], offering excellent cover for riflemen barring an advance from the south. On this spur, which is over 1,000 yards wide, were several straggling fir copses. Krithia Spur, which nowhere has a width of more than half a mile, was more open and less broken, and along its eastern side, close to [the Achi Baba Nullah], ran the straight ribbon of road from Krithia to Sedd el Bahr. Kereves Spur was the highest and the most important of the four, as well as the most irregular in shape. Curving to the south in front of the position at that time occupied by the French, some of whose trenches were on its lower slopes, it effectually shut out all view of the Kereves ravine.[5] (Official History)*

During the campaign a series of roads also ran north-east up the peninsula. The most important of these was the Krithia Road which followed the course of the present road from Seddulbahir to Alçitepe, entering the latter on the east. Parallel to it, a mile across to the west, was the West Krithia Road, set about 400 yards in from the Aegean coast. It started at the Base Camp and ran up as far as Pink Farm where it split into two. The right fork went on to Grey Tree Farm, while the left followed the old pre-war route past Twelve Tree Copse towards the village, this time coming in from the west. At the foot of the Aegean cliffs a third road was eventually cut from Tekke Burnu to Gully Beach,

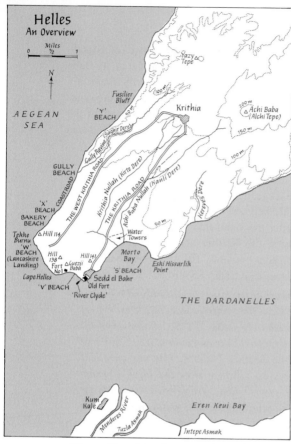

the entrance to Gully Ravine, which provided the safest route up to the trenches on the left of the line, being both unobserved by the Turks and protected from random gunfire by the lee of the cliffs. Above it on the cliff-top was another, more vulnerable road. It is along the route of this road that the present western road runs between Lancashire Landing Cemetery and the sharp turn inland near the path down to Gully Beach. After this it cuts sharply across to Pink Farm Cemetery before it assumes the course of the old West Krithia Road, following the left fork into the village. Together these roads and deres formed the only definite landmarks in what was otherwise a smooth and featureless landscape.

The Helles Plain

From the inland slopes of Guezji Baba today there is a long, clear view forward over the intervening ground to the peak of Achi Baba, with the final front line resting just below the distant horizon. An avenue of grass runs round the memorial, past the faint rows of names, towards a small hedge and the forward edge of the hill. In summertime beyond the hedge the scrub, as it was in April, 1915, is largely wild thyme. The prickly branches reach out across the bare earth of the paths and when the fragile leaves are broken underfoot the warm smell of the herb drifts upwards on the eddies of the wind. Each footstep pulls and breaks them, stirring up fresh tides of aromatic perfume that turn like frothing waves upon the smooth rocks of the shore. It is a calm, refreshing smell that seems to capture all the quiet and steady solitude of the inland battlefields at Helles. From here up to the very edge of Alçitepe all is natural and old. There are no houses, no soldiers, no swimmers on the beach. Everything is simply the way it was; the way it has always been, except during the ten months of the campaign.

The scrub paths lead for about a hundred yards across the rounded summit of the hill until it falls away quite suddenly down towards the main road. Beyond this the fields leads on for another two hundred yards before they too drop down a gentle incline on to the lowest stretch of ground at Helles which runs directly inland from Morto Bay towards X Beach in a broad fertile strip. This low ground is ringed in to the south-west by the hills along the coastline and to the north-east by the spurs that climb gradually up the 700 feet to Achi Baba. Hidden on the horizon in a perpetual cloud of mist, this distinctive peak is not quite central, but set off slightly to the right-hand side of the view, and surrounded just below the summit by a raised plateau. From there two spurs gradually taper down towards the level of the sea on either side.

Describing the same view in May, 1915 Ellis Ashmead-Bartlett captured the shape of the hill in his despatch about the Second Battle of Krithia.

> 'The mountain itself has a peculiarly forbidding aspect. It most nearly resembles an old Chinese idol, with a great, round, stupid-looking head and two long arms stretching out on either side to the sea.'[6]

It is an image that still fits today, with the distant hill quietly dominating all the ground to the south-west of it not by its power or size but through its mysterious, brooding inscrutability. Across the spurs which run down from it, swathes of golden corn glitter as the sunshine catches them, lodged between the shadowy bands of trees. The colours are rich and hard, exaggerated by sharp contrasts and an iridescent light. It is a scene alive with natural vitality that in the early summer must be one of the most beautiful views in the Mediterranean.

In the same despatch Ashmead-Bartlett went on to describe the same colourful beauty that also existed here before the battles destroyed it.

> In the morning the plain which is embraced by the arms of Aki Baba is a beautiful and fertile garden. You gaze down upon a landscape of dark green, light green, and bright yellow. It abounds in green fields covered with a coarse grass and is dotted with trees. There are, besides, many scattered ferns.

A WONDERFUL GARDEN

In a short ride across it you will find yourself amid olives, Turkey oaks, witch elms, apricots, almonds, Scottish firs and small tamarisks. On the cliffs are great bunches of yellow plantagenesta and yellow poppies. You ride over fields and through gardens in which flowers abound in a reckless and beautiful profusion. There are white orchids and rock roses, while mauve stock and iris abound. There are fields of poppies, white marguerites, and blue borage, intermingled with deep purple vetches, brick-red pea and yellow clover, pink and white campions, and asphodel.[7] (Ellis Ashmead-Bartlett)

It was not only the vegetation that was so lovely. Private Denis Buxton wrote home at this time explaining that 'three nights ago ... instead of

The first day's objective: Achi Baba, in the centre of the horizon, from the summit of the high ground above the Helles beaches. The village of Krithia, now called Alçitepe, lies beneath it to the left. (1915/1988) (Q13546)

guns to keep me awake, there was a warbler singing in a tree nearby whenever I woke. There were Pigeons, Kestrels, Magpies, Rollers, Blackcaps, Tits, and a Red throated Warbler.'[8] It was indeed an enchanted garden.

Within a fortnight of the landing the first two Battles of Krithia swept across it, destroying all the fragile, natural beauty. Two months later, on 31 July, Ashmead-Bartlett revisited the area accompanied by another journalist who had also been subsequently attached to the MEF, H. W. Nevinson. In his history of the campaign Nevinson included the notes he made immediately after the visit giving a clear picture of the then squalid scene that they encountered at the start of the journey near Hill 141.

> *One passes through what was lately a garden of wild flowers, fields, vineyards, and scattered olive trees, but is now the desolation which people make and call war. It is a wilderness of mounds and pits and trenches, of heaped-up stores and rows of horses stabled in the open, of tarpaulin dressing-stations behind embankments, of carts and wagons continually on the move, of Indian muleteers continually striving to inculcate human reason into mules. Except for a few surviving trees, hardly a green thing remains. Over all this wilderness a cloud of dust sweeps perpetually, and on the result of war flies multiply with a prosperity unknown to them before.*[9] (H. W. Nevinson)

The rich and hopeful beauty of Gallipoli had been submerged beneath the fighting. Dust blew where previously the perfume of the flowers had turned; instead of hardy scrub barbed wire spread across the banks. Lines of dug earth disfigured the smooth contours of the slopes and everywhere there was clutter. Yet, as soon as the war had gone, the perennial flowers returned to re-occupy their devastated homeland, burying these deep scars beneath new life and colour. By 1923 the scrub was thick again. When working on the cemeteries A. E. Cooke encountered 'short stubby shrub, poppies in bloom everywhere ... wild pomegranates, a few olive trees, wild boar, and goats.'[10] Slowly, with the returning population, this fertile, wild growth was tamed and replaced with deliberate crops. The range of colours gradually shrank beneath the spreading agriculture until it reached the carefully cultivated state it is in today and if, as a result of this, it no longer dazzles with the old, unkempt beauty of a cottage garden, it does still retain the feeling of lovely enchantment. Helles is again a wonderful place to see.

The Krithia Road

Leaving behind the Helles Memorial, the road curves back along the balcony of the V Beach amphitheatre to Seddulbahir. On the edge of the village a track leads off to the left away from the direction of the beach towards Doughty-Wylie's grave and beyond it the flat top of Hill 141 which stretches inland for half a mile towards the low ground. In the centre of the village, the road turns left to begin its long haul up to Alçitepe. Beyond the overgrown Ottoman cemetery, with its distinctive slender headstones, the road levels out at its lowest point. There, opposite the roadside fountain which stands above the Krithia Nullah, a white sandy track cuts off it to the left. Twenty yards along it, hidden in the scrub, is the old stone bridge that used to carry the Krithia Road before the modern concrete strip. In the summer the nullah beneath it is almost completely dry. Where the sun shines harshly on it the water evaporates; but under the shadow of the old bridge a pool of stagnant, black water remains, home to a crowded colony of terrapins who topple off their warm stones whenever anyone approaches down the grassy banks nearby.

The soft sandy strip carries on, parallel to the bank of the nullah. Forty yards along it a trail of stones, lying neatly across the curve of the bed, shows the site of the second old bridge clearly marked on the wartime maps. Looking along its course, a discernible path runs straight across the corner of the opposite field, linking up exactly with the course of the road that now leads to S Beach and Morto Bay. Turning round to see where this road would have led a rough tractor track climbs up between the overhanging trees onto the summit of Hill 141. A bank of piled earth, thickly covered with grass and scrub, runs round the inland edge of the plateau until, after about fifty yards, it tumbles into the first sign of the British occupation. A large hole, about five feet square and three feet deep, stands right on the edge of the hill. Along the front facing inland, and along both sides as well, a small parapet of stones adds another foot in height, and across the centre of the base running from the front to the back there is a shallow ridge. A short distance beyond it there is a similar hole in a similar position and still further on another set squarely in the corner of the hill above the Krithia Road. This last one has a parapet of earth instead of stone and the ridge along the centre is taller. They look like gun pits; but their size and position suggest that they might have been for machine guns and their teams. These positions along the edge of the hill, which would have been less thickly wooded then, would have created a series of enfilading positions overlooking the low ground at the foot of the plain.[11]

Behind the hole dug into the corner there are also the remains of a communication trench which used to lead back along the top of the hill parallel to the road as far as Doughty Wylie's grave. Shallower now, but still in places three feet deep, the banks are scattered with wild oats whose stalks rustle in the wind. In 1915 this area stood at the rear of the Royal Naval Division's lines. The ploughed earth was then covered in dug-outs and slit trenches just deep enough for a man to sleep in. Beyond the Krithia Road, between it and Morto Bay, where the swimming was so fine, stood another of their rest areas known as Orchard Gully in the fields which now lie behind the Motel Abide. It was down to these places that the remains of the exhausted battalions came after the battles of May and June.

The area offered a welcome degree of protection. Orchard Gully was blocked from direct front line observation by its position on the edge of the low ground and throughout the campaign there were a number of trees along the banks of the two nullahs. Sub-Lieutenant Douglas Jerrold, an officer in the Hawke Battalion, remembered later in life the relaxing atmosphere of these rest areas during the overwhelming heat of the summer months.

We were still in our old rest-camp, dug with so much unnecessary enthusiasm on the first night of our arrival. We slept in little oblong dug-outs like coffins and the lucky ones had a water-proof sheet or two strung together to provide shade during the day. We lived and ate under an olive tree, silvery white with dust. I remember no rain, only the heat of the sun and the bitter cold of the June nights. And above all, the flies. Later on, the nights were perfect, made for talk or drink or love. We had to content ourselves with talk, and in consequence talked a good deal too much in self-protection.[12] (Sub-Lieutenant Douglas Jerrold RNVR)

It was at night, here, that tensions seemed to drift away, disappearing with the sun. Then, gathered round in little groups, the men would sit and listen to the sounds of night. So impressive were these disembodied noises that Ordinary Seaman A. R. Peters, a soldier in the Howe Battalion, jotted down the sensations in his little red pocket book.

Dull explosions of bombs and crackle of rifles over towards Achi Baba accompanied by flashes and occasional flare lights. Stars glint but give feeble light as there is no moon. Nearer round

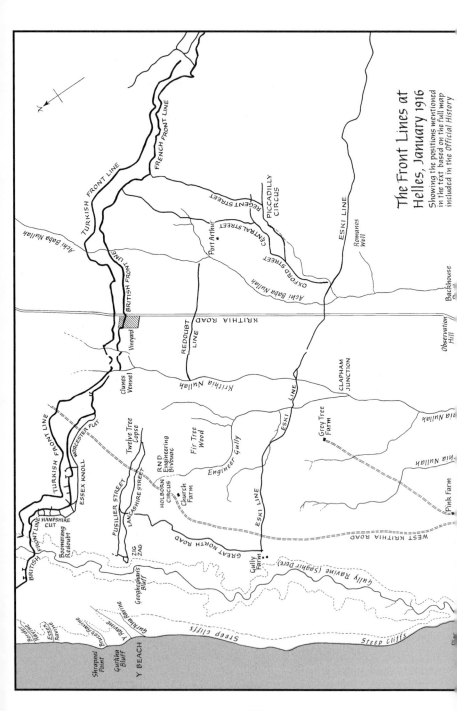

The Front Lines at
Helles, January 1916

Showing the positions mentioned
in the text based on the full map
included in the *Official History*

the camp the trees look gaunt and tall and they seem to listen to
the numerous sounds and noises. Everywhere noises in the form
of shouts, talking, songs, a few round songs, all making
themselves heard. Lot of laughing going on. Even the animals
carry on a conversazione with neighing and a stray dog barks.
Owls are not the sole owners of the trees as in England at night.
Birds twitter and crickets go tick tick ticking round.[13] (Ordinary
Seaman A. R. Peters)

From the top of the bank near the last pit there is a clear view across
the strip of low ground that lies at the base of the Helles plain. The
Krithia Road runs up towards Skew Bridge Cemetery, set back slightly
from the verge, before it begins the short but steep climb up the hill
known as Observation Hill. The whole area is flat and open, broken
only by occasional spinneys of trees, with the road to S Beach leading
off to the right. At the start of the campaign five tall towers stood along
the right edge of this road, immediately beyond the junction. After one
of his early trips up to the line before the Second Battle of Krithia,
Buxton made a note in his diary of these strange structures. 'We went
out early to one of the RAPs (Regimental Aid Post) the one we usually
go to, under the side of a little cliff, by a big walnut tree, near this end
of the 5 pillars, huge blocks of white masonry 60 or 80 feet high: I
can't say for what purpose they were built.'[14] Three weeks later to
Compton Mackenzie, who passed them on his way to the RND
Headquarters, they appeared 'like factory chimneys emerging from
groves of trees'.[15] To him their purpose appeared to be the same as it
did to Nevinson who believed them to be the remaining 'lofty piles of
an ancient, perhaps Byzantine, aqueduct ... probably at one time
conveying water to a more ancient town than Sedd el Bahr. Later in the
campaign they were destroyed, but for some months they formed a
conspicuous landmark.'[16] Nothing discernible remains in the
hedgerows and thickets of scrub which now line the road, but the fact
that they stood there can be seen from old photographs of this area in
the background of which they feature prominently.

See Maps
on page 76
and
page 70

Moving back to the old bridge it is only a short distance beyond it
to the road junction where the first of the towers used to stand. Turning
round to look over in the direction of the hidden Aegean Sea across the
intervening plain the significance of the high ground around the
beaches is clear for the first time. From Guezji Baba the drop down on
to this lower level is not immediately appreciated; but from the Krithia
Road only the very top of the Memorial is visible behind the thickly
wooded forward slopes of Hill 141. From further up the road, towards

Skew Bridge Cemetery, avoiding the obstacle of these trees, the view is clearer. The distinctive shape of Hill 138 stands in the centre, with the whole of the Memorial visible to the left and, beyond it, to the right, the distant wall of Lancashire Landing Cemetery.

Skew Bridge Cemetery was named after the wooden bridge that stood behind it across the Achi Baba Nullah and first established at the end of the Second Battle of Krithia. After the war a number of smaller cemeteries were moved into it from places like Orchard Gully, where the RND's 3rd Field Ambulance was situated, and from Backhouse Post further up towards the front. Across to the left of the cemetery's gate, a few yards up the side of Observation Hill, is the start of a long communication trench that runs parallel to the road. It is generally about four feet deep and very broad. The usual scrub lines its course, but spread randomly along it there are a number of larger trees. After about a hundred yards a large, deep pit opens up on the right of the trench in the centre of which there is a rusted mortar set in place on its concrete platform. Continuing out of the top left-hand corner of the pit, the trench deepens by another one and a half feet before another, smaller chamber with a deep narrow entrance leads off again to the right.

Climbing out of the corner of this chamber on to the natural height of the surrounding land a thick line of pine trees bars the way forward. Instead, following the trees round to the right, they lead into a rough, scrubby field bordered on the far side by a steep bank which drops down into the broad valley of the Achi Baba Nullah. It was in this valley that the RND had its divisional headquarters. Moving back away from the top of the bank the trees again begin to thicken. Beneath their trunks there is a short cliff of earth, covered in the most part by pine needles and falling creepers. Set into this cliff, looking out towards the valley, are a series of eight, almost identical dug-outs. On the outside

Bivouacs of the Royal Naval Division in Howe Rest Camp on Hill 141 above the strip of low ground that runs in from Morto Bay. Through the scrub to the left of centre in the old photograph the tips of two of the water towers can just be seen. **(1915/1988)** (Q14801)

The view across the low ground at Helles from the extreme inland edge of Hill 141 looking forward to Achi Baba, with the five water towers clearly visible on the right of the old picture alongside the road which now leads to S Beach and the Turkish Memorial. (1915/1988) (Q14796)

they are about ten feet long and two feet deep, but scooped out deeper inside the entrance to a depth of between three and four feet and in the back wall of each there is a little shelf. It is not certain who lived in the dugouts or at what time; but nearby, lower down on the valley floor, was Backhouse Post on the edge of the RND reserve lines.

Soon after the road levels out to begin its long straight run to Alçitepe, the trees which have flanked it since Skew Bridge suddenly stop. Moving away from the road to the right, across the now wide open field, the ground begins to drop gently towards the Achi Baba Nullah. Following it back towards Achi Baba, after about two hundred yards its course splits. Beyond the offshoot to the right, there is a ditch, about three foot deep, full of tall, hard grass that is quite separate from the nearby streambeds. It would appear to be the overgrown remains of a RND communication trench marked, on the January, 1916, map, as running along this same course. Called Oxford Street, it ran from the point where the offshoot branched off the Achi Baba Nullah up to the deep trench junction known as Piccadilly Circus from where Regent Street continued on into Leicester Square and the support lines. These trenches were very deep, over six feet, and during the summer their sides were fired like brick. Today this shallow, green ditch leads nowhere and nothing can be confirmed. At its head there is no great open space that might show the site of Piccadilly Circus and the tall grass stops abruptly when the ploughed earth fields take over once again. There are few signs of the British presence. Only the nullahs remain, their courses marked by files of trees along their banks, enabling approximate readings of the ground to be taken; but even these provide no real help in pin-pointing where the old trenches used to run.

Alongside the left of these fields the Krithia Road runs perfectly straight for nearly a mile, climbing almost imperceptibly past two recently built private houses until it starts to curve right near the Vineyard which was once marked by a little sign that has long since vanished. On the opposite side of the road, along the length of Krithia Spur, the fields are also now cultivated. Yet, during the campaign all of this area was almost completely bare with only a thin covering of grass binding together the dusty soil, but very few trees remained. It was a desolate place - the antithesis of the beautiful plain one now sees - and it was across this ground that the 2nd Australian Brigade made their charge during the Second Battle of Krithia.

The fields are now bisected by two long avenues of trees that flank the rocky track leading up to Redoubt Cemetery. The cemetery, named after a line of Turkish redoubts that once ran right across Krithia Spur from the Krithia Nullah to the Achi Baba Nullah, was established near the point where the tip of the Australian charge breached this line. In it there is an English oak tree planted by his parents in memory of 2nd Lieutenant Eric Duckworth of the 6th Battalion, Lancashire Fusiliers, who was killed on 7 August. Beyond the end of the avenue can be seen the trees which line the banks of the Krithia Nullah. A quarter of a mile beyond the old stone bridge that sits on the edge of the low ground the main nullah turns from its easterly course through 90° towards the north. It then runs up towards the village roughly parallel to the road with three smaller offshoots cutting off to the left into Fir Tree Spur. In his account of the campaign Nevinson included a description of a journey up to the front line, giving an interesting picture of life in the line at Helles during the summer months. He began by leaving the Headquarters of the 42nd Division and entering the Krithia Nullah just after it had turned north in order to avoid the parallel communication trench.

The peculiarity of this watercourse is that there is visible water in it - a trickle of filthy greenish water unfit for washing or drinking; but still the men wash where it has settled down in the large holes made by 'Jack Johnsons' or 'Black Marias' which have pitched in its bed. One point where the watercourse divides is inevitably called 'Clapham Junction'. But Lancashire names have been given to the main trenches and 'dumps'. Burnley, Warrington and Accrington have given names to the narrow clefts which are the homes of the Lancashire men, and a long communication trench, constructed by the Turks with great ingenuity, has now become Wigan Road. Like all this part of our position, that trench was captured in the fighting of June 4-6, relics of which, in the shape of the dead who cannot be reached for burial, still lie exposed in certain places among our own lines, so keen is the watch of the Turkish sniper. The 38th Brigade is all Lancastrian too. In its headquarters, General Baldwin was giving a discourse to his officers. A young Captain Chadwick, of the machine-guns, showed the way round the trenches. Through periscopes, or by raising the eyes for a few seconds above the parapet (for I found it hard to judge distances through a periscope), one could see the Turkish black and white sandbags only forty or fifty yards from our front, and follow the long lines and mazes of trenchwork round the base of Achi Baba. ... In the midday heat, the men who were not 'standing to', were quietly engaged in cooking or eating their dinner. They cooked on little wood fires lighted in holes scooped out in the trench side, and their tin 'canteens' served for cooking pots and plates. So there these sons of Lancashire stood, almost naked in the blaze of sun, jammed between high walls of white and parching marl; some were cooking, some having their dinner from the pans, some crouching in any corner of shade that could be found, some engaged upon war's inevitable occupation of picking lice off the inside of their clothes. I don't know what work they had done before - weaving, spinning, mining, smelting, I don't know what

*- but they were at an unaccustomed sort of work now, and yet
how quickly they have adapted themselves to so strange a life in
so strange a land!*[17] (H. W. Nevinson)

It is possible, standing in the shade of the trees beside Redoubt
Cemetery looking back down the centre of the Helles lines in July or
August, to feel the presence of these vanished Englishmen nearby. In
the intense quiet that hangs over the peninsula here there is no
distraction. Maybe a group of farm workers toils in the distance,
silently throwing full loads of hay up onto a trailer. Or, if the sun is hot
and overhead, they might instead be sitting in the shade of a nearby tree
peeling a watermelon they have just plucked from the ground. Work is
slowly done and rest is keenly taken. Scarves are pulled down over
eyes and sleeves are buttoned at the wrist. Except in what they do and
the danger in which they do it, these workers are not so different from
Nevinson's soldiers.

Gully Ravine

After it has skirted the site of Bakery Beach immediately beyond
Lancashire Landing Cemetery, the main road from Seddulbahir passes
X Beach on its left. About a mile further on the road turns sharply
inland. Directly in front of the bend stand the tall pine trees that mark
the head of Gully Ravine. Leading off to the left a rough track leads
first across to the sea before turning to the right to run parallel to the
coastline. As it turns it also starts to fall, dropping down beside an ever
steepening cliff on the right. To the left a clear view unfolds of the sea
with the faint shadow of Imbros, the home of GHQ, discernible on the
horizon. Ahead stands the distinctively shaped mouth of Gully Ravine
where the 29th Division had their headquarters from May until August.

Before reaching the mouth of the main ravine a smaller gully
reaches down to the sea across the end of the path. Its sides are equally
as steep but it only runs inland for a few hundred yards before it ends.
The area in front of these two gully mouths was known, for obvious
reasons, as Gully Beach and ran along the shoreline between the end
of the Beach Road and the road that was built in July up to Y Beach,
the fifth of the original landing beaches on 25 April. A landing at Gully
Beach, then labelled Y2, had been rejected because the mouth was
clearly heavily fortified. In the centre of the beach, just beyond the
mouth of the main ravine, was a single pier at which the trawlers plying
from beach to beach used to call. The beach had no breakwater and

consequently disembarking there was sometimes a precarious business. Today the remains of the pier are clearly visible in the sea, causing the shallow water to froth as it breaks over the submerged obstacles and beside it, the rotten ribs of the prow and stern revealing its complete length, lies the wreck of a barge driven aground.

Behind the beach the shoreline is rocky and covered in lengths of dried seaweed. The smell of these rotting, brown strands permeates the whole of the shore and when they mat together they form a soft, spongy carpet that sinks beneath each footstep into the wet sand beneath, oozing out new rivulets of rancid water. The sea is rougher than that inside the Dardanelles and on the beach a strong wind blows. But inside the mouth of the ravine it stops immediately. In its place a hot, heavy blanket of air descends and the frenetic energy of the sea subsides. Looking again from here across to shadowy Imbros the water begins to reflect this oppressive stillness and the brightness of the sun begins to catch on the waves far out to sea. In July 1915, after the 13th Division had been temporarily landed at Helles, 2nd Lieutenant Charles Baxter wrote home to his mother from Gully Beach, giving his address as 'A Sea Side Holiday'.

The headquarters of the 29th Division at Gully Beach looking up the coast across the mouth of the smaller ravine. Note the substantial pier running out from Gully Beach into the sea and the distinctive headland which stands at the entrance to the main Gully Ravine. **(1915/1988)** (Q61082)

How lovely the sea is, isn't it? It is all a mixture of yellow and the brightest emerald green and the darkest blue black. In the distance, just showing through the morning mist, another land lifts its inevitable sand and rock into high yellow dunes and precipices, and a long way further off the outline of a huge mountain shows slightly bluer than the pale blue sky behind. And in front of all the blue green and yellow of the sea spotted with white foam and streaked with purple lines where the sea-weed lies beneath the water.[18]
(2nd Lieutenant Charles Baxter)

The entrance to Gully Ravine is formed, looking up the ravine, on the right by the wall of the smaller ravine and on the left by the steep,

The remains of a boat driven ashore beside the pier at Gully Beach in September 1919 and August 1988. These features can also be seen in the background of the other pictures of Gully Beach. (Q13917)

narrow shoulder of land that runs parallel to the sea for about a hundred and fifty yards before it joins the wider mass of land forming Gully Spur. Along the seaward edge of this shoulder as the campaign progressed a number of small encampments were built and in early August the 88th Field Ambulance moved their main base from W Beach to the side of this cliff.

> *The new camp is about 400 yards up the coast from Gully Beach. It spreads about 150 yards along the face of the cliff which has here been terraced by former occupants. Next the sea, and splashed by the waves is the road to Y, then the waggons and mules and kitchen, then on the first terrace store-tents and bivouacs; about half-way up on a big terrace two hospital tents, then more bivouacs. It faces due west so that is shady for half the morning, but very hot in the afternoon. However, there is usually a good breeze down the peninsula. The cliff is 60 to 100 feet high here, I should say. Bathing very handy, but the water is shallow and rocky a long way out.*[19] (Private Denis Buxton)

Looking today along the seaward edge of this shoulder, from the beach its course appears to maintain the level of the crest onto Gully Spur until the coast turns more sharply to the north-east and disappears. But from the top of the wall of the smaller ravine the view along the inland edge of the shoulder destroys this impression. There is no broad summit along the top of the shoulder; instead the inland wall also falls away as steeply as the one above the sea, creating a sharp drop down onto the floor of the ravine. Only a thin strip actually runs forward to the edge of Gully Spur along the top. Along the inland edge the ground is scooped out forming a deep band of black shadow on the bright yellow sand and at its head the ground falls down in a fan shape, the base running round from the beach into the bed of the ravine. Along this fan more dug-outs and tents were pitched.

In the scrubby bushes strewn across the entrance there are numerous signs of the old occupants. Buried in the hard earth are many green bottle necks, the exposed glass turned opaque by the constant grating of the sand carried in the wind. Also there are pieces of the glazed, khaki earthenware rum bottles marked on the dark brown neck SRD for Supply Reserve Depot.[20] Everywhere across the Peninsula hundreds of pieces of rum jar are to be found. In the ploughed fields on Kereves Spur where no other signs of the RND remain, these

The base of a rum bottle found in Gully Ravine. (July 1987)

Panorama of the entrance to Gully Ravine in September 1915 populated by the men of the 42nd (East Lancashire) Division and the same view in August 1988. Around the large open space set immediately inside the entrance the shape and appearance of the surrounding hills have changed very little and the scrub bushes today still hide many signs of the troops who once lived there. **(1915/1988)** (Q13400a)

small thick pieces of jar lie discarded on the banks along with the larger stones. Along the length of Gully Ravine, varying in size from two inches square to the whole of a base seven inches across, like the trail in a paper chase these pieces lead the way forward towards the front line. It is the same at Anzac on Russell's Top and in Shrapnel Valley, at Suvla near West Beach and Lala Baba. These pieces of rum bottle provide proof after eighty years, as clear as writing on a wall, that Tommy Atkins was here.

Gully Ravine formed an enduring impression on all those who came into contact with it, not just as a result of the fighting there on 28 June, but because for most of the campaign the Gully became an important thoroughfare along which men passed on their way in to and out of the trenches on both Gully and Fir Tree Spurs. Inside its relative protection, but still exposed to

Gully Beach looking north along the coas road, showing the dug-outs that were buil along the seaward face of the cliffs in th summer. The road continued around th headland on the left in the direction of ` Beach. (1915/1988) (Q13649)

shells fired blind and spent bullets dropping down from the higher levels above, the engineers, medical corps and all levels of transport lived permanently, while before them the infantry streamed perpetually in both directions. It inspired a powerful sense of fate in all travellers who passed along it, a feeling that was increased manifestly by the melodramatic nature of its scenery.

After almost literally falling down into it for the first time Buxton made a note of the impression the high walls and long shadows made on him.

The cliffs must have been over 100 foot high, nearly

perpendicular, & except for a band of hard sandstone near the top covered with bright green bushes, brooms & hollies & rhododendrons etc. The yellow sand & the green bushes made a very pretty show lit up by the evening sun.[21] (Private Denis Buxton)

In a despatch devoted entirely to Gully Ravine, Ellis Ashmead-Bartlett expanded upon a similar idea, adding further details of how the inside of the Gully appeared.

But for the grimmer business of war, you would naturally stop and admire the surprising beauty of the scene, which resembles the Highlands in its rugged grandeur. The heat in summer is, however, almost unbearable, because no sea breezes penetrate its depths, and the sun beats down on this war-worn road with pitiless severity. But there is plenty of good water for men and horses, parched by the sun and the sand. These springs are carefully guarded against pollution, and are known and beloved by every thirsty warrior to, or on his way from, the trenches. There are some which, flowing from the interior of the hills, enter the valley in a tiny, trickling stream, clear as crystal and icy cold. Crowds of perspiring, dusty, thirsty men will wait indefinite periods in a long queue, each with his water-bottle in hand, for the privilege of obtaining a draught from one of these springs, which are valued more in Gallipoli than the choicest brand of champagne would be at home.... Along the road in every spot sheltered by the overhanging cliffs from the sun you will find hundreds of weary men who have just come from the trenches, and who have flung themselves down to snatch a few hours' sleep whilst they may. They lie there unconscious and indifferent to the shells bursting overhead and the stream of stray bullets which come 'sizzing' along. A man drops and is immediately carried to the dressing station, but no one takes the smallest notice or even seeks cover, for prolonged experience has had the effect of making nearly all indifferent or fatalists. In the ravine you are constantly coming upon lonely graves, each marked with a cross and a name, marking the last resting-place of some soldier who has fallen in one of the early engagements, or who has been killed on his way to the front and who has been buried just where he fell.[22] (Ellis Ashmead-Bartlett)

The start of the ravine, where the sea breeze occasionally still makes itself felt, is open and the watercourse about four to five feet deep. It leads on, completely dry in the summer, past the far end of the wide, open space inside the entrance, before twisting to the right in the first of hundreds of bends and disappearing into the close, oppressive silence that hangs over most of the route up to the front lines. Despite the dry grass and the thick banks of scrub there is no sense of life once inside the narrow corridor of Gully Ravine. Instead, a heavy stillness sinks lethargically down as the wind passes over the towering walls without disturbing the contained air at all. Nothing moves; no air currents disturb the dust or branches and overhead the round sun

Inside Gully Ravine: while not intended as an exact match these two pictures clearly show how the banks of the gully along its inner reaches have changed almost beyond recognition in direct contrast to the open space immediately inside the entrance. (1915/1988) (Q14848)

The wide open space found in Gully Ravine approximately threequarters of a mile up the ravine from the entrance. The thick covering of pine trees on the banks and the carpet of fallen cones and needles shows how difficult it is to pinpoint accurately the many positions, such as Aberdeen Gully, which ran off it in 1915. (July 1987)

continues to shine down brightly. It is like walking through a greenhouse.

After leaving behind the wide open space a separate path develops distinct from the bed of the gully. Sometimes it is easier to follow one and sometimes the other. They meander in and out, criss-crossing, as the path moves from bank to bank across the depths of the bed. The appearance of the Gully is radically different now from in 1915. Then, whilst covered in patches of scrub and plants, the sides were clear of trees and there were many paths up to the tops of the banks. Now, every surface is covered by thick belts of pine trees that not only obscure the banks, but also increase the claustrophobic nature of the atmosphere. Along the bed pine cones are littered in abundance and the fallen needles form a thick, hostile carpet.

After a few hundred yards the first spring is reached, dropping a clear trail of water down the rock surface into a black pool where a frog starts and disappears out of sight. Throughout the course of the ravine, as Ashmead-Bartlett observed, these water sources appear; some flow, whilst others drip, and many have been covered with small shelters. Three quarters of a mile beyond this first one the ravine opens up again into a wide bowl with an area of approximately one acre. The stream splits around it forming a raised island and at the far end a clear track climbs up to the right through the trees onto Fir Tree Spur. Beyond it the sides close in once again and the narrow course continues.

Over the next mile the journey is very tedious. There is nothing to see but pine trees and underfoot the soft sand clings to each footstep. A number of tributary gullies, their size obscured by the trees, run off to the left onto Gully Spur. It was in two of these side gullies that the 88th and 89th Field Ambulances established their dressing stations after the 29th Division had moved its headquarters to Gully Beach. The Reverend Oswin Creighton, as the chaplain of the 86th Brigade, was attached to the 89th Field Ambulance and he included a description of the Dressing Station in his diary entry of 14 June:

> *It is about 500 yards from the firing line in a little gully called Aberdeen Gully (as the 89th come from there), which runs off from the big gully. A narrow path about fifty yards long had been cut out of the bed formed by a stream, now dry. The path runs up into a little natural amphitheatre in the cliff, about fifteen yards in diameter. The sides of the gully are almost precipitous, but it has been widened enough at places to make a dressing-station, cook-house, and officer's mess, and the amphitheatre is also used as a dressing-station if necessary. It is absolutely safe, but bullets have a way of dropping anywhere, and a man got one in his arm last night, and one was at the foot of my dug-out this morning. My dug-out is reached by a little flight of steps partly cut out of the soft rock and partly made of sand bags. It is only just long enough for me and is cut into the rock with a piece of corrugated iron as cover. It is very snug and away from people, and I sleep on pine branches.*[23] (Reverend Oswin Creighton)

A short distance beyond the last of these side gullies the walls of the main gully rise even more steeply as the gap between their tops closes. A series of abrupt turns leads the bed through this tall straight sided section, past the hidden route up onto Fir Tree Spur known as the Zig Zag, until the edge of Gully Spur levels out again in the long flat slope of Geogheghans Bluff on which was situated the main burial ground in the Gully. Through another set of sharp bends the bed begins to rise perceptibly over increasingly rough ground. The smooth sandy path has by now disappeared, leaving only the bed itself and a surface remoulded each year by the passage of the winter rains. Shortly the

The remains of the British front line prior to its advance during the Action of Gully Ravine on 28 June 1915 leading up on the right along Frith Walk onto Fir Tree Spur. (July 1987)

Fusilier Bluff, the northernmost point of the British line at Helles, looking down to the Aegean Sea with the Turkish line on the opposite side of the gully on the right. **(1915/1988)** (Q14851)

front line of early June is reached. Two thick earth barricades, still three feet high, run across the bed with clear trenches cut out of the banks continuing up onto both of the flanking spurs. The distance from there to the small side gullies is just under half a mile.

Beyond these early front lines the gradient lessens and the sand becomes soft and hot again as it was nearer the beginning. The height of the banks is much shorter now, only about twenty feet, and they are no longer steep. Soon the final support line is reached, faintly discernible in the green shadows of the deep ditches that climb up onto the tops of the two spurs. Twenty-five yards further on a line of parched white rocks run down one bank and up the other, crossing the bed like stepping stones. They are the remains of the British front line still stacked in places like a broken drystone wall. A short distance beyond ran the Turkish front line.

At this point the two and a half-mile journey which takes as many hours is complete. Beyond the Turkish lines the ravine flattens out on either side and between the sparse scrub bushes the way is clear to climb up easily onto Gully Spur. Across the bare earth fields which now curve over the surface of the spur the front line led through Forward Inch to Fifth Avenue, the northernmost point reached by the British at Helles where it fell back down to the Aegean along Fusilier Bluff. Today in front of the junction of Fusilier Bluff and Fifth Avenue a squat, pink Turkish monument surrounded by trees commemorates the successful containment of the British on Gully Spur on 28 June 1915 and the heavy losses that the Turks suffered on this part of the Helles front. Like most Turkish monuments it is accessible by road. Just outside Alçitepe the old West Krithia Road from Pink Farm forks right into the village and left to pass instead behind the busy fields. The track dips down into the shallow bed which is all that remains of Gully Ravine, climbs back onto the crest of Gully Spur and heads down the coast to the monument.

Walking south-west from there along the top of the coastline a number of steep tracks lead down the cliffs to the sea, until one reaches Y Beach. A force of about 2000 men from the 1st Battalion King's Own Scottish Borderers (KOSB), the Plymouth Battalion RMLI and the fourth company of the South Wales Borderers were landed here unopposed on 25 April. A reconnaissance party was even able to cross Gully Ravine in the area of the final front line and approach Krithia unchallenged. 'For eleven hours they were left undisturbed by the enemy, and throughout that period, they alone were equal in numbers to all the Turkish forces south of Achi Baba.'[24] Despite this advantage, they remained static in the defensive line around the top of the beach that they had been ordered to take up while awaiting the expected advance from the south. It was not until 1.00 pm that the first Turkish troops arrived and three more hours before serious opposition began to inflict casualties on the landing party. All efforts by the commander of the force to establish contact with 29th Divisional HQ, pre-occupied with the trials of V Beach, failed to break the silence and overcome their isolation and a totally unexpected and successful landing began to degenerate without reason into a desperate defence of a beach-head. By 11.00 a.m. on 26 April, the whole force had been evacuated and all advantage lost. The recapture of the beach and its ravine was to prove costly and drawn out many weeks later and no other British soldiers were to get so close to Krithia until 1919.

Y Beach was actually at the bottom of two ravines. The furthest up the coast road which ran north from Gully Beach was called Y Ravine and led up onto the top of the Spur, its northern wall was formed by Gurkha Bluff. A short distance back down the coast road was the second called Gurkha Ravine. Around the top edges of these two ravines today are the remains of trenches set back in the trees; but the way down both to the beach is precarious. The sides are steep and the earth brittle; without the protruding roots and rocks it would be virtually impossible. The nature of this climb and of the beach itself was cleverly caught during the later stages of the campaign in an ironic verse written by Winston Churchill's brother.

> *Y Beach, the Scottish Borderer cried,*
> *While panting up the steep hillside,*
> *Y Beach!*
> *To call this thing a beach is stiff,*
> *It's nothing but a bloody cliff.*
> *Why beach?*[25]
> (Major Jack Churchill)

As at X Beach it is not difficult to see why the landing was unopposed.

Turning round to walk inland the ground rises slightly before it rolls gently down to the edge of Gully Ravine near the final British and Turkish front lines. It was across these fields that the Action of Gully Ravine took place. Little of the fighting on 28 June took place in the Gully itself. Instead the intention was to seize all the Turkish trenches running across Gully Spur south-west of the small tributary nullah half a mile behind the Turkish front, together with the Boomerang Redoubt across the Gully on the slopes of Fir Tree Spur. A fortnight after the attack Lieutenant Colonel Stoney, who had been promoted since the V Beach landing to command the same battalion of the KOSB which had landed in April at Y Beach, wrote home to his brother and described his battalion's part in the Gully Ravine attack.

> It was quite the best 'stunt' we have had so far. I am sorry to say we have again suffered very heavily.... The Regiment have done most awfully well and those that are left are as keen as anything. By this last show we have fairly secured our left flank and have it well pushed forward and the sea beyond it. We have captured a large number of rifles and ammunition. They did not mean to be turned out of these 5 lines of trenches which we occupied. I should have like to have seen them running away up the Gully.[26] (Lieutenant Colonel George Stoney)

His description is a fair one. Casualties were heavy and parts of the attack not successful; but in terms of success at Gallipoli it was also the best so far.

As has happened with most of the other trenches at Helles, all discernible signs of the trenches on Gully Spur have disappeared. But the narrow slope is sparsely covered and it is easy to walk unhindered over the ground of the attack to work out what little distance it had to cover and also at what cost. Directly across the Gully a thick patch of scrub marks the site of the Boomerang Redoubt. Walking back along the course of Fifth Avenue to the pink Turkish memorial, from the crest of the spur looking south a clear view unfolds of the whole of the Helles area. On the immediate right is Y Beach with the densely wooded coastline of Gully Spur drawing away until it ends in Gully Beach. Beyond the thin green line of Gully Ravine is the Aegean coast with the three main beaches at the tip running right to left: X, W and V. Between them the crests of Hill 138 and Guezji Baba, beneath the obelisk of the Helles Memorial, are clearly visible; while, in front of the faint dark line of the Asiatic coast, the invisible sweep of Morto Bay leads leftwards to the Turkish Memorial above S Beach. It is a wide, all encompassing panorama, that can be enjoyed again on the crest of Fir Tree Spur, and it reveals how everything the troops at Helles did, from unloading on the beaches to moving up into the front line, could be seen by the Turks from the higher ground they held around the foot of Achi Baba.

The West Krithia Road

Turning inland by the path which leads down to Gully Ravine, the road from Lancashire Landing runs round for four hundred yards into Fir Tree Spur to Pink Farm Cemetery. Pink Farm, correctly called Sotiri Farm in Turkish, was named by the British troops after the terracotta colour of the soil in the surrounding fields and situated alongside the West Krithia Road. A cemetery grew up there after the First Battle of Krithia on the site of the two plots now found immediately inside the gate and this was enlarged after the war. Today it is a quiet, isolated spot. Inside the walls a steady pall of silence falls over the ground as the bank of tall, surrounding trees muffles the melancholy roll of the distant sea and blends it with the soft breath of the wind. Like an invisible shell placed over an ear, the warm and extra-sensory hiss of the air shuts out the remaining quiet of the cultivated fields until there is nothing.

In this eerie dome of silence the ground is carefully landscaped with the dead ground between the headstones populated by a variety of shrubs. The upper level of the cemetery is marked by two rows of Special Memorials set over the graves brought in after the war from other small cemeteries like Gully Beach and 29th Divisional. Another such cemetery was 52nd Divisional, originally situated 'just West of the West Krithia road, on a line due East from X Beach'.[27] One of the graves moved from there was that of Lieutenant Colonel Stoney. He was killed, along with one of his subalterns, 2nd Lieutenant J D Mill, on 15 October when a high explosive shell penetrated his dug-out in the rest area of the 52nd Division to which the 1st KOSB had been attached. The day after his death a friend from the battalion sent his brother an evocative account of his funeral.

> *Last night at Stoney's funeral the pipes played the Flowers of the Forest - a plaintive dirge in an impressive setting. The sun had set over the Aegean, the sky was overcast & grey, the moon in her second quarter casting a faint radiance on the land and seascape. Against this background was silhouetted the figures of hundreds of the Battalion grouped around to pay a last tribute of*

respect to a fine commander. The only point of light was that of the chaplain's electric torch turned on the pages of his prayer book.[28] (Captain C S Stirling Cookson)

At a time of many deaths the attendance of such a large number of his men was an impressive tribute indeed. Stoney is now buried in this cemetery and commemorated by Special Memorial number 204 and J D Mill by number 179.

Outside the cemetery the road resumes the old course of the West Krithia Road parallel to the coast and leads off along the crest of Fir Tree Spur. It crosses the invisible Old or Eski Line, the fortified reserve line that ran across from Gully Ravine to the Kereves Spur, and moves into the front line zone. To the left of the road, three quarters of a mile beyond Pink Farm, is the last of the Helles cemeteries, called Twelve Tree Copse. In many ways it is like Pink Farm Cemetery but larger and includes a Memorial to the Missing New Zealand troops who were killed at Helles, mainly during the Second Battle of Krithia. Yet it had no existence during the campaign but was formed entirely by the subsequent relocation onto this single, more accessible, site of a number of other nearby cemeteries, principally those of Fir Tree Wood, Clunes Vennel and Geogheghan's Bluff. The highest, third level, was formed principally by graves from this latter place which was originally sited on the flat, raised plateau on the west bank of Gully Ravine just behind the early June front line. During the campaign 925 men were buried there, a large proportion of them casualties from the fighting on 28 June.

All of these bodies, exhumed after four years, were re-buried in the upper level and commemorated with Special Memorials. There are about 470 of these in this one plot but two of them, in the corner of the uppermost line, bearing a common English surname seem to span the extremes of the Gallipoli soldier. First there is 16827 Private E Smith, age 37, killed in the diversionary attacks on 6 August

WHO DIED
FOR HIS KING, COUNTRY
WIFE AND LITTLE ONES

Beside him, with an ornately carved copy of the medal replacing the standard plain cross in the top left-hand corner, is a Victoria Cross winner. 2nd Lieutenant A V Smith, the only son of the Chief Constable of Burnley, was killed aged 24 in the last weeks of the campaign on 22 December and originally buried in a battlefield cemetery above Y

Beach near where he died. The citation for his decoration in the London Gazette of 3 March 1916 reads:

> *For most conspicuous bravery. He was in the act of throwing a grenade when it slipped from his hand and fell to the bottom of the trench, close to several of our officers and men. He immediately shouted out a warning, and himself jumped clear and into safety, but seeing that the officers and men were unable to get into cover, and knowing that the grenade was due to explode, he returned without any hesitation and flung himself down on it. He was instantly killed by the explosion. His magnificent act of self-sacrifice undoubtedly saved many lives.*[29]

His epitaph is taken from Tennyson's 'Crossing the Bar':

SUNSET AND EVENING STAR
AND ONE CLEAR CALL FOR ME

Between them Class, Society and Education stand like a gulf, and yet, together in this half-forgotten cemetery, linked like two sides of a sovereign they stand for England.

Behind Twelve Tree Copse the fields of Fir Tree Spur climb slightly up before rolling gently down again towards the edge of Gully Ravine some four hundred yards away. Above the banks of the ravine here the scrub is impenetrable. Moving along the side of it, away from the early June front line, after a short distance it begins to thin, spilling on to the edge of the fields, until finally it is possible to enter. Scrambling over waist-high gorse one stumbles over abandoned pieces of battlefield debris. A bent and rusted British water bottle, still half enamelled but with no sign of its khaki jacket, lies on the earth. Beyond it lies another legacy of the campaign as a crisp white shape sticks sharply out of the ground. Beside it there is a second bone, and a little further on two more that fit together like the fibula and tibia from the same leg. Over seventy

The headstones of 2nd Lieutenant A V Smith VC and Private E Smith in Twelve Tree Copse Cemetery. (August 1988).

years these broken and fragmented limbs, left to disintegrate, have dried out and grown more fragile. The short-lived but heavy autumn rains together with the strong eroding winds have removed the top-soil which covered them and resurrected others buried in the nearby shallow pits. One man, Everyman, Tommy Atkins or Yorick, the bones still point the way into Gully Ravine.

The way down into the Gully or up from there into the front line trenches near here was along the side of a long path that meandered over the steep sides of the ravine and was naturally called the Zig-Zag. The distinctive shape of the path is not visible from the bed of the ravine; but it is possible to force a path through the scrub, following the gaps between the trees, to reach the edge of the cliff down which it ran. It is only really when looking down into the Gully from this height, perched precariously above the steep cliff-face, that the real depth of the ravine can be seen. From the head of the Zig-Zag two support trenches ran across to Twelve Tree Copse called Fusilier and Lancashire Streets; between them and the front line four hundred yards ahead ran a complicated network of British trenches. In a letter to his mother written a fortnight before the big fight advanced the line along the Gully Guy Nightingale, who had been promoted to Captain since the Landing, gave a vivid description of what life was like in this part of the line.

The trenches are absolutely awful - very badly made - narrow, not bullet proof, and smell absolutely revolting from dead bodies. We are occupying Turkish trenches which we captured but there is an absolute maze of trenches. We are all round the Turks and they are all round us too. The Dublins trenches have their back to Achi Baba and face our base, the Turks being between them and us! We share several trenches with the Turks, with a barricade between and throw bombs at each other over the top! The whole place is up and down hill not in the slightest bit like the trenches in France. To get to our trenches we go four miles up a deep nullah with sides 200 feet high. There is a great barricade up right across the nullah at the furthest point we hold. To get into our trenches we go up a zig-zag track and enter a hole in the cliff which leads into our support trenches and from them there are innumerable communication trenches leading into the firing line. Of course you can't show your head above the trench for a second, but have to look through periscopes or through peep-holes. Between the trenches are any amount of dead and decomposing bodies of our own men and Turks lying on the heather. The smell is awful, though we throw down quantities of chloride of lime and creosote. We are always sapping and digging day and night, and so are the Turks, who in places are about 30 yards away, and in others 100, and where we share trenches only the other side of the barricade.[30] (Captain Guy Nightingale)

Although confused, all of these trenches were precisely named and recognised. The battalion which occupied a new trench for the first time would give it a name and usually this was associated with their county or town. The Official History explains that 'it is easy to imagine that names like "Border Barricade" and "Hampshire Cut" commemorate brave deeds by the regiments concerned, but it is not so easy to realize that they designated portions of fire trench. But in 1915 ... the name of say "Essex Knoll" for a fire trench caused no more confusion than that of Haymarket or Knightsbridge for a London street.'[31]

It is difficult now to look out over the quiet, passive fields and see Hampshire Cut, Worcester Flat, or Essex Knoll. Even Fir Tree Wood has gone. All that remains is the slight, barely perceptible curve in the crest of the spur which is otherwise flat, over which the 88th Brigade attacked on 4 June during the Third Battle of Krithia. In the distance a sleek white minaret glistens like a marker flag less than one thousand yards away in the old village of Krithia. As with the RND trenches on Kereves Spur, careful searching reveals nothing. Determined to find invisible traces imagination overpowers reason. Ditches become the washed-out courses of communication trenches; hedges cover-up the remains of lost redoubts. Possibilities expand and begin to live a life of their own until the nature of the random guessing reasserts itself and the demand for empirical evidence returns. Only the chunks of shining rum bottle clinging to the clods of earth are there to satisfy this. To the west of Twelve Tree Copse, in a large scrub lined hole, man-made and unreclaimed, two bits of russet metal are cradled in the branches of a tree. The hole is too far north to be Holborn Circus, too far west to be the RND Engineering Bivouac. There are no clues, no signs as to what went on there and where it used to lead. Nearby the Great North Road has been ploughed back into the soil. Turning east to look across to Krithia Spur, one sees just the ghost of the old front line weaving across the undulating ground, its sorrowful course staked out by the cemeteries' trees, there Twelve Tree Copse and beyond Redoubt beside the Krithia Road. In them it seems the men of Helles wander still beneath the ground, *Hic et Ubique.*

Chapter Four

ANZAC COVE

April to August

The initial aim of the ANZAC landing on 25 April was for a covering force to land and establish a line from the north of Gaba Tepe to the peak of Chunuk Bair with its left flank falling back down to the sea near Fisherman's Hut. The remainder of the Corps would then follow up and advance through this position towards the pivotal hill of Mal Tepe and its surrounding area. From there the Australians and New Zealanders would be able to threaten the northern face of the Kilid Bahr Plateau and Turkish communications around it, matching the pressure being placed against its southern flank by the British landing at Cape Helles. Lieutenant General Sir William Birdwood, the GOC ANZAC, insisted on commencing the landing in the dark to achieve greater surprise and security, despite the Navy's grave concerns about the risks that this entailed. Consequently the covering force, comprised of the 3rd Australian Brigade under the command of Colonel Ewen Sinclair-Maclagan, was set to land at 4.30 am along the beach to the north of Gaba Tepe that had been lettered Z in conjunction with the pattern at Helles.

**Lieutenant General
Sir William Birdwood**

**Colonel Ewen
Sinclair-Maclagan**

1500 men were to be placed in groups of 500 on board three battleships while the remainder were put into seven destroyers. Of the three 'mother' battleships, the anchor ship on the southernmost flank, HMS *Queen* holding the men of the 9th Battalion, was to be positioned one mile north of Gaba Tepe. 800 yards further north, HMS *Prince of Wales*, containing the 10th Battalion, was to be in the centre of the line. Another 800 yards to the north opposite the beach that became known as Anzac Cove, HMS *London* holding the 11th Battalion was to stand off the northernmost flank. Four tows from each ship, numbered south to north 1 to 12, were to land the men, each one being composed of either a picket boat or a steam pinnace

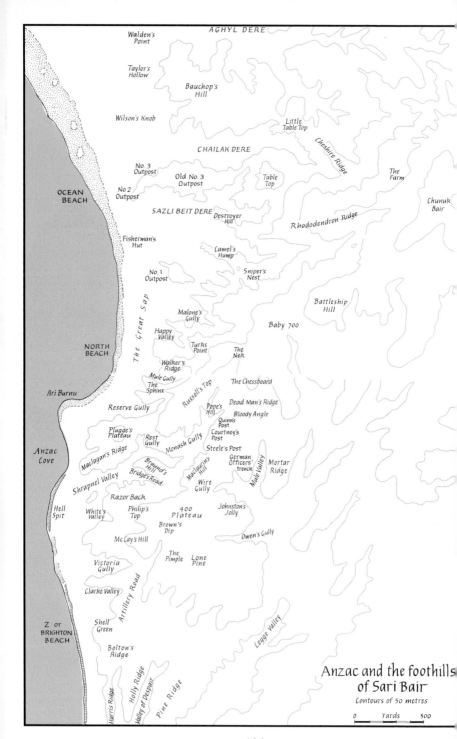

Anzac and the foothills of Sari Bair

Contours of 50 metres

0   Yards   500

and three pulling boats to be rowed ashore for the last few hundred yards. They were ordered to approach the shore in line abreast, each tow 150 yards to the north of the one on its right with No.1 Tow on the southern end, commanded by Lieutenant Commander John Waterlow RN, responsible for guiding the whole line in on its correct bearing. Once the boats in the first wave had reached the shore and disembarked their soldiers, they were to return to the destroyers, which by then would have advanced through the line of battleships to anchor as close to the shore as possible, allowing the remaining men of the brigade to be towed ashore in a similar way to the first wave.

At 3.30 am the tows began to move slowly in towards the shore through the darkness. However, between this point and the moment that they reached it something happened that was to land them in considerable confusion in the wrong place, much further north than had been expected. The subsequent official explanation was that the current off Z Beach had slowly drawn the whole line to the north as it headed in along its correct eastward course. As the first evanescent fingers of the lightening sky began to pick out the outline of the coast, Waterlow supposedly looked to his left and saw the headland of Ari Burnu, a mile to the north of the beach his tow should have been approaching. Surprised, he mistakenly believed it to be Gaba Tepe and that the current had carried them south and not north. He immediately re-set his course, and consequently that of the whole line, and began to move sharply north to where he believed Z Beach to be. Commander Charles Dix RN, in command of the northernmost tow, saw this change of course occurring and, realizing that it would result in the covering force being landed at least two miles north of the ground identified as suitable for the invasion, began to turn his tow towards the south, cutting in front of the other tows, and shouting to them to follow. Those nearest to him naturally began to do so and the organisation of the line was thrown into total disarray as the two outer tows started to converge on the same point around Anzac Cove.

In his book *Gallipoli*, Robert Rhodes James, using the evidence of an Australian veteran, Major H V Howe, also suggests that the tows might have been moved north deliberately in accordance with a change of plan made on the previous night by Rear-Admiral Cecil Thursby, the senior naval officer in command of the Anzac landing.[1] But there is no official evidence to support this. The Çanakkale tour guides offer an even more ingenious explanation based on the local tradition that a Turkish soldier from Gaba Tepe swam out on 24 April to move a marker buoy intended to guide HMS *Queen* into position on the southern edge of the line. In this way they are able to claim that the Turks themselves prevented the success of the landing, and not the intervention of Fate. Unfortunately for the veracity of this fable the *Queen* was never dependent on a buoy. The most plausible explanation did not emerge until sixty years after the campaign when extracts from the private accounts of two of the key participants, both of which can now be read in full at the Imperial War Museum, first appeared in print.[2] With one corroborating the claims made in the other, these complementary descriptions of the landing suggested that the northward movement occurred as a result of misplaced initiative and a failure to obey without question written orders, a combination of human failings that appears much more convincing than the intervention of the current.

No.2 Tow, immediately to the north of Waterlow in No.1, was commanded by Midshipman J Savill Metcalf RNR of HMS *Triumph*. Having collected his men from HMS *Queen* and been towed in from the early rendezvous alongside this ship in his correct station, shortly after 3.40 am when the tows were released Metcalf received a verbal order from the bridge to 'Go Ahead' to his position in the line of tows. This he proceeded to do but slowly, aware of the need to keep No.1 Tow in sight on his starboard. Immediately another peremptory order to 'Go Ahead' followed and this time, fearing that otherwise his actions might be interpreted as cowardice, Metcalf reacted by moving off full speed ahead. In the darkness it was difficult for the boats in the line to maintain visual contact with each other and instead of remaining spaced 150 yards apart they quickly bunched together with only 50 yards distance between them. In the process the overall length of the line was significantly reduced. After leaving the lee of HMS *Queen* Metcalf soon lost sight of No.1 Tow to starboard but remained in touch with No.3 to port.

> *About a quarter of an hour later I realized we were heading very close to the north side of Gaba Tepe which, because of its height, is very conspicuous. Knowing that there were Turkish troops there, and we would get an enfilading fire all along the starboard side as well as from ahead, I was confident that we must be heading for a wrong place. There was no one to consult and I felt the lives of the men I was towing were my responsibility. Without any delay I altered course two points to port to get away from Gaba Tepe. After a quarter of an hour, finding the tows to port had conformed, I again altered course a point and a half to port.*[3] (Midshipman J Savill Metcalf RNR)

This represented a change of course for his tow of nearly a mile.

This movement is confirmed by Waterlow's own diary. Approaching the shore, also from HMS *Queen*, Waterlow initially believed he was following his correct bearing in towards a dark mass in front of him which he assumed was Gaba Tepe. However, as the outline of the hills cleared he became aware of another prominent headland to the north and began to wonder whether, in fact, this was Gaba Tepe, much as he was held to have done in the official explanation.

> We began to vacillate - our faith in our course was more shaken by the fact that all other boats were steering more to the northward. At last I altered course to the northward also and steered for the high land we could clearly see. We had to assume that the 'Queen' was in her correct billet, and working on that assumption this prominent headland could not be Gaba Tepe. So my uncertainty increased - but still the boats steered to the northward. At last I altered course and went down the line astern trying to draw them to the southward with me. This failed, and I was now convinced that my prominent headland was not Gaba Tepe. It was too high, and also on its summit there was not visible the ruined building which surmounts Gaba Tepe. I then tried to urge the boats to the northward where a good beach was visible - then again to the southward, but efforts in every direction failed ...... The dawn began to glow and our prominent headland loomed larger and larger against the pale saffron light, - the one place on the whole coast on which we should have decided not to land. However, we were approaching the shore and the dawn was growing so fast that at last in despair I dashed straight for the frowning cliffs now straight ahead.[4] (Lieutenant Commander John Waterlow RN)

In the tows themselves the midshipmen who commanded most of the steam boats and the troops who followed in the pulling boats were aware only of a distinct zigzagging in their course. As they moved east the outline of the hills in front of them gradually became lighter. At the head on No.8 Tow Midshipman Eric Bush RN later noted the final moments of the approach.

> When the flotilla was within 300 yds of the shore the Turks gave the alarm. Immediately star shells burst over the flotilla & verey lights were fired from the shore. Rifle & maxim fire at once broke out. In the distance on the shore a bugle call could be heard 'Calling the patrols'.... The picket boats who were

sounding with their boat hooks found bottom. Immediately they slipped their tows, who got their oars down and pulled for the shore.[5] (Midshipman Eric Bush RN)

To the north of Bush the first two companies of the 11th Battalion who had disembarked from HMS *London* at first knew nothing of these events, sensing in the darkness only the weaving of the tows. But then, just as the steam pinnaces were disengaging from the cutters and the soldiers were preparing to row, the mistake was noticed. But it was too late.

A terrific hail enveloped us and cut the water to foam. We knew we had been spotted. [I didn't] bother to row. I threw my oar over board and got over the side of the cutter at once. For, to remain all massed together (50 men in each cutter) was providing an excellent target for old Jacko the Turk; although he, from his trenches, could not in that light see individuals very clearly. He concentrated his fire on the boat loads of men. So it was imperative to 'scatter' and over the side and into the sea we went. ... At last I reached the shore. ... The next and immediate thing to do was to get across the few feet of shore to the base of the cliff for cover, and off I went. Now, I could only stroll; so, leisurely, I went along and when I reached that welcome cover down I dropped [gasping] for breath. I thought of my heavy smoking which [had] made me so short winded. I got beside a big bush. The soil being sandy was worse and a kind of thyme grew in profusion all around and in the morning dew gave forth a perfume. I afterwards learnt to loath [it] and shall always do so now. The bullets came by thick. They came past my ears so close I felt the air move as they whizzed past and whispered 'wzip, zip, ZIP'. This description of the sound is exact and it made your eyes blink, so close they came. After regaining my wind I got rid of my pack and crawled up and up, gradually becoming cased with mud on my wet garments.[6] (An Anonymous Soldier of C Company, 11th Battalion AIF)

Further off the coast, in accordance with the original plan, the line of seven destroyers had sailed past the three battleships a short distance behind the first tows. These destroyers carried the remaining men of the 3rd Brigade, including the whole of the 12th Battalion. On board HMS *Chelmer* the other two companies of the 11th Battalion were disembarking into the ship's boats when they began to hear the sound of rifle fire along the shore. Soon they too were heading in, exactly as the first wave had done only minutes beforehand.

We were supposed to land on a shelving shore, with cultivated ground, and an orchard running almost on to the beach. Judge my horror, when in the half light I saw we were being towed direct for a narrow strip of beach, with almost inaccessible cliffs rising straight from the beach to a height of 200 feet. ... At last our boat grounded and I jumped out as I thought into 2 feet of water. It was up to my neck, and under I went. I got up scrambled into about 2 feet of water and waved the boys on and they all jumped out quickly enough who could ... We climbed up the beach and lay doggo for a few seconds while everyone took off his pack and got a breather. Then, round a winding, precipitous path, up, up, up, we charged. Not a rifle had been loaded (by strict order) and our boys did not waste their breath cheering, until we got to the top. Then a wild coo-ee and the bayonet.[7]
(Captain Dixon Hearder)

In the confusion of the landing the precise order of the 3rd Brigade's battalions had been randomly shuffled like a pack of cards. Most of the boats in the first wave had landed between Ari Burnu and Hell Spit, respectively the northern and southern arms of Anzac Cove, and none landed south of Hell Spit on Z Beach. Yet the men who followed up so quickly from the destroyers remained close to their intended positions and added to the confusion by enthusiastically throwing themselves into the maelstrom. Inland from the Cove the steep, rough-sided face of what became known as Plugge's Plateau presented a daunting first objective, but immediately the men surged forward off the beach onto its lower slopes.

There was not two men of the same battalion together. The men did all on their own initiative, which was greatly to their credit. They crawled, climbed, ran and struggled over boulders, hills, valleys and dales, ever going up and up this enormously high mountain like a cliff, for it was a fearful height up ... Up and down we went, up, up, for ever it seemed; this time to the summit which at last we reached and then we dashed along after the Turks who we could see clearly now in the rising of the sunlight. Here a tremendous report came echoing all around. We, for the moment, wondered what had happened. The ground seemed steady. Then it dawned on us. It was the warships that had commenced to back us up. The good old Triumph *had sent 10 inch flyer to Jacko at Gaba Tepe fort and then another in quick succession. The Turks hastened a bit and we also took a faster run and, the result of this splendid 'music'? We let go a mighty*

British cheer and 'cooeed' to our cobbers below who 'cooeed' back. This Australian cry must have put the fear of Allah on to Jacko, for he doubled his efforts at running and so did we.[8] (An Anonymous Soldier of C Company, 11th Battalion AIF)

Having stormed and conquered Plugge's Plateau almost by instinct, the triumphant soldiers of the covering force next encountered a sudden drop on the far side. All around them the ground fell away in steep precipices into a twisting, scrub-lined valley. Yet again they charged; slowly dispersing themselves amongst the craggy offshoots of the main valley. 'Down we went slipping and scrambling and sliding, following the track of a stony gorge, while our friend the enemy poured in rifle fire and shrapnel.'[9] Slowly, largely as a result of the mistake in the landing, but compounded by the complexity of the ground which ran off the beach, the attack lost all cohesion and co-ordination. All possibility of establishing a central command was lost as the men of the 3rd Brigade, followed during the course of the day by the rest of the 1st Australian Division as well as the New Zealand and Australian Division, became intermixed and spread about the hills and gullies above the beach. The tremendous energy of the landing was gradually dissipated by chaos, whilst the bewildered Turkish garrison slowly re-grouped and began to fortify the main objective of the high ground inland.

By the time the Australians and New Zealanders were sufficiently reorganised to contemplate moving off, they found themselves besieged within a ragged horse-shoe around Anzac Cove; for the next three months there would be no significant change in the course of the line and each attempt to break out would fail.

The minute scrap of territory which the Anzac corps had

Australian troops landing at Anzac Cove on 25 April 1915. (Q112876)

captured, and which was to be its home for the next three months,
had a total length of rather less than 1½ miles. Its greatest depth
from the front line to the sea-coast was only 1000 yards. Its
perimeter was open to almost every objection as a position for
defence. Its sea-base, only a thousand yards from the trenches,
was the open beach, exposed to north-west and south-west
winds. Its anchorage was under direct hostile observation from
the coast on either flank.... But only those who visit the actual
ground, and look at the incredible position from the old Turkish
front line can fully appreciate the spirit of the troops who held
it.[10] (Official History)

The Anzac position is best thought of as a fortress built in a hollow with the result that the highest battlements remained below the level of the surrounding hills. With the sea behind it in the west, a ridge climbed slowly up from the south near Gaba Tepe to cross first over a broad, flat plateau and then along a narrow wall to the east before it cut back at 45⁰ from the northernmost point to fall down towards sea level, forming a shape like a large number 7. The fortress had a keep and a raised platform from where the action could be viewed; it had bivouac barracks, dressing stations and cemeteries. All it lacked was a sanctuary where the garrison could go and feel safe, relieved of shell-fire for a short while. However, despite this, the garrison grew 'accustomed to think of the place as home, and of the conditions of our life as natural and permanent.... The men continued to make the trenches impregnable and were contented. It was in some ways a curiously happy time.'[11]

Anzac Cove to Plugge's Plateau

The road from Gaba Tepe runs north beside the long, flat sands of Z Beach, eventually named Brighton Beach by the Anzacs after the beach outside Melbourne. It would have been a fine place to land an army, leading off to the east across the relatively gentle slopes of Second Ridge (later named Bolton's and Pine) to Third Ridge (named Gun) which was the inland objective of the covering force. The beach ends in the rocky, scrub covered headland of Hell Spit, an apparently innocuous mound that, from the south, gives no warning of the precipitous and scarred terrain hidden to the east. Between the mound and the sand of the beach, is the quiet steppe of Beach Cemetery. The spontaneous confusion of the headstones shows that these graves are still the original ones in which the dead were buried in 1915. This is the first indication that at Anzac the cemeteries are different from those at Helles. There is a subtle but significant change of tone, manifest in the way the graves cluster together in little groups. No longer are they arranged in perfect rows of upright soldiers. Instead they are standing easy, relaxed and nonchalant, as if still talking and smoking cigarettes, Anzacs even in death.

This style is commonly the case here. Unlike the large, orderly cemeteries formed at Helles after the war, at Anzac, because of the different nature of the ground, the cemeteries remained largely where they had been established. In *The Unending Vigil* Philip Longworth explains that, when they were being built,

Ari Burnu Cemetery after the initial work of the Graves Registration Directorate had been completed but before the then Imperial War Graves Commission had erected the headstone blocks. Behind the old cemetery is the wreck of the steamer *Milo*, sunk to form a breakwater. Beyond this to the left are the outlines of No.1 Outpost and (slightly further back) No.2 Outpost. (1919/1987) (Q14391)

> *'the special feeling the Australians and New Zealanders had for Gallipoli was reflected by the junior architect on the spot who called for the whole of the Anzac area of the Peninsula to be made "a consecrated ground", the cemeteries being retained unwalled "simply in the positions in which they were found".*[12]

On the whole this basic idea seems to have been followed, with little of the exhumation and reburial which afforded the opportunity to introduce a new sense of order at Helles. Instead, the whole of Anzac was declared a protected area in which the undiscovered bodies of the dead would be allowed to remain undisturbed. To the Turks this presented few problems as there had never been any farming there and the hills made it virtually impossible to build. So when it was decided to open up the peninsula and encourage visitors, at Anzac the cemeteries had remained much the same as when they were first established and the original aspiration had been brought about almost by chance. The declaration of the area a National Park has merely embraced this original idea and ensured that it will continue. Although it was realised from the first that they would have to be walled as security against the vicissitudes of the weather, most of the cemeteries are still tucked carefully into the corners of the hills and on the flat, protected plateaux of the rear slopes where they evolved. They are many, and small, and retain their more intimate, impromptu wartime character.

The headstones too seem different, with the inscriptions revealing a characteristically more direct and sentimental approach. Reading them is like discovering a series of private letters that were never intended to be publicly read. The standard British tone, *Dulce at Decorum Est*, has been rejected as insufficient. Instead in the wind over Beach Cemetery a thin, fragile voice whispers that

WHEN DAYS ARE DARK
& FRIENDS ARE FEW
DEAREST HOW I LONG FOR YOU

Still at Lone Pine

SISTERS, FLORRIE, ALICE, ROSIE MISS YOU DEARLY
MISS YOU 'WILL'

A mother is proud of her son, even though he was only a private, and the family of 559 Private J Owens killed fighting in the trenches now hidden beneath the Lone Pine Cemetery speak to him in Welsh

BYDD MYRDD O RYFEDDODAU
AR DORIAD BOREU WAWR.
(There shall be a thousand wonders in the breaking of the dawn.)

They are searing flashes of real feeling, of grief mixed with pride and loneliness; they are fresh and personal, the voice of a new people.[13]

Rounding the headland beyond Beach Cemetery one comes abruptly to Anzac Cove lodged between Hell Spit and Ari Burnu. It was this beach that was the main entry point for both men and provisions. Throughout the whole campaign its sands were covered in stores and jetties, the first to be built in June being named Watson's Pier after Lieutenant S H Watson of the 2nd Australian Field Company who supervised its construction. Thrust out into the sea, across them working parties toiled day and night to unload the ships. All approaching sea-traffic could be seen from Gaba Tepe in the south and Lala Baba to the north on Suvla Bay, and artillery fire from well-known guns such as Beachy Bill was liable to strafe the beach at any time. Yet despite its vulnerability the beach remained 'packed with stores, ammunition, transport, animals and human beings as thick as bees round a hive.'[14]

Bearing this picture in mind, with its untidy clutter and thronging population, particularly on 25 April, it seems certain on approaching that it will be a decent sized beach. It is not; perhaps 175 yards long, its depth is now a mere 15 yards. The drop down on to the beach is too steep to descend, falling sheer over brittle cliffs of compacted sand; but in 1915 the slope climbed up more gradually towards Plugge's Plateau. The construction of the new road has changed its shape and absorbed a little of the meagre space around the beach, lifting up the bottom of the bank to place it

116

Anzac Cove, looking north along the level of the beach to Ari Burnu. It is interesting to note how much the building of the bank to support the new road has changed the depth and appearance of the beach. **(1915/1987)** (Q13603)

further up the slope and form a level carriageway along the back. Driving along this, the beach vanishes before it has been properly seen. Passing through Hell Spit, you see Ari Burnu ahead, turn to look behind, turn back again to see the beach and it has gone. It is the first of many astounding sights at Anzac; that this tiny pebble-strewn beach, shaped like an archer's undrawn bow with the sea as straight as the string, lies at the centre of both the legend and the fortress.

At the centre of the bow the ground above the beach is shielded from direct observation by Plugge's Plateau. Named after Lieutenant-Colonel A Plugge (pronounced Plug-ee), Commanding Officer of the Auckland Battalion, the plateau is a large, rectangular piece of flat ground pointing gently up towards the east that sits firmly on a pedestal of steep slopes which drop down to sea level. Along the seaward faces of these slopes run a jumble of gullies and crags, like a thick screen of ivy around the base of a neglected statue. It was into this confusing tangle, then named First Ridge, that the first Australians charged. The rough,

The headquarters of the New Zealand and Australian Division above the centre of Anzac Cove on the lower slopes of Plugge's Plateau. (1915/198...
(Q13828)

uneven nature of the ground can be seen most clearly from the road beside Ari Burnu Cemetery, looking up on to the plateau over the nearest deep ravine called Howitzer Gully. Towards the top of the steepening slopes the vegetation ends and the sheer, brittle cliffs rise up bare towards the level platform. It takes but a little imagination to realize just what an achievement the storming of Plugge's Plateau really was.

In the centre of the beach, raised off the level of the sand onto the rocky hills, Birdwood had his Corps Headquarters for the first eight months of the campaign. Unlike the Corps Commanders on the Western Front, at Anzac Birdwood was forced to live under the same conditions as his men. Shot in the head in May, buried in the front line in July, even his dugout here was under the same shell-fire which strafed the beach and his ADC, Lieutenant Brian Onslow, was eventually killed whilst sleeping outside it on the ledge that he himself liked to use when it was safe. Looking up towards the summit of the plateau from the centre, another deep gully leads away into the undergrowth. The base is lined with shrunken holly trees, the sides carpeted by hard and painful tendrils of scrub. Yet this difficult road once pushed a wide and steady course towards the headquarters of the New Zealand and Australian Division. With the scrub cut back the path was much wider, with space even for ranks of mules. It was one of the major routes off the beach, leading to the dugouts where the Division's Commander, Major-General Sir Alexander Godley, and his staff were bivouacked at the base of the plateau's steeper slope. Nothing remains of the sandbags and sheets, but the outlines of the terraces where the dugouts were cut can still be seen in the lines of bushes that encircle the base in parallel rings.

Rising out of the concrete ditch that surrounds Shrapnel Valley Cemetery, a short distance inland from Beach Cemetery at the seaward end of the main route up to the line, a narrow path climbs up the pointed shoulder of land that grows out of Hell Spit. Named MacLagan's Ridge after the commander of the covering force the shoulder curves up and round towards the summit of Plugge's Plateau. The steep climb is an interesting one, for it is only from the slopes of this ridge that one can really see the size of Anzac Cove and appreciate

Anzac Cove seen from the path that climbs up MacLagan's Ridge to Plugge's Plateau Cemetery. (August 1988)

just how small it actually is. Halfway up the path, as it begins to turn towards the left and level off, there is a view down into a third deep ravine called Bully Beef Gully. At the end of the path is the small, quiet Plugge's Plateau Cemetery. Around it, in the collapsed trenches that weave aimlessly over the plateau and in the empty holes of the dug-outs on the rear slopes where hares now live in quiet seclusion, there is ample evidence of its tactical importance as the last line of defence above the beach.

From the inland edge of the plateau there is a clear view down into Shrapnel Valley, also known as Shrapnel Gully, as it winds its way from Hell Spit to its junction with Monash Gully, also referred to as Monash Valley, named after the then Colonel John Monash, Commanding Officer of the 4th Australian Brigade.* Although overgrown and difficult to follow a clear and obvious track still leads up to the front line along the course worn by the Anzac soldiers. Sir Ian Hamilton described the route in a letter to Lord Kitchener.

> *Walking up the path at the bottom of a deep valley to the trenches, you find notices stuck up warning you to keep to the right or left of the track. If you know better you are almost certain to be shot. It is an extraordinary thing the half of the road being comparatively quite safe, the other most dangerous.*[15]

Major-General William Bridges, Commanding Officer of the 1st Australian Division, was one who knew better, being mortally wounded by a sniper on 15 May when he refused to hide behind the sandbag traverses in Monash Gully.

Immediately beneath the sheer drop of the inland face of Plugge's Plateau another valley curls round to the left away from Shrapnel Valley. This is Rest Gully, so called because in the early days the protection offered by its three high walls provided the best shelter for the troops; but, like Birdwood's dugout, even this was not inviolable, just better than the front line. Like the headquarters' sites too, in Rest Gully there is still evidence of the terraced dugouts that were once cut into the hills which 2nd Lieutenant Ivor Powell recalled quite clearly later in his life.

> *Those so called dugouts are no more than holes scraped out of the crumbling cliff side, and numerous twigs, presumably the roots of a prickly shrub, protrude from the roof. Each root is festooned with flies, and it is a feat of leger-de-main to consume a morsel of food without swallowing a mouthful of them. In addition to the flies there are voracious fleas which batten on each night.*[16] (2nd Lieutenant Ivor Powell)

*The use of Gully or Valley to describe these two continuous features varies from source to source. As Shrapnel Valley Cemetery is also referred to in this book, in order to maintain consistency Valley has been used for this end of the valley, while to make the distinction absolutely clear the top half has been called Monash Gully.

The northern wall of Rest Gully was formed by a sinuous ledge, with precipitous slopes dropping down on either side, called Razor Edge, which led across from Plugge's Plateau to the southernmost tip of Russell's Top. From Ari Burnu and the beach just north of there, naturally called North Beach, Razor Edge looks like a continuation of the flat top of Plugge's Plateau. Many of the 11th Battalion who landed on North Beach, believing this to be so and appreciating the need to seize Russell's Top, ran straight off the beach and climbed the steep barren cliffs in front of them. On reaching the top they discovered Razor Edge to be only about a foot wide. Although carrying a full pack and under sporadic fire, they scrambled along the narrow ridge and on to the high ground beyond. It is still possible to walk carefully along the same route, over the clogging scrub and jumping the gaps; but hard to imagine attempting it in the half-light of dawn, under fire and with a heavy pack on one's back.

Once the line at the head of Russell's Top had been secured the ground between the sea and the arc of Plugge's Plateau, Razor Edge, and Russell's Top was designated a second rest area called Reserve Gully, mirroring Rest Gully on the opposite side of Razor Edge. The Official History explains that although this new area was protected from direct Turkish fire it was still 'less than 800 yards from the enemy's front line. In such a position there was no rest from the noise of the battle and no respite from daily fatigues.'[17] It was to this area that the 4th Australian Brigade was withdrawn at the end of May after

A gully at Anzac on the northern flank of Plugge's Plateau. (1915/1988)
(Q14345)

holding the line at the head of Monash Gully since the landing. They were visited there on 2 June by Godley who was accompanied by his Divisional Staff including Captain Aubrey Herbert.

This morning I went to Reserve Gully with the General. Monash's Brigade is resting there for the first time for five weeks. The General, looking like a Trojan hero, made them a fine speech from a sort of natural throne in the middle of the sunlit amphitheatre, in which they all sat, tier after tier of magnificent-looking fellows, brown as Indians.[18] (Captain Aubrey Herbert)

Throughout the campaign stores were piled up along North Beach just as they were in Anzac Cove and the slopes of Reserve Gully became covered with habitations. In particular at the seaward end hospital tents collected in the protective shadows of the hills like Bedouin caravans at an oasis. Dugouts were carved out of the cliffs; new paths cut in the scrub. Even the YMCA staked their claim. The piers that ran into the sea directly in front of them were used to load the wounded on to hospital ships and eventually they were brought here from as far afield as the Aghyl Dere at the far northern end of Sari Bair. Private Harold Thomas who, despite being an ordained minister in the Church of England, served from August on as a private in the 3rd East Anglian Field Ambulance at Suvla, had to carry casualties from this distant point to the piers at Anzac. In a private memoir he later recalled the cluttered scene he found here in the late summer.

Besides the hospital tents perhaps the most striking features of the landscape were the enormous dumps of ammunition and 'rations' - mountains of bully beef and biscuits towered up foursquare to the sky; nearby were 'dumps' for all kind of stores, one pathetic pile being formed of dead men's kit, haversacks, water-bottles, belts, broken rifles and all the flotsam and jetsam of the battlefield. As I write I see the whole scene again; innumerable and strenuous activities in a confined space frowned on by towering cliffs from which came the increasing roll of musketry and machine guns and sometimes from whose edges fell the puff of shrapnel or the smoking trail of a big H. E. shell. Strings of mules with squatting Sikh drivers, Australians and New Zealanders almost invariably stripped to the waist and burnt black with the sun, Tommies in soiled khaki, some still smart and brisk others hollow eyed and weak in the knees with faces lined with pain just 'carrying on' until dysentery 'outed them' altogether. Imagine Wells's Mr Polly contemplating the scene and trying to find the words for it. 'Cosmopolous' he would

North Beach from the northern edge of Plugge's Plateau. In the foreground of the old picture, taken after the August offensive, are the tents of No.1 Australian Stationary Hospital at the entrance to Reserve Gully and in the distance, at the end of Happy Valley, those of No.13 Casualty Clearing Station. Near this latter point in the modern picture, on the right of the road, can be seen the clearing of Canterbury Cemetery and a short distance beyond this the workshops of the CWGC in front of No.1 Outpost. **(1915/1988)** (Q13618)

certainly have called it and 'dusti turbuloferous' in all probability.[19] (Private Harold Thomas)

Peering down towards North Beach today from the junction of Razor Edge and Plugge's Plateau all this has gone. Not even the faintest spectres can still be seen. The contours and the paths are all submerged beneath an even cover of brush. Only the road shaves a strip of emptiness beside the coast. From Anzac Cove, looking up, the scrub on Ari Burnu and Plugge's Plateau is wide-open and varied, creating patterns and textures that look much like the pitted ground they hide. Things appear similar to the way they were. But from above, on the hills, distance and height blend the bushes together in an opaque wash of colour that masks the features beneath. It is an example of just how much the face of Anzac has really changed whilst apparently staying the same.

Russell's Top to Baby 700

Before reaching Gaba Tepe the road from the Çanakkale ferry that skirts the northern flank of the Kilid Bahr Plateau passes the new Turkish War Museum which opened in 1985. Beyond it there is a crossroads. To the left a road leads across the centre of the southern half of the peninsula to Alçitepe and the Helles battlefields. From around two kilometres down this road, turning back to look north towards Sari Bair there is a long clear view of the ridge as it climbs up through Anzac to Chunuk Bair. Taking the right turn at the junction a second road begins a lengthy climb up this range of hills. Around the base of the lower slopes of Second Ridge the ground is wide open with small orchards of trees breaking up the expanses of green pastureland. Rising gently at first but soon becoming steeper, the road follows the crest of the larger, inland spur of Second Ridge called Pine Ridge past the statue which shows a Turkish soldier carrying a wounded Anzac officer to his own lines for treatment. Based on an actual reported incident, it symbolises the respect that the two adversaries had for each other. Levelling off on the south-eastern flank of 400 Plateau, the road first bends left round the Lone Pine Cemetery and then

Statue on Pine Ridge depicting a reported incident when a Turkish soldier returned a wounded Anzac officer to his own lines. His actions symbolised the respect and lack of personal animosity that all sides had for each other throughout the campaign. (April 1998)

right past that of Johnston's Jolly. After the course of Second Ridge narrows once again it passes two more small cemeteries before it forks. To the right it climbs still further up past the crisp, clean new brickwork of the Turkish 57th Regiment Cemetery and the Commonwealth cemetery on Baby 700 to Chunuk Bair. But to the left it circles round across the head of Monash Gully towards the Nek, ending near a small Memorial to another Turkish sergeant who stood his ground and was killed in the early days of the campaign, Mehmet Çavus. With the Anzac cemetery a short distance beyond it, there the metalled road stops and a dirt track takes over. Dusty in summer but thick mud after it has rained, the track extends the route as far as the cemetery at the head of Walker's Ridge. In front is North Beach, with Ocean Beach further up on the right. To the left is the familiar shape of Plugge's Plateau, buried in the undergrowth above Ari Burnu. Underfoot runs Russell's Top.

Russell's Top is the long flat plateau which forms the north-western wall of Monash Gully. On the map it is shaped like a right arm extended on a table with the palm facing up and the fingers closed, pointing towards Anzac Cove. Razor Edge links up with the index finger and the broad expanse of muscle narrows to a point at the elbow where the Nek leads off to the right. Along the edge of this, facing out to sea, runs an arc of ominous cliffs in the centre of which, erect and solitary, stands the Sphinx. Possibly the most distinctive feature of this seaward wall, the Sphinx is an outcrop of rock in two parts, a head and a supporting wall, and can be seen all the way from the borders of Suvla. From there it looks exactly like its Egyptian namesake, with a clear line between the head and shoulders and the back wall, and for troops just arrived from Egypt it must have seemed a familiar sight.

From the north one can also see most dramatically the hostile cliffs, bleak when the sun powers down from overhead and more dangerous still when it casts deep, expressionist shadows among the pitted ravines, that run back from the Sphinx to Walker's Ridge around Mule Gully. The view of the gully from sea-level is one of rugged hills and scrubby spurs that squash together in a chaotic heap, clambering over each other as they reach up to the plateau on top; the climb looks difficult but not impossible. However, staring down into the narrow twisting gully from the summit induces a feeling of nauseous vertigo. Out of the hard, sheer cliff a host of knobbly vertebrae twist and turn their rocky way down from the Sphinx and Russell's Top towards the beach. It is a testament to the energetic determination of the Australian soldiers on 25 April that, after landing in the second wave, Lieutenant

Colonel Lancelot Clarke ordered the men of his 12th Battalion, together with some remnants of the 11th Battalion who had landed in the first wave, to attack this ground from the beach and drive the Turks off the summit to relieve the pressure on a small group of men who were crouched at the foot of Walker's Ridge. Almost incredibly, Clarke and fifty of his men actually succeeded in reaching Russell's Top along this route. He was killed shortly afterwards.

Once on the high ground, his men linked up with those who had stumbled over Razor Edge. Together they began to drive the outnumbered Turks back across the flat ground of Russell's Top via the Nek towards Baby 700, the first peak in the chain of hills that led up to Chunuk Bair. By 10.00 am they had pushed on as far as the rear slopes of Battleship Hill, the peak beyond Baby 700; but at this point the initiative passed from Australian to Turkish hands. The retreating Turks had been met on the slopes between Chunuk Bair and Battleship Hill by the Commander of their 19th Division who had been ordered to defend these hills. Appreciating the threat that their seizure by the enemy would pose, he decided to move up his whole division and had preceded it there to assess the situation. 'Fortunately for the Turks the commander of the 19th Division was none other than Mustafa Kemal Bey, the future President of the Republic; and that Man of Destiny was at once to show an outstanding genius for command.'[20] He immediately

The bleak, hostile cliffs surrounding Mule Gully seen from the junction of Russell's Top and Walker's Ridge with the rear profile of the Sphinx in the centre and Ari Burnu Cemetery on the protruding tip of coastline on the right. (April 1998)

stopped the stragglers and ordered them to turn and stand. When he discovered that they had little ammunition, he decided on bluff and told them to fan out across the hill with their bayonets showing. The Australians saw this change of attitude, hesitated and the momentum of their advance was arrested. Soon Kemal's own men, with the three battalions of the 57th Regiment in the vanguard, began to arrive and the Turks were able to start pushing the Anzacs back down towards Baby 700.

Throughout the day this hill changed hands five times and by mid-afternoon the Anzac units were made up of men from seven battalions with no senior officer to exercise an authoritative command. By 4.00 pm the Turks, still mostly drawn from the one division and under the leadership of Kemal, were once again pressing hard at its summit and this time they won it decisively and retained it for the whole campaign. The forward units of Australians had been annihilated. Those who could fell back through the Nek to Russell's Top. There they dug a weak line, whilst behind them, at the head of Walker's Ridge a stronger line was established. In roughly these positions the lines became set. The Turks regained possession of the Nek, but the Anzacs remained on Russell's Top. Brigadier General Harold Walker, Birdwood's chief staff officer who had replaced the sick Colonel Francis Johnston in command of the New Zealand Brigade at the landings, was placed in command of the left flank which now ran back from the Nek and down the crest of the ridge that eventually bore his name. The whole area became heavily fortified with deep trenches running along Russell's Top and down Walker's Ridge. Only a few weeks later the trenches there had already 'become a perfect maze'.[21] The two sides faced each other squarely across their impregnable defences. It was a stalemate. The Anzacs would never be turned out; but neither would they ever be able to move forward.

The trench system that developed at Anzac was quite different from anything experienced elsewhere in the war. The nature of the ground, the lack of space, the enthusiasm of the Anzac diggers, all combined to produce trenches that remained unique. What struck visitors most was their depth. The hot weather that blossomed in May dried out the sandy soil until, as hard as stone, the Anzacs were able to dig it out much more easily and much deeper than the sticky clay and high water table of Flanders allowed on the Western Front. The main communication trenches soon became over six feet deep with room to spare at the top and an ironic standard was devised to describe the optimum size. 'The men call an ideal trench a Godley-Braithwaite trench; that is, tall

General Birdwood and General Godley in one of the deep Anzac trenches. (Q42322)

enough for General Godley and broad enough for Colonel Braithwaite.'[22]

These sandy channels wove for miles over the flat ground of Russell's Top and 400 Plateau, the flat expanse of ground that lay behind the line on the opposite side of Shrapnel Valley, and along the narrow ridges in between. Dugouts were scooped out of the side and smaller, lateral trenches cut across creating the avenues of the maze. The digging went on throughout the summer, long after the positions had become unassailable. The men who dug them began to take an intense pride in their work, as if aware that they were creating a permanent monument. In the preparations for the assault on Sari Bair a trench was dug near No.2 Outpost that became known as Millionaire's Sap, 'so called because it was made by six Australians, each the son of a millionaire'[23]. However, in the middle of its construction their regiment was relieved. But the men 'refused to go down with their battalion until they had finished their job, as they wished it to be known as their job and no one else's.'[24]

As the builders exhausted the space available behind the lines they simply went deeper, beneath the ground in front of them. It was more than just mining. They developed a technique, as used at the start of the attack on Lone Pine, of tunnelling out a complete new line beneath the ground and then blowing out the roof to deliver 'rather a nice surprise packet for Mr. Turk'.[25] On 12 October Hamilton visited Russell's Top with his ADC and nephew, Lieutenant Alec McGrigor. Both of them recorded what they saw in their diaries.

> *By jove! The Australian trenches are a perfect eye-opener, and are simply magnificent. They are certainly the most wonderful thing I have seen on the Peninsula. There is a wonderful system of subterranean passages being bored right up to the Turks' lines; I was taken down one place opening on to a crater which is less than 20 feet, not yards, from the Turkish trench.[26]* (Lieutenant Alec McGrigor)

> *Ex-westerners say that in France they have nothing to touch these Australian tunnellings. In one place they are boring into a crater only 20 feet from the Turkish trench. There is nothing unusual in the fact, but there is in the great depth they are going down so as to cross the danger zone far below the beaten tracks of mines and counter-mines. On the steep slope in another place there is a complete underground trench running parallel to, and only a short bomb throw from, a Turkish trench. We went through it with a lantern. Sandbags, loopholes, etc., all are there, but blind! They are still veiled from view by several feet of clay. Tomorrow night the Anzacs are going to chip off the whole upper crust of earth, and when light dawns the Turks will find a well equipped trench, every loophole manned, within bombing range of their own lines.[27]* (Sir Ian Hamilton)

Even at the last hour they were still digging. A week before the evacuation Birdwood, then in command of the whole peninsula, visited his old lines at Anzac. He wrote, in great distress, to Hamilton about the continuing enthusiastic efforts of the men to make their lines fit for winter, describing how they had dug chambers twenty feet deep with several entrances so that if one was closed by a mine or explosion, another would remain open. They were displaying great ingenuity, as they had always done. In the creation of this astounding network the men of Anzac had revealed their greatest strength. Ask them to dig and they would dig deeper. Ask them to build and they would build larger. It was all a challenge, a serious game. And they won.

These unique trenches are still extant. Over the broad expanse of Russell's Top today they still weave a confusing maze of thick, sharp leafed bushes that fill up most of the depths, giving the impression of an even surface. But there are sections that can still be followed from inside for about thirty yards. Their original depth is still obvious, for, despite eighty years of infilling and erosion, they remain at least three feet deep, often more. Unlike the wide, grassy remains on Vimy Ridge and Beaumont Hamel, their sides are steep and neatly cut. Tin cans, open and full, lie scattered about, and although their present state would suit neither Godley nor Braithwaite no doubt both would be able to find their way along the routes they followed then.

The easiest way onto the plateau is beyond Walker's Ridge Cemetery where the dirt track from the Nek curves round its wall. Branching off it a narrow path winds its way into the scrub. Briefly skirting the top of the very steep cliffs, it plunges deep into the thickets, wandering along the top of the dusty parapets. At each meeting and division of the trenches the path disappears, to be replaced by a similar one that goes off in a new direction. Finding one's way about is tricky and the Cross of Remembrance at the back of the cemetery acts as a useful reference point. Keeping to the right, though, eventually brings one to the back of the Sphinx. From there, taking care to stand well back, one can gaze down into the violent shadows of Mule Gully, cast across the ground that Clarke and his men climbed.

A bit further on the tip of Russell's Top is reached where Razor Edge drops away towards Plugge's Plateau separating Rest Gully on the left from Reserve Gully on the right; from this angle the crossing looks more difficult still. Moving back into the centre of Russell's Top, the flat ground leads over towards the edge of Monash Gully. At first the drop down into this looks steep, but gradually appears to flatten off towards the bottom of the bed. Along the bank a number of lifeless trees have fallen, adding a new colour to the varied shades of green and straight ahead, across the gully, the rear slopes of Second Ridge mirror the scene.

Walker's Ridge Cemetery stands about two-thirds of the way back along the length of Russell's Top and from it a rocky escarpment falls away towards the sea along the crest of the ridge itself. To the right a breathtaking panorama of the foothills of Sari Bair sweeps along the coast to Suvla. When the sun is glinting on the placid sea and the small clouds of dust are swirling across the fields beneath the tractors of the invisible farmers, when the shimmering magic of the Salt Lake contrasts with the blue-black outline of the Kiretch Tepe Sirt, it is a magnificently beautiful view. Walker's Ridge runs on a level with the high ground of Russell's Top only for the first fifty yards of its north-westerly course before it starts to drop gradually down. A narrow path, about eighteen inches wide, can be carefully followed along the crest, and from it the ridge appears to be similar in shape to MacLagan's Ridge, except that it has a secondary, smaller ridge curling back into Mule Gully.

The junction of Walker's Ridge and Russell's Top comes a hundred and fifty yards behind the Nek where the Anzac left flank ended. The front line here was a long cul-de-sac which dropped down to its final end at Turks Point above Happy Valley, straddling the western end of the narrow funnel that led on to the slopes of Baby 700. Once it had been lost to the Turks on the afternoon of the first day the Nek was never recaptured. The most concerted attempt to do this formed the basis of the Peter Weir film, *Gallipoli*. On the whole this fine film clearly recreates this one episode, while simultaneously managing to evoke much of the pathetic tragedy and ironic humour that characterized the campaign. But it is seriously flawed in the implication that the death of the 234 men here was a direct result of the British troops sitting nonchalantly on the beach at Suvla. In fact although the Suvla campaign was happening simultaneously, and on the early morning of 7 August the British troops there were beginning their attack on Hill 10, it bore no direct relation to the Anzac attacks at the Nek and Lone Pine.

The attack on the Nek was a feint attack designed to support the combined Australian and New Zealand assault on Sari Bair. It was hoped that by the time the Light Horsemen attacked, the New Zealanders would have captured Chunuk Bair and be working their way down through Battleship Hill to Baby 700. The attack on the Nek would be against an enemy already heavily engaged in their rear. They would therefore be split and forced to defend themselves on both fronts. This would have reduced the strength of the formidable defences which they had constructed on their narrower end of the Nek. In the end it was the failure of the Anzac troops engaged in the assault on Sari Bair that allowed the Turks holding the Nek to concentrate their fire power on the Australian Light Horse to such devastating effect.

The attack was carried out by the 8th and 10th Australian Light Horse, troops newly arrived. The events were much as they are portrayed in the film and in the resulting massacre died many men from Victoria as well as 'the flower of the youth of Western Australia, sons of the old pioneering families, youngsters - in some cases two and three from the same home - who had flocked to Perth at the outbreak of war with their own horses and saddlery in order to secure enlistment in a mounted regiment of the A.I.F.'.[28] The Turks had built a redoubtable double line of trenches, equal to anything the Anzacs had yet constructed, that was only twenty-five yards wide and just sixty yards from the Australian jumping-off trench. Set into it were at least five machine guns. The majority of the dead fell 'in an area smaller than a tennis court' just beyond the front line trench.[29] Three months after the attack McGrigor visited this part of the front and described the bodies that were still clearly visible. 'One can see many of the men still lying out there in the 'No Man's Land' with packs on their backs and water bottles complete; the bodies, though, are now mere skeletons. One body was within 30 yards of our parapet, and could never be got at.'[30] The cemetery has virtually no headstones because of this. The bodies could not be buried until 1919 and out of 326 buried in the cemetery 316 are buried as unknown soldiers. It is an empty, arid rectangle with an area of 948 square yards.

Men of the Australian 10th Light Horse in their trenches.

Thirty yards back down towards the Australian position from the cemetery's rear wall the old Anzac front line, from where the ALH charged, still runs down the narrow width of the saddle to Turks Point. The surviving trenches, still deep enough to enclose a standing man, have been revetted with heavy timber props in the standard artificial style used to preserve key points such as this and the redoubt around the Yahya Çavus Memorial above V Beach. Yet although this will no doubt ensure their long term survival, it also removes something of the mystique exuded by the remains of the real, unadulterated trenches that can still be found in abundance elsewhere. Using the Anzac line and the ground in front of it, it is still possible to work out the events of the attack. Crossing the scrub beyond the trench, barely forty paces wide, the wall of the cemetery is reached. A further sixty paces beyond it stands the Memorial to Mehmet Çavus with its flag-poles and surrounding trees. Combined these landmarks provide a salutary reminder of how very short the ground was over which the charge was made.

The main road curves away from the Nek, between the top of Pope's Hill set off to the right and the Chessboard to the left, before rejoining the road from the museum at the start of its climb up to Chunuk Bair. About two hundred yards beyond the junction it reaches the main monument that has been built in the Anzac area by the Turks in recent years. The 57th Regiment, which Mustafa Kemal deployed to such great effect on the morning of 25 April, was principally drawn from Anatolian Turkey rather than the further reaches of the Ottoman empire and considered to be the most efficient and strongly motivated element of the 19th Division. Over the weeks that followed the landing it became the focal point of the dogged Turkish defence along this northern flank of the Anzac line, throwing itself repeatedly into the fray and incurring very heavy casualties. In the process it acquired an almost legendary status. Today, near the Chessboard, a fitting and sensitively laid out cemetery has been built largely to record the deeds of this Regiment. Across to the south-east, near Scrubby Knoll in the centre of Third Ridge, can be seen one of the few genuine Turkish graves from 1915. It contains the body of Yarbay (Colonel) H Avni Bey, the commanding officer of the 57th Regiment who was killed on 13 August. It is fitting that his men should also now be permanently commemorated on the battlefield where they died.

As at Helles above S Beach, a number of symbolic headstones have been erected. But the power of the cemetery derives not from these individual markers, but their combined strength. They form a collective memorial to all the Ottoman soldiers who died at Anzac, or Ariburnu as it was known to them. In a fine uplifting perspective, a wide open archway draws the eye of visitors across the neat rows of headstones to a slender three storey tower lodged at the cemetery's head. In contrast to the homogenous Occidental style of the Commonwealth cemeteries that surround it, the Turkish memorial strikes a distinctively eastern note and delicately highlights the cultural differences that separated the two sides. Directly opposite the gateway to the cemetery is a statue of the last surviving Turkish veteran of the campaign shown holding the hand of his granddaughter who has brought flowers to honour the dead. Hüseyin Kaçmaz served for eleven years in the Turkish army, fighting first at Gallipoli, then in the Balkans and between 1919 and 1922 the War of Liberation. In April 1991 he flew to London to attend the Anzac Day parade at the Cenotaph in Whitehall and two years later attended the opening ceremony of the Turkish Memorial here at Anzac. He died in Ankara in September 1996 aged 106.

The statue of Hüseyin Kaçmaz, the last surviving Turkish veteran of the Çanakkale War, and his grand-daughter attending the opening of the 57th Regiment Cemetery in 1993. (April 1998)

Around two hundred yards beyond the 57th Regiment Cemetery the road reaches Baby 700 which during the campaign was one of the key Turkish observation posts and is now ironically marked by an Anzac cemetery formed entirely after the war by the concentration of individual graves and bodies found on the battlefield. From the summit of Baby 700 the flagpoles of the Mehmet Çavus Memorial on the Nek and the tower of the 57th Regiment Cemetery on the Chessboard can easily be seen, marking out the extremities of the Turkish line that contained the apex of the Anzac position. Beyond them a wide panoramic view unfolds of the whole battlefield. Looking back up towards Baby 700 from almost anywhere in Anzac, these two features seem to crown the head of the high ground that looks down onto Russell's Top, Second Ridge and Monash Gully. This is the view that

The Turkish 57th Regiment Cemetery positioned at the northern apex of the original Anzac line beyond Quinn's Post near the Chessboard. (April 1998)

the visitor must see to appreciate the vulnerability of everyone contained within the fortress walls; as astounding as the size of Anzac Cove is the ease with which the Turks could watch the heart of Anzac beating.

Pope's Hill to Steele's Post

Like the delta of a great river, Pope's Hill stands at the head of Monash Gully while round its base two small, shadowy streams diverge. On the afternoon of 25 April Lieutenant-Colonel H Pope was ordered to bring up his 16th Battalion to bridge the gap that had opened up between the ends of the lines at the Nek and the northernmost point reached on Second Ridge, a position later called Quinn's Post, and for the rest of the campaign, although never linked in any continuous way to either side, an outpost line ran across the top of the hill. At first it could only be reached out of Monash Gully but later on a tunnel called Bully Beef Sap was built to provide a more permanent link between its base and the plateau on Russell's Top. Looking down towards it from Russell's Top today, Pope's Hill is difficult to discern because its scrub blends like the skin of a chameleon with the background of Quinn's Post beyond. But from that reversed position a bare earth cliff reveals the outline of the hill as it rises up out of Monash Gully. Capped by a slight scrubby plateau, despite climbing gently upwards, the hill fails to reach the level of the surrounding high ground, remaining just below it in a lee of shadow.

From the road that runs along this higher ground just above the top of the hill itself there is a clear view down into Monash Gully. The high banks pull away like outstretched arms, with the right arm of Russell's Top slightly higher than the left of Second Ridge. At the far end, the junction with Shrapnel Valley that can be seen from Plugge's Plateau is just obscured by Braund's Hill. But above it looms the vast, flat expanse of 400 Plateau with the dominating memorial of Lone Pine to the left. It is the first in a series of panoramas that link up the different features of the Anzac line into one single, coherent position.

A gap of about 150 yards existed throughout the campaign between Pope's Hill and Quinn's Post. All attempts by the Australians to fill it were thwarted by the heavy fire from Baby 700. But, likewise, the Turks were also prevented from exploiting the gap by the severity of the cross-fire from the Australian positions on either side. The nature of this dangerous no-go area inspired a number of evocative names to describe the different parts of the gap. Above Pope's Hill, between it and Baby 700, was the Chessboard, named after the complicated network of intersecting trenches, where the 57th Regiment Cemetery is now situated. To the south on a small, flat hilltop jutting out into Monash Gully on the same level as Pope's Hill was Dead Man's Ridge, the name referring to the bodies of the Royal Marines who lay across it after the failure of their attempt to capture it on 3 May. At the south-eastern end of this, beside the point where Second Ridge also narrowed down to a saddle of land similar to Russell's Top at the Nek, was Bloody Angle. All of these areas, although unoccupied, were securely held by carefully positioned machine guns.

Running south from there along the backbone of Second Ridge were the three independent posts that formed the northern half of the front line. A useful mnemonic as to the order in which they ran is that QuinN's Post was to the North, Courtney's Post in the Centre and Steele's Post in the South. All three were named after the officers who established the outposts there in the days following the landings, Lieutenant Colonel R E Courtney and Major T H Steel being in the 14th Battalion and Major Quinn the 15th. The name 'post', which they were given, is misleading because it suggests a small, isolated position held by only a few men; but in fact these positions were usually held by up to a battalion each, with most of the garrison housed in dug-outs on the rear slopes above Monash Gully and only a few holding the large bays which formed the line.

At first each of the posts was isolated, like Pope's Hill; but slowly over the course of the ensuing months tentative communications were established between them, although these never became really secure. The opposing Turkish positions were similarly held and the trenches of both sides were so close along the narrow ridge that there was room for only one trench each. Often the same trench was held by both sides, a hurriedly built sandbag traverse being the only barrier between them, and distances between the lines varied, sometimes being as great as thirty to forty yards, sometimes as little as five. Today the parallel courses of these two lines run invisibly along each side of the road.

During the first week of May, while both sides were settling down to the conditions of siege warfare, tensions were high along the ridge. The Turks soon resorted to bombing, having a plentiful supply of cast iron bombs. But the Anzac supply was meagre and mostly based on jam-tin bombs manufactured down on the beach. To begin with the contest was very one sided; but slowly the Anzacs improved, learning out of necessity the delicate art of throwing these home-made bombs. Precautions were also taken in the form of netting barricades to ward off the less energetic attempts to lob bombs into their trenches and the situation gradually eased; but it remained difficult throughout the campaign. However, the slightly freer atmosphere did allow the more playful soldiers to develop competitive games with the Turks. One such game was described by Birdwood in a letter to Hamilton after one of his trench inspections.

> As I say, I went through both these Posts, and found all the men keen as possible at nearly every loophole and sniping whenever they got the chance. In places they had got periscopic rifles up where they were able to enfilade some distant Turkish trenches, and regular matches were going on between them in the Turk shooting line. One Turk had deliberately waved a wash-out with his spade, but unfortunately for himself, raised his head shortly afterwards, and at once got a bullet through it. Another man waved a small flag also making a wash-out signal, but in putting his hand over the parapet he got a bullet through it, and dropped the flag like a hot potato![31] (Lieutenant General Sir William Birdwood)

On 19 May the Turks launched a strong attack against the whole of the Anzac line, but it was these posts that bore the brunt. It was a fierce and bloody fight that came to be called the Defence of Anzac. 'The assailants came on so thick, the ground to be covered was so narrow ... that the Anzacs had but to fire point-blank into the half-visible darkness before them, and at every shot an enemy fell. Many Australians mounted the parapet, and, sitting astride upon it, fired continuously, as in an enormous drive of game.'[32] For many it was a welcome opportunity. The frustrations of trench warfare that had been built up, the tensions of living so close to a largely invisible enemy, old scores from the landing, all could finally be released. Ashmead-Bartlett described how, in response to Birdwood's questioning after the attack, 'another happy warrior remarked: "You put 'em up for us, General, and we'll shoot all you want".'[33] But after a while for most the thrill began to pall. As the Turks kept surging forward in their hundreds and the sporting drive became a nauseous massacre, even the Anzacs found it hard to go on having fun.

Australians and men of the Royal Naval Division using a periscope rifle at Anzac. (Q13427)

Opposite Courtney's Post a small group of Turks did succeed in breaching the Anzac line where it was being held by the 14th Battalion and from their anonymous ranks another Anzac legend arose. While an officer maintained covering fire on the front, Lance-Corporal Albert Jacka worked his way behind the group of Turks and stormed their trench. Quickly he shot five of them and polished off the remaining two with his bayonet and the first Australian of the war had won a Victoria Cross. In the illustrated war newspapers it became a favourite scene, a fitting popular symbol of the Australians' achievements at Gallipoli which had so caught their imagination.

After the attack had finally exhausted itself, thousands of Turkish dead lay thick upon the inland slopes that ran

Lance-Corporal Albert Jacka VC.

away towards Mule Valley. It was soon appreciated that a temporary armistice would need to be arranged if, in the intimate proximity of the two lines, the Australians were to avoid being forced down into Monash Gully by the stench and filth of the decaying bodies. Captain Aubrey Herbert set about the arrangements in characteristic style, visiting Hamilton at GHQ on Imbros the next day and Sahib Bey, the Turkish general, two days later. A cease-fire was arranged for 7.30 am on 24 May, to allow for the collection and removal of all the offending bodies except those that had become part of the actual defences. No trench improvements were to be made. In his diary Herbert recorded this unique occasion in considerable detail, beginning with his walk along the line from its southern end.

We walked from the sea and passed immediately up the hill, through a field of tall corn filled with poppies, then another cornfield; then the fearful smell of death began as we came upon scattered bodies. We mounted over a plateau and down through gullies filled with thyme, where there lay about 4,000 Turkish dead. It was indescribable. One was grateful for the rain and the grey sky. A Turkish Red Crescent man came and gave me some antiseptic wool with scent on it, and this they renewed frequently. There were two wounded crying in that multitude of silence. The Turks were distressed, and Skeen strained a point to let them send water to the first wounded man, who must have been a sniper crawling home. I walked over to the second, who lay with a high circle of dead that made a mound round him, and gave him a drink from my water bottle, but Skeen called me to come on and I had to leave the bottle. Later a Turk gave it back to me. The Turkish Captain with me said: 'At this spectacle even the most gentle must feel savage and the most savage must weep.' The dead fill acres of ground, mostly killed in the one big attack, but some recently. They fill the myrtle-grown gullies. One saw the result of machine-gun fire very clearly; entire companies annihilated - not wounded, but killed, their heads doubled under them with the impetus of their rush and both hands clasping their bayonets. It was as if God had breathed in their faces, as 'the Assyrian came down like the wolf on the fold.'[34] (Captain Aubrey Herbert)

Strict rules were supposed to govern the conduct of both sides. Neither were to collect dead from positions that would allow the bearers to observe closely the other side's lines. There was a great deal of anxiety over the collection of rifles from the dead; but eventually it was agreed that both sides could remove them without the bolts, although some claim the Australians went out on patrol the night before and had already brought the best ones in. Rumours of infringements were rife. It was reported that Turkish staff officers were walking about the lines dressed as Red Crescent men, even that both Mustafa Kemal and Liman von Sanders, the German Commander-in-Chief, used the same ruse to take personal looks around. On the right of the line between Steele's Post and Wire Gully a group of German officers were seen and from that time on the position was known as German Officer's Trench. But although both sides were wary, all things went well.[35]

> Our men gave cigarettes to the Turks, and beyond the storm-centre at Quinn's Post the feeling was all right.... The burying was finished some time before the end. There were some tricks on both sides. Our men and the Turks began fraternizing, exchanging badges, etc. I had to keep them apart. At 4 o'clock the Turks came to me for orders. I do not believe this could have happened anywhere else. I retired their troops and ours, walking along the line. At 4.7 I retired the white-flag men, making them shake hands with our men. Then I came to the upper end. About a dozen Turks came out. I chaffed them, and said that they would shoot me next day. They said, in a horrified chorus: 'God forbid!' The Albanians laughed and cheered, and said: 'We will never shoot you.' Then the Australians began coming up, and said: 'Good-bye, old chap; good luck!' And the Turks said: 'Oghur Ola gule gule gedejekseniz, gule gule gelejekseniz.' (Smiling may you go and smiling come again). Then I told them all to get into their trenches, and unthinkingly went up to the

Removal of the Turkish dead at Anzac on 24 May during the burial armistice. (Q42315)

Turkish trench and got a deep salaam from it.... At last we dropped into our trenches, glad that the strain was over. I walked back with Temperley. I got some raw whisky for the infection in my throat, and iodine for where the barbed wire had torn my feet. There was a hush over the Peninsula.[36] (Captain Aubrey Herbert)

A small Turkish Memorial now stands on the site of Turkish Quinn's commemorating not only the heavy losses of 19 May and the failure of the attack to drive the invaders into the sea as they had intended, but, ironically, also their eventual success in containing the Anzac forces within their original line.

The three posts are spaced about 200 yards apart, each occupying a small lobe sticking back into Monash Gully. In the centre of the line, from Courtney's Post, the distance north and south to the other two can be seen from the position of the two cemeteries that now stand on these outer positions. Behind them, on the rear slopes, where the broken dugouts and overgrown trenches that climbed the steep bank out of Monash Gully have collapsed and fallen in, the ground is too dangerous to explore, except for a few yards around the northern edge of Quinn's Post Cemetery. In summer the dry scrub becomes very brittle, failing to bind together the soft earth which is eroded more each year, and it crumbles quickly underfoot. But it is possible to stand carefully at the top and gaze down at the rough, undulating ground trying to understand how a battalion of men could be billeted there.

Monash Gully to Lone Pine

Running south from Steele's Post the road bends inland slightly at German Officer's Trench, before it crosses over another narrow neck of land, called MacLaurin's Hill after Colonel H N MacLaurin, the Commanding Officer of the 1st Australian Brigade, who was killed by sniper fire near here on 27 April. Beside the road a small path leads down away from Wire Gully on the left as far as the isolated Fourth Battalion Parade Ground Cemetery. It is a steep, meandering path, once called Bridges Road after the Commander of the 1st Division, with a few steps cut out of the earth to aid descent, and from it one can see straight down the extended length of Shrapnel Valley to Hell Spit. The cemetery, established on a piece of relatively flat ground where companies could collect on their way in to and out of the line, rests on the side of a ridge named Braund's Hill after Lieutenant Colonel G F Braund, Commanding Officer of the 2nd Battalion, which leads off

MacLaurin's Hill at a right angle into the centre of the valley beyond. Above the cemetery the crestline of Braund's Hill reaches down towards a small knoll from where the ground falls away sharply to the right, dropping and bending round, like a hook. Inside the hook, on the right flank of Bridges Road, there is a wide, open gully like a small copy of Rest Gully and at its end a squat plateau towers above the paths and valleys that surge around its base.

From here the most comprehensive view of Anzac unfolds, in a complete panorama of the inner keep. Directly in front are Hell Spit and Beach Cemetery, with the outline of Plugge's Plateau rising gently up to the right to its crest from where Razor Edge continues off to the right across the top of Rest Gully on to Russell's Top. Jutting out above the climbing slope of this is the rear of the Sphinx's outcrop. At the far end a straight line of rock, possibly Bully Beef Sap, runs down the inland slope to the foot of Pope's Hill above which to the left is the Nek Memorial. On the higher ground to the right, beyond Pope's Hill and the small plateau of Dead Man's Ridge, is the ground of the Chessboard and the 57th Regiment Cemetery; between Dead Man's Ridge and the cemetery of Quinn's Post, Bloody Angle. Then, running back from Quinn's Post the rear slopes of, first, Courtney's and then Steele's Posts merge into those of MacLaurin's Hill out of which runs Braund's Hill. On the opposite side of Bridge's Road, with Johnston's Jolly and Lone Pine on its inland edge, 400 Plateau sweeps round to the sea, tumbling down over Philip's Top and McCay's Hill into White's Valley to arrive again at Hell Spit. In one single sweep, as can be done at Helles from Gully Spur, most of the tiny Anzac fortress can be see from one position. But whereas at Helles to see clearly what was happening on Hill 138 from Fifth Avenue an observer would have needed binoculars, at Anzac the slightest movement could be seen by the naked eye along the barrel of a sniper's rifle.

Through the centre of this panorama creeps the long, dry watercourse that ends at the foot of Pope's Hill. It starts beside Shrapnel Valley Cemetery at Hell Spit, where the track is about a foot wide and heavily overgrown, passing under the interwoven branches of holly trees and is not easy to follow. It twists along, with small tributaries cutting off it in both directions, rarely leaving the cover of the overhanging branches that all but obscure the sides of the hills towering over it. But from the top of the hills the trail of its sandy soil can be easily traced. Across from MacLagan's Ridge, on the edge of 400 Plateau, the opposite bank of Shrapnel Valley is thickly covered. It was on this area, at the mouth of the valley, that the shrapnel rained heaviest in the first few days of the fighting and which 'to the last ... was so harassed by rifle fire that it retained its thick coating of scrub, as being too dangerous for dugouts or any movement of man.'[37]

There, where the bed is wide, a number of small tributaries, like White's Valley, Bridges Road and Rest Gully, branch off the main Shrapnel Valley before it reaches its junction with Monash Gully. As it approaches this point, the hills on either side start to rise up more steeply, squeezing the path into a narrower course. As it moves from valley to gully the path changes direction, turning north-east to run almost parallel with the sea. It passes between the tall sides of Russell's Top and the base of the hooked plateau as if through a gorge and turns an S-bend first to the right and then to the left before opening out on to the smooth rounded slopes behind the three posts of Second Ridge. It is a single, continuous road that still meanders round the traverses that General Bridges ignored.

Here the Anzacs lived from April to December, stacked precariously on top of each other like residents in decaying tenement flats, 'practising the whole art of war'.[38] There they slept beneath the stars and the whispering whistle of spent bullets. In among today's fallen trees, on slopes that they wore bare by constant tramping, they washed, sang and played two-up. They lived a kind of life that no one had ever lived before and would never live again, a unique community of men.

> *Men staggering under huge sides of frozen beef; men struggling up cliffs with kerosene tins full of water; men digging; men cooking; men card-playing in small dens scooped out from the banks of yellow clay - everyone wore a Bank Holiday air; - evidently the ranklings and worry of mankind - miseries and concerns of the spirit - had fled the precincts of this valley. The Boss - the bill - the girl - envy, malice, hunger, hatred - had scooted far away to the Antipodes. All the time, overhead, the shell and rifle bullets groaned and whined, touching just the same note of violent energy as was in evidence everywhere else.*[39]
> (General Sir Ian Hamilton)

In the beginning the men all seemed fit. When not in the line they worked long hours carrying stores up from the beach. The sun was hot and, then as now, in the depths of the valley the wind was slight. To keep as cool as possible the Anzacs began to peel off and discard their clothes.

> *Since the Dervishes made their last charge at Omdurman no such naked army has ever been seen in the field. The British Tommy likes to move and work and fight with the majority of his*

worldly goods round him, no matter what the state of the temperature. *The men in our front trenches sit with their packs on, sweating in the broiling sun, and will dig trenches without removing a garment. But to find an Australian in the hot weather wearing anything except a pair of 'shorts' is extremely rare, whether he be in the trenches, in a rest camp, or on fatigue. One by one they throw aside their various articles of clothing. First the coats go, then the shirts, then underclothes, a very large*

Early dug-outs and bivouacs at Anzac lodged on the rear slopes of the hills only a short distance beneath the front lines. (HU53361)

number throw aside their boots and putties, and only a lingering
feeling of decency still kept alive by memories of the mixed
bathing season at Sydney preserves the 'shorts,' which, starting
at full-length trousers, eventually arrive half-way up the thigh. In
this primitive costume the Australians and New Zealanders lived
and worked and fought on the peninsula. Their huge frames and
giant limbs became burnt by the sun to a dull brick red.[40] (Ellis
Ashmead-Bartlett)

There they lived, colonels next to privates, Monash next to Jacka.
From there they went down to the sea to bathe, to clean off and forget;
from there, when they could, they carried their mates to the cemeteries
on the shore. It was a teeming place; a city of life and death, where the
tides of energy and spirit washed incessantly over the hills. Today
although the waters have receded, along the banks this invisible spirit
still lies like flotsam from the wreck of a magnificent ship. The sun is
bright, the languid air still prevalent. There is laughter in the wind and
animation in the slow movements of the scrub. One can feel the
stripped down, sunburnt soldiers strolling up the long neglected paths,
along the trenches to the shallow remnants of the old front lines; and
in their presence life remains at Anzac.

From MacLaurin's Hill the road crosses the centre of 400 Plateau
towards Lone Pine, following the approximate course of the front line.
It was on the large open expanse of the plateau that some of the fiercest
of the fighting took place after the landing as the troops who landed
after the covering force were sent to the right in an attempt to break out
into Legge Valley and on to the slopes of Third Ridge beyond. The
inland edge of the plateau is made up of two lobes, divided by Owen's
Gully. The first and smallest is Johnston's Jolly. 'The name was due to
a repeated saying of Colonel J. L. Johnston (11th West Australian
Battalion) that if only he could bring howitzers instead of field guns to
bear on it, he would have a "jolly good time there".'[41] Today a small
cemetery to the east of the road, containing mostly men killed in the
first days of the campaign, stands on the site of the Turkish front line.

Opposite to it a thin line of trees forms a screen along the top of the
drainage ditch that runs alongside the road. Through the overlapping
shadows one can see the light, open ground of the western half of 400
Plateau. Scrambling over the ditch almost anywhere, a vast network of
surviving trenches is soon encountered. Frequently up to four feet
deep, they wind their back towards the distant sea, twisting, turning,
climbing, falling through the crisp, dry undergrowth. The whole of this
part of the plateau is still riddled with the trench system of that part of

the Anzac front line known as the Pimple. Wide channels cut through the surface towards Brown's Dip with countless lateral alleyways linking them together. All around the debris lies. To the south the wide protuberance of Bolton's Ridge spreads out like a shelf above Brighton Beach. It falls slowly away towards Shell Green Cemetery where, on the flat field around it, the Anzacs once played cricket and in the late summer coloured flowers covered the ground.

Looking inland from the Pimple the tip of the Lone Pine Memorial, positioned over the Turkish trenches that were captured in the attack, reaches out above the handful of trees that survived the fire. This view shows the extent of the Australian advance - about 200 yards. The attack on the Turkish positions along this part of the line, stretching as far north as German Officers Trench, was another of the subsidiary attacks linked to the offensive at Sari Bair. From May to July this southern lobe was known to the Turks as Kanli Sirt or Bloody Ridge; but the environmental effects of their trench improvements reminded the Australians more of a popular song back home, 'Lonesome Pine'. So they gave it that name, inspired by 'a solitary tree which the Turks had left standing alone out of a small wood or fringe of firs lining their side of the ground. They had cut down the rest for their dugouts or head cover, and in fact the solitary pine itself was felled just before the attack, or even on the very morning, but the place kept its name.'[42] Before the attack the line curved forward in a salient round this point. The distance from there to the Turkish trenches was about 150 yards, and in order to cross it and by-pass the worst of the clogging, waist-high scrub that grew around the wire in no-man's land, the Australians employed their system of hidden front lines. A new line of underground trenches was secretly tunnelled out, complete with an instant communication trench. Immediately prior to the attack mines were blown along this to open it, and the infantry attacked from these new, unsuspected positions.

Trench debris found in the extant trenches near the Pimple on the seaward half of the Lone Pine plateau. (July 1987)

The preceding bombardment lasted for three days. It had been carefully planned so that its successive stages, shrapnel to destroy the wire and heavy shells to soften the Turkish line, would not alert the Turks to the coming attack. After an hour of intensive bombardment, at 5.30 pm on 6 August, four waves of troops attacked the Turkish position. It was then that they unexpectedly found the whole of the opposite front to be fortified with thick lengths of roofing timber. But the Australians had achieved such a degree of surprise that many passed right over and leapt into the communication trenches beyond, entering the line from the east. While some began to haul off the roof timbers, others fired blindly into the widening gaps and through the sandbagged loopholes. A fierce fight quickly developed in the dark, overcrowded trenches, with sections being cleared only to be reclaimed by bombing parties hours later. This intense fighting lasted for over two days. Much of it focused on a small, previously unnoticed gully that ran off the main position into Owen's Gully called the Cup and it was not until 12 August that the Australians had sufficiently consolidated the achievement to call it won.

> Throughout these days of incessant fighting the spirit of the Australian troops was beyond praise, and so great, and almost embarrassing, was the anxiety of the rank and file to take their share in this historic action that at one period the unique precaution had to be taken of posting piquets in the communication trenches leading to Lone Pine to prevent unauthorized men from going into the fight. Reserve troops would wait in long queues for a chance of pushing their way forward, and sums of five pounds and upwards were freely offered, and offered in vain, by employed men in rear to take the place of friends going up to the front line. No less than seven Victoria Crosses were awarded for gallantry at Lone Pine.[43]
> (Official History)

Hamilton recognized this gallantry in his final despatch in terms reminiscent of those used to describe the landing of the 29th Division at Helles in April.

> The irresistible dash and daring of officers and men in the initial charge were a glory to Australia. The stout-heartedness with which they clung to the captured ground in spite of fatigue, severe losses, and the continual strain of shell fire and bomb attack may seem less striking to the civilian; it is even more admirable to the soldier.[44] (General Sir Ian Hamilton)

Such was the reputation that these men won for Australia to match that gained upon the cliffs above Anzac Cove. It was a foretaste of what they were to do on the Western Front. Finally at Lone Pine the flame of Australian national pride had found its own triumphant furnace.

It is here, to this place, that the Australians now come. For over the field of their last great attack at Gallipoli the Memorial to all their missing dead has been erected. Underneath the bleak white terraces, buried like the dead, run the vanished trenches. The Cup has also been covered over by the landscaping and building; but, beside the edge of the road its tip still falls into the trees of Owen's Gully. From all the heights of Anzac, the Memorial dominates the view like a folly set in an ornamental scene intended to add perspective and depth. It is built out of limestone like a large, exaggerated version of the Cross of Remembrance that stands behind all the cemeteries. But here there are four relief crosses, facing all the points of the compass. It is an impressive but subdued structure, taking its reflected grandeur from the names along the memorial wall which, unusually, have been carved and painted to give each letter a rich, blood-red heart. Building the memorial on this commanding spot was no easy matter, the builders having to 'construct an aerial ropeway two and a half miles long to carry materials from Ocean Beach'.[45] However, the result is a fine, impressive tribute to the men who disappeared into the ground beneath.

The cemetery that unfolds towards the Australian line is widely spaced and about the same size as the large British cemeteries at Helles. It is one of the few such cemeteries built retrospectively at Anzac and split into two distinctive plots. The easternmost, beneath the memorial, is the original Lone Pine Cemetery of 46 graves, enlarged by the later concentration in it of a number of individual battlefield graves. The other western plot beyond the avenue that cuts across between the entrances was moved there from its original position in Brown's Dip. It had been started there at the head of Victoria Gully

The Lone Pine Memorial at Anzac, built over the trenches taken at such cost in August, recording the names of all those Australian soldiers who were lost in the main Anzac area from April to December but who have no know grave and those New Zealanders who also died there prior to the start of the August offensive. (April 1998)

after the August attack, but the site proved to be unstable. So its two plots were moved after the war and placed as one at the other end of the larger cemetery on Lone Pine. Ironically this practical act has significantly helped to develop the cemetery's atmosphere. By doubling its size, the concentration has imbued it with a greater sense of distinction that matches more closely its position at the foot of the Memorial.

From the terraces above the Memorial wall there is a clear view forward to Third Ridge. A concrete plinth now marks the high ground of Scrubby Knoll reached on the morning of 25 April by Lieutenant Noël Loutit with a small scouting party. From there 'he could see only $3\frac{1}{2}$ miles away, the gleaming waters of the Narrows - the goal of the whole campaign'.[46] It was the closest that any Allied soldier would get. At the south-western end of Third Ridge the journey from Brighton Beach is completed by regaining sight of the slight raised headland of Gaba Tepe.

That is Anzac.

A total area, from Gaba Tepe to Walker's Ridge and from Anzac Cove to Quinn's Post, of about 3 square miles; or, as Alan Moorehead described it, 'not much bigger than Regent's Park'.[47] At Ari Burnu the Turks have erected one of their characteristic concrete memorial plinths. It was unveiled on Anzac Day, 1985 by the Australian Minister for Veterans' Affairs to commemorate the seventieth anniversary of the landing and proclaims in English a statement sent by Mustafa Kemal, by then known as Atatürk, to greet the Anzac visitors of 1934.

> *Those heroes that shed their blood and lost their lives ... You are now lying in the soil of a friendly country. Therefore rest in peace. There is no difference between the Johnnies and the Mehmets to us where they lie side by side here in this country of ours ... You, the mothers who sent their sons from far-away countries wipe away your tears; your sons are lying in our bosom and are in peace. After having lost their lives on this land they have become our sons as well.* (Atatürk)

Positioned there, it acts as an explanation to all visitors as to why Anzac is calmer and less haunted than the ground at Helles. The dead lie still within the ground, undisturbed and respected; it is their bones that lie buried not their past ordeals. At Anzac no ploughed and cultivated earth has been allowed to douse the flame.

The memorial plaque at Ari Burnu, unveil on 25 April 1985, which bears the messag sent by Mustafa Kemal Bey, by then known Atatürk, to greet the British and Anz visitors of 1934. Memorials bearing the sam words were also unveiled on the same day Wellington, Canberra and Albany. (July 198

Chapter Five

THE AUGUST OFFENSIVE

Exactly a week after the landing the Anzacs made one final attempt to move forward, with an attack on Baby 700 from the head of Monash Gully. The attack was a failure and, as a result, Sir William Birdwood began to consider alternatives to another direct assault against the Turkish line. Ten days later, on 13 May, he laid down in a letter to Sir Ian Hamilton the foundations of the plan that would eventually become the assault on the Sari Bair Ridge in August. Birdwood explained his belief that a headlong assault, like that which had recently failed at Helles, could be avoided by carefully moving his men up the coast to outflank the Turkish defences before turning them sharply inland to climb the steep hills of Sari Bair. Independently, unauthorized reconnaissance of the hills was being undertaken by the New Zealand Mounted Rifles who had just taken over Nos.1 and 2 Outposts, the two small posts that had been established along the northern shore beyond Walker's Ridge after the landing. Led by Major P J Overton a scouting party entered the complicated foothills to the east and discovered two essential facts. First, it was possible to follow the deres up on to the higher slopes inland and, second, at that time there appeared to be no Turkish defenders barring the route. At ANZAC headquarters, the significance of these discoveries confirmed Birdwood's premise and, after a detailed map of the whole Anzac area was discovered on the body of a Turkish officer killed in the Defence of Anzac, his belief was finally able to be translated into a definite plan.

The scheme submitted to GHQ on 30 May was smaller in scale than that which was finally executed. Birdwood explained that he hoped to turn the Turkish positions by simply 'making a big sweeping movement round my left flank to the Sari Bair Ridge.... My plan would be to attack the ridge with three brigades of a total of about 8000 men and occupy a position Hill Q - Chunuk Bair - Battleship Hill.'[1] Significantly, the highest peak, Koja Chemen Tepe, was not at that stage included as it was believed to be isolated from the other three peaks by steep precipices. The plan recognized that the nature of the ground would make the assault a difficult one; but it was hoped that it would still be within the capability of the 29th Brigade of the Indian Army. Like both Birdwood and Hamilton, they were veterans of the

Indian North-West Frontier and considered experts in the kind of country then under examination. This one unit was all that Birdwood felt he would need to expand his Corps into one capable of both holding Anzac and attacking on the new front.

To Hamilton it was a very attractive scheme. For a comparatively small investment he was offered great strategic rewards. From the three main peaks of the ridge the Anzacs would have a clear view eastwards to the Narrows, northwards to Suvla and directly to the south along the main Turkish positions opposite the old Anzac position. Positioned there, Birdwood's troops would be firmly astride the southern end of the Peninsula; a fact that Mustafa Kemal had appreciated so quickly on the morning of 25 April and continued to stress to his superiors throughout the following months. Above all, it was Kemal who understood most clearly the value of the Sari Bair range. For, 'it was not distance that counted on Gallipoli, nor even the number of soldiers or the guns of the fleet; it was a simple issue of the hills.'[2]

On 8 June Hamilton heard from Lord Kitchener at the War Office that the three remaining New Army Divisions - the 10th (Irish), 11th (Northern) and 13th (Western) - were to be made available to him to allow a renewal of the offensive. This fact significantly altered the situation. There now existed the possibility of a larger operation instead of just a localised attack out of Anzac. The alternatives were re-examined. Of them all Birdwood's plan remained the most promising; but now, with more men available than had been expected, the new attack from Anzac could be expanded. The most advantageous extension appeared to be at Suvla Bay to the north.

Since the appearance of the *U21* the security of the fleet had become impossible. However, it was felt that Suvla Bay, about two miles long and just over one mile wide, could eventually be secured against submarine attack by a net across its mouth and a permanent naval presence re-established. Opening off the bay the flat, cultivated plain was protected by a ring of high hills which, if taken and secured, would offer the army a similarly secure base unlike any other available on the peninsula. It appeared that the whole Suvla area was only lightly defended. A dynamic attack inland against these hills would provide both an additional threat to the weakened Turks at Anzac and protection to the exposed left flank of the Australians and New Zealanders as they wheeled round over the foothills of Sari Bair. The seizure of the Suvla hills would then allow the final line to be extended up from Anzac through the new line to the Gulf of Saros.

While these matters were being debated a more significant decision was being taken, one that would eventually decide the outcome of this new attack. Who was to command the operation at Suvla? The three divisions had been organized into the IX Corps and as Corps Commander Hamilton had in mind either Lieutenant Generals Sir Henry Rawlinson or Sir Julian Byng. Kitchener would not consider either, but insisted the choice be made from the senior generals who remained in Britain. This raised a delicate problem for the 10th Division had been raised by Lieutenant General Sir Bryan Mahon, and it was felt that he should be allowed to lead his division into battle. Mahon had no wish to command the IX Corps and Hamilton did not want this either; but any alternative commander would have to be senior to him. There were only two possibilities: Lieutenant General Sir John Ewart and Lieutenant General Sir Frederick Stopford.

Ewart, Hamilton felt, was now the wrong shape for Gallipoli and he had been desk-bound for too long to endure the peculiar hardships of command on the peninsula. Stopford had served his whole life in the Army 'and his courtesy and personal charm had won him the affection of all who came in contact with him. But in 1915 his health was far from good, and he had never before commanded troops in war.'[3] He had been in retirement for over five years and neither his character nor experience suited him to the command. Yet as a result of his seniority he remained the only serious candidate.

Stopford arrived at Mudros on 11 July, but was not shown an outline of the plan for eleven days. By then it had been expanded further and in addition to the new landing it had been decided to add two feints, one at Helles at the Vineyard and the other at Anzac at Lone Pine. Birdwood's simple plan was now a great offensive, like 'a chain reaction, a succession of explosions from south to north';[4] but in this expansion its integrity had been lost. During the wait for the IX Corps the Turks had begun to take notice of the unprotected deres that led up on to Sari Bair and two months of lethargic weather, debilitating sickness, and tense and unfit living conditions had also changed the character of the men who were to carry out the most arduous element, the assault on the hills.

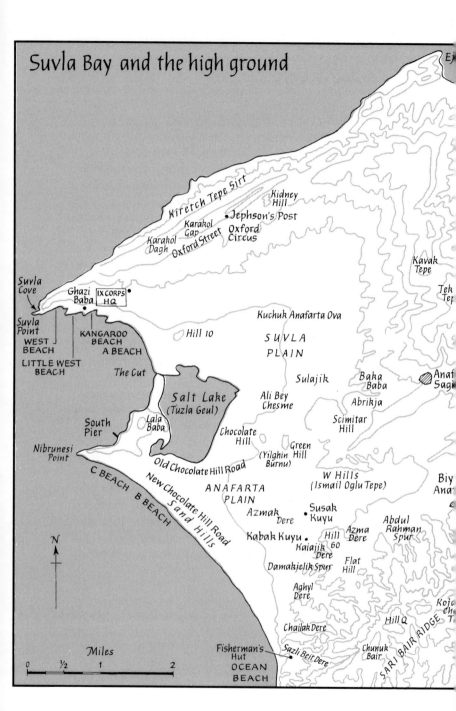

Suvla Bay and the high ground

Ej

Kiretch Tepe Sirt

Kidney Hill

Jephson's Post

Karakol Gap

Oxford Circus

Karakol Dagh

Oxford Street

Kavak Tepe

Tek Tep

Suvla Cove

Ghazi Baba   IX CORPS HQ

Suvla Point

WEST BEACH

KANGAROO BEACH

A BEACH

LITTLE WEST BEACH

The Cut

Hill 10

Kuchuk Anafarta Ova

SUVLA PLAIN

Sulajik

Baka Baba

Anaf Sagi

Salt Lake (Tuzla Geul)

Lala Baba

Ali Bey Chesme

Abrikja

South Pier

Chocolate Hill

Scimitar Hill

Nibrunesi Point

Green Hill (Yilghin Burnu)

Old Chocolate Hill Road

ANAFARTA PLAIN

W Hills (Ismail Oglu Tepe)

Biy Anα

C BEACH

B BEACH

New Chocolate Hill Road

Sand Hills

Azmak Dere

Susak Kuyu

Abdul Rahman Spur

Kabak Kuyu

Hill 60

Azma Dere

N

Kaiajik Dere

Flat Hill

Damakjelik Spur

Aghyl Dere

Koj ch T

Chailak Dere

Hill Q

Miles

0   ½   1   2

Fisherman's Hut

Sazli Beit Dere

Chunuk Bair

SARI BAIR RIDGE

OCEAN BEACH

Chapter Six

THE ASSAULT ON SARI BAIR

The Sari Bair, or yellow hill, Ridge is made up of the north-easterly range of hills, approximately two miles long, that climbs gradually up via a series of peaks from the northern end of the Anzac positions along Second Ridge. It culminates in the highest peak on the peninsula east of the Narrows named Koja Chemen Tepe, known more simply by its height in feet as Hill 971. Looking north from the base of the Lone Pine Memorial, the eastern slopes of the ridge show a gentle face. Starting first at Baby 700 they roll along past Battleship Hill towards Chunuk Bair (850 feet), the central and most important feature of the range. Barely discernible is the further climb of fifty feet from there to Hill Q which is characterized by two distinctive peaks. Beyond this the slopes move slightly back to the east before they make the final climb to Hill 971.

This gradual rise from Baby 700 to Hill 971 of just 90 yards and its direct course through a string of equidistant peaks can be best appreciated from across the Salt Lake at Suvla. From there one can also see the radically different face of the western slopes, a maze of deres hewn from the rock by the water that flows from the crestline in winter. These deep deres merge into three main valleys that lead parallel off the hills to the west. In the south, the Sazli Beit Dere enters the sea just below Fisherman's Hut, called Balikji Damleri in Turkish. 400 yards to the north lies the Chailak Dere and 1000 yards beyond this the Aghyl Dere, the widest and deepest of the three. These ravines are the main routes down from the slopes to the sea. Further round to the north-west two more lead down in the direction of Anafarta, skirting round the small knoll of Hill 60 with the Kaiajik Dere to the south and the Azma Dere to the north.

In between each of these deres there is, of course, a spur of high ground. Once again the Gallipoli landscape can best be simplified by using the model of a right hand, this time with the palm flat on the table with the fingers widely spaced. The little finger represents the Abdul Rahman Spur, pointing north-west with the peak of Hill 971 on its knuckle. Next to it the third finger is the Damakjelik Spur leading up to the peaks of Hill Q. Between the tip and joint of the middle finger is Bauchop's Hill, with Cheshire Ridge between the joint and the knuckle. Finally, with Chunuk Bair between the knuckles of the index and the middle fingers, along the index finger the spur of Rhododendron Ridge runs down through the Pinnacle and then the Apex towards the peak of Table Top on the joint. The thumb, some distance to the south-west, leads down through Battleship Hill and Baby 700 to Walker's Ridge at Anzac.[1]

Yet this simplicity is deceptive. In June Hamilton noted in his diary that 'the ground between Anzac and the Sari Bair crestline is worse than the Khyber Pass';[2] but little detailed reconnaissance of it was actually possible. The hills could be observed from the sea and Major Overton's forays were able to confirm many of the loosely held opinions; but most of the final, adopted plan was based on map work. With regards to Sari Bair this was as good as guessing. For the clarity of a map, like the simplicity of a model, belies the actual small-scale complications of the ground.

The plan was based on a pincer movement in which two columns of assaulting troops would swing round on to the hills along the three main deres. The Left Assaulting Column was intended to march north, turn east and attack Hill 971 and Hill Q by climbing up the Aghyl Dere. The Right Assaulting Column aimed to converge on the peak of Chunuk Bair along the Sazli Beit and Chailak Deres. The initial obstacles at the entrances to these routes were to be cleared previously by two corresponding covering forces. The Left Covering Force was to set out three hours before its assaulting column to clear the northern bank of the Agyhl Dere by seizing the tip of the Damakjelik Spur and fanning out to protect the column as it swept up towards the higher ground. The Right Covering Force had a more specific objective. Half were to move into the Chailak Dere to clear the wire barricades; having done this they were then to wheel to the left on to the first hill of the spur, subsequently called Bauchop's Hill after Lieutenant Colonel Arthur Bauchop of the Otago Mounted Rifles who was killed in the attack. The remainder were to assault the first two hills that overshadowed the Sazli Beit Dere. In the middle of May the Canterbury Regiment had pushed a detachment inland from No.2 Outpost on to a round plateau that thrust up from the surrounding low hills. They had called the new post No.3 Outpost. But on 30 May the Turks had recaptured the hill and turned it into a very heavily defended fortress. The New Zealanders were forced back down towards sea level where they established a new No.3 Outpost, just north of No.2. The first action of the Sari Bair assault would be the recapturing of the Old No.3 Outpost.

The assault began late on the evening of 6 August and although the first attacks were successful it soon became clear that the operation was too ambitious and the men incapable of matching it. Delays began to occur, even in the work of the covering forces. The assaulting columns, marching over longer routes and through more complicated country, began to lose their way among the dead ends of the maze. Isolated Turkish snipers, lodged in invisible, inaccessible positions, held up whole bodies of men. There was no way round until each could be removed. Above all, debilitated by sickness and strain, the troops stood little chance of reaching the high ground. Skill and expertise were irrelevant as stamina and morale began to flag with first light. By dawn on 7 August, when they should have been upon the summit starting their push back down the ridge towards Baby 700 and the Nek, the assaulting columns still found themselves on the shelf of almost level ground at the head of the deres, still 200 feet below the crestline. From the Right Assaulting Column the Canterbury and Wellington Battalions launched one final effort along Rhododendron Ridge, reaching the Apex by 8.00 am. On their left they established tentative

A tin of biscuits being opened by soldiers from the 14th Sikhs, part of the 29th Indian Brigade which played such a central role in the assault on Sari Bar. (Q13651)

contact with the Gurkhas from the Left Assaulting Column who had reached the plateau known as the Farm. Beyond the Aghyl Dere the 4th Australian Brigade had climbed onto the Damakjelik Spur and established themselves along the crest, known to the Turks as Yauan Tepe or Flat Hill, which led down to Hill 60 but they could go no further.

Plans were drawn up during the day for a new attack in which the troops would move to seize the crestline, fulfilling the intentions of the original plan. Some reinforcements were sent forward, but substantially the situation remained as before. At dawn on 8 August the second assault began. The New Zealanders at the Apex expected a heavy fight for Chunuk Bair; but their initial advance was unopposed. The summit was empty and the Wellington Battalion, under Lieutenant Colonel William Malone, established themselves in the old Turkish positions. But, to the south the Turks on Battleship Hill soon realized what had happened and began to enfilade the New Zealand line from the Apex to the summit. As casualties increased, the Turks gradually began to return, forcing the New Zealanders off the summit on to its rearward slopes. But still the Wellingtons held. To their north a new attack on Hill Q had not been successful. Many of the new troops who had been sent up to join it during the night had lost their way, as the assaulting columns had done the night before, and arrived too late to attack with the men who had been in position overnight. Only the 1/6th Battalion, Gurkha Rifles, commanded by Major Cecil Allanson, moved forward, finding the slopes below Hill Q to be as empty as Chunuk Bair. They established themselves 100 yards below the summit and Allanson brought up reserves from the disorientated troops he found below him; but there was little more they could do that day.

A third attack would be necessary on 9 August to capture Hill Q and raise the line so that it could link up with Chunuk Bair. A new column of troops was established to attack up the slopes between Hill Q and Chunuk Bair from the Farm. But, as had happened before, the advance of the column was delayed and it failed to reach its jumping off point in time for the attack. Unaware of this, on the slopes of Hill Q, Allanson's Gurkhas waited throughout the night for the naval bombardment of the Turkish line to begin. When, just after dawn, it finally lifted, the Gurkhas and a handful of New Army stragglers were ready to scramble forward over the short distance to the summit. They surprised the Turks and slowly began to push them back down the western slopes towards their rear lines. Casualties along the crestline were severe, but in front of them, 'like a white serpent sliding between the purple shores', lay the Narrows.[3] Then, suddenly, everything went wrong as shells started to fall among the triumphant soldiers as they pursued the retreating Turks. The Gurkhas' Medical Officer described what happened several years later.

The noise of the battle became more and more deafening when it was suddenly interrupted by six massive explosions of shells fired by the Navy, who evidently mistook our Gurkhas for Turkish troops.... The results of those six mighty explosions, Allanson said, were ghastly, at such close quarters, and led to a sudden retreat of the troops to the line from which they started. The blast was so tremendous that, although protected by the ridge, I was blown backwards heels over head out of the fox-hole, but I was not hurt.... Allanson stayed a little while on the ridge, gazing, as he said, on the 'Promised Land', but soon saw that the attack had failed, and that the Turks were massing for a counter-attack.[4] (Major Selby Phipson)

For many years controversy raged about who had fired the shells. The troops themselves, as Phipson says, believed them to be naval. In a letter to Hamilton on the next day Birdwood explained that 'it was a very dull morning and probably very difficult to see, and some of the ships landed some of their fire just too low'.[5] But Philip Schuler, the Australian correspondent, doubted whether, had they been fired from a ship over the summit of Hill Q, they could have landed so close to the crestline. In *The Dardanelles Campaign* Nevinson followed up this idea with the suggestion that the shelling had more likely been from an Anzac field gun intending to catch the Turks as they retreated down the rear slopes. On balance this would appear to be the clearest explanation; but the possibility of a naval error resurfaces in the light of Robert Rhodes James's reference to the unrecorded shelling of the Wellington Battalion on Chunuk Bair on the previous day.[6] Whatever the explanation, as Birdwood continued to Hamilton, 'on such a piece of bad luck ... we have lost so much'.[7]

On the morning of the following day, 10 August, at 4.45 am, under the inspirational leadership of the ubiquitous Mustafa Kemal, the Turkish forces on Sari Bair launched their counter-attack in two dense waves that swept over the summit of Chunuk Bair. One ran down the Pinnacle and attacked the Apex, to be stopped there by the New Zealand machine-guns, the few troops still beneath the summit and near the Pinnacle being annihilated. The second poured down the steep slope on to the small plateau of the Farm. There a grim battle developed between the scattered remnants of the column from the previous day and the men spurred on by Kemal, until both sides were too exhausted to continue. No official account of this fight exists because no officer involved survived to tell the story. 'The Farm plateau, forsaken by both sides, was held by the dying and the dead.'[8]

This was the effective end of the fighting on Sari Bair. No new offensives could possibly be launched in the immediate future. Where the units had come to rest would be the final line. It ran from the Apex on Rhododendron Ridge across Cheshire Ridge to the Damakjelik Spur. None of the objectives had been achieved. The now Major Aubrey Herbert, who had commanded the Maori detachment in the Right Covering Force, concluded that 'it's on the same old lines, on the hills we are the eyebrows and the Turks are the forehead'.[9] The crestline remained as far from capture as it had always been. It had beckoned like a massive door promising that through there lay the road to the Narrows and its seizure had been the only way forward at Anzac.

Baby 700 to Chunuk Bair

Gazing down towards the Aegean from the crestline of Sari Bair today, the intervening hills appear almost unfathomable. In order to understand the events that took place amongst them, visitors must first establish the intricate relation of the deres to the spurs; only by taking careful note of the shapes and positions of each can they then make any sense of them at all. Yet from the top of the hills there is little chance of doing this. At the beginning of its account of these operations the Official History tried to convey this problem to its readers.

> No account of the operations ... can hope to convey any adequate idea of the extreme difficulties of the undertaking if the reader does not first try to visualize the bewildering nature of the country through which the troops were to move. The spurs and gullies are so contorted, so rugged and steep, and so thickly covered with dense prickly scrub, that their passage is difficult enough, even in peacetime, for an unencumbered tourist provided with a good map and setting out in the full light of day. In August 1915 the only available maps were very inadequate, and these arduous routes had to be traversed at night by heavily laden men, who were harassed by an invisible enemy and led by guides who themselves had little real knowledge of the ground.[10]

Eighty years after Aspinall-Oglander himself returned with a map in peacetime, it is once again virtually impossible to distinguish the individual features of the landscape.

A thin scattering of pine trees weave their way across the upper reaches of the deres and the seaward face of the crestline, obscuring further the essential contours of the ground. By the time of the fire the trees had grown so thick that they formed a heavy blanket which completely smothered the landscape, replacing the severe, hostile rock formations with an incongruous uniformity. From the edge of the Chunuk Bair summit no clear view could be had down to the coast, or even further afield to Suvla. But with most of these trees now gone, even though the scrub has once again covered the earth itself, one can see the longer vistas across the intervening hills. Yet even so this provides little elucidation.

> No analysis or map or description can adequately express the roughness and complexity of that desert jungle, the steepness of its cliffs and spurs and edges, or the bewilderment of its dry watercourses, creeks, fissures, and ravines. Neither in the British island or in Ireland is there a scene to compare with it, because in our islands the frequent rain and prevailing moisture smooth off the edge, fill the ravines with water, and cover even the crags with moss and ferns or grasses.[11] (H. W. Nevinson)

The summit of Chunuk Bair, where the New Zealanders established their position on 8 August, is a triangular plateau with the highest point situated in the northern vertex. It sits directly in the centre of the range with the modern road passing along its eastern edge. The road starts its climb at the fork lodged between Quinns's Post and the 57th Regiment Cemetery. Where the left road swings round to the Nek, the right rises up past Baby 700 before swinging round between it and Battleship Hill. Just beyond this feature stands a statue commemorating the heroic efforts of Talat Göktepe, the Director of the Çanakkale Forest Service, who died fighting the fire on 25 July 1994. At the start of the campaign both Baby 700 and Battleship Hill were held to be part of the same peak, 700 feet high, so the two were distinguished by individual names; the larger one appearing like the prow of a battleship emerging from the hillside, the smaller one a 'baby' beside it. However, like so many details on the original maps, this was not entirely accurate and in fact the two were separate hills with Baby 700 '50-100 feet lower than Battleship Hill, which overlooked it'.[12]

It was on these lower slopes that the Australians' forward parties encountered Mustafa Kemal on the morning of 25 April, coolly awaiting his reinforcements. His decisive action here was the first of a series of brilliant strokes that helped to counter the Anzac threat along this northern section of front. His subsequent anticipation of

Birdwood's plan and awareness of the vulnerability of the hills, helped keep him alert to the possibility of an attack upon them. In the penultimate paragraph of his Epilogue Aspinall-Oglander acknowledged this central role of Kemal, 'that "Man of Destiny"'.[13]

> It was that officer's ready grip of the situation on the 25th April which was primarily responsible for the failure of the Anzac corps to gain its objectives on the first day of the landing. It was his vigorous action on the 9th August, when entrusted at a moment's notice with the command of the northern zone, that checked and defeated the long-delayed advance of the IX Corps. And, twenty-four hours later, following a personal reconnaissance, it was his brilliant counter-attack at Chunuk Bair which placed the Turks in undisputed possession of the main Sari Bair ridge. Seldom in history can the exertions of a single divisional commander have exercised, on three separate occasions, so profound an influence not only on the course of a battle, but perhaps on the fate of a campaign and even the destiny of a nation.[14] (Official History)

Having established his reputation on Gallipoli, Kemal was able to lead the uprising against the Treaty of Sevres in 1923, drive out the Greeks in the War of Liberation and reclaim Gallipoli along with Turkey's other European territory. From there he progressed further, reshaping the whole political structure of the country to found the present day Turkish Republic and add to his name the title Atatürk, Father of the Turkish people. Throughout the country his picture appears and his reputation endures, a reputation founded and galvanized here on the slopes of Sari Bair.

Beyond Battleship Hill, where Kemal had his headquarters for the early part of the campaign, the road reaches a T-junction. Turning left it swings round to approach the summit of Chunuk Bair and the two

The ring of Turkish memorial plaques on the lower slopes of Chunuk Bair. Note the tip of the New Zealand Memorial on the higher summit of the hill emerging from the trees on the left. (August 1988)

sets of memorials to be found there. The first, on the south-western end of the plateau, is the imperfect ring of curved, concrete columns that form the Turkish Memorial. They give the impression that the Memorial is intended to commemorate the achievements of Kemal as much as the Turkish soldiers who died on the Anzac front. The five columns have been placed in a rough semi-circle to symbolize the fingers of a hand reaching up towards the sky, 'praying and thanking to GOD', and the inscriptions describe, in sequence, the successful defence of the ridge from 25 April to 10 August.[15]

Between the Turkish Memorial and the higher peak beyond, a steep dirt track runs off the crest of the hill to the left along the course of Rhododendron Ridge. At first the ridge was 'called Canterbury Ridge' but soon the more familiar name arose, derived from the flowers that grew profusely upon it.[16] Nevinson explained that at the time of the assault the surface was 'brilliant with the crimson oleander, which our men call rhododendron'.[17] However, in 1962 Mr R. J. Alexander of the CWGC told Robert Rhodes James 'that he had never seen oleanders on the Peninsula, and considered that the flowers were almost certainly a small bright red flower which grows in profusion early in the summer'.[18]

From the Apex, initially known as 'the Mustard Plaster', as the track starts to fall off precipitously down towards the Chailak Dere, there is a clear view northwards along the sides of Chunuk Bair.[19] In the centre of the view is perched the forlorn handful of graves that make up the Farm Cemetery. Most of those killed in the bloody battle on 10 August were never found. Following the disappearance of the trees in the fire the cemetery's wall can be seen once again from the summit, nestling quietly at the foot of the slope down which the Turkish counter-attack swept.

Beyond the Farm the middle finger stretches out over Cheshire Ridge towards Bauchop's Hill. In the small dip between them, near the joint, a 'plateau of about one acre jutting right up into the sky in a most peculiar formation (such as one sees in Saxon Switzerland) with

No.2 OUTPOST   TABLE TOP

Chunuk Bair to No.2 Outpost from the western edge of the summit, with Rhododendron Ridge running from the Apex (extreme left) to Table Top (the slight scrub covered rise in the centre) which in turn leads first to Old No.3 Outpost and then No.2 Outpost (the small peak to the left of centre before the crestline begins to fall away to the sea). (April 1998)

apparently sheer sandstone cliffs on all sides' identifies the peak of Little Table Top.[20] Across to the left, beyond the Chailak Dere, the similarly shaped but larger Table Top stands out bleakly between the end of Rhododendron Ridge and Old No.3 Outpost. In this country lay the Anzac line. Hewn out of the rock, the hilly terrain invested the trenches with unique properties. Even compared to old Anzac the gradients were steep and the angles acute. Following Godley from his headquarters in No.2 Outpost Herbert plied the route regularly. He found it 'a weary business walking through these narrow mountain trenches'. Yet he also found variety in the way they were kept up. 'The trenches are curiously personal. Some are so tidy as to be almost red-tape - the names of the streets, notices, etc., everywhere - and others slums.'[21]

No doubt he would have found the line of rather overclean and well constructed trenches that have been rebuilt on the edge of the hillside for the interest of visitors to be an ironic example of rarely achieved perfection. The line is based on the formidable redoubt that the Turks built around the base of the peak once the summit had been cleared. After touring the Anzac line beneath this part of the front in September Hamilton described to Kitchener the heavy fortifications that were rapidly being constructed on the summit:

164

> *The approaches along the upper north-western slopes were formerly quite clear of any entrenchments, whilst the top itself had never a spade struck into it. Now there is a mass of works on the top surrounded by a long loop of a communication trench about 100 yards down the slope on our side; beyond this again a string of sandbag redoubts joined together by communication trenches.[22]* (General Sir Ian Hamilton)

He may have had in mind Birdwood's earlier ironic parallel of Chunuk Bair to the landscape of South Africa that they had both encountered there. 'As the little American Attaché said to me at Colenso when he saw the Boer position, 'Say, is there no way round?' That is rather what it has come to here.'[23] Near the northernmost end of the redoubt Mustafa Kemal came dangerously close to being fatally wounded when he was hit by shrapnel. His life was saved by the watch that he kept in his breast pocket. Near the spot where this occurred, replacing a modest notice that formerly recorded this fact, there is now a massive new statue reflecting his undiminished stature as a Turkish hero.

Turning round to climb back from the forward edge of the slopes to the actual peak of the hill, the graceful form of the Chunuk Bair Memorial rises up. It is an elegant obelisk of glistening stone, visible from both the Narrows and the Aegean, with a wide base on which stands an octagonal column that strikes a stark contrast to the epic grandeur of Kemal's statue beside it. On every other face of the column

The Farm Cemetery beneath the seaward face of Chunuk Bair looking north to Suvla Bay. Beyond the level plateau of the cemetery lies first the scrub covered mound of Cheshire Ridge, with the Chailak Dere tracing a barren course to its left, and then the flatter outline of Bauchop's Hill, with the Aghyl Dere beyond. In the middle distance the features at Suvla lead left to right from Nibrunesi Point through Lala Baba (directly in front of the bay) across the Salt Lake (filled with water) to Chocolate and Green Hills (known collectively as Yilghin Burnu). On the horizon the Kiretch Tepe Sirt climbs gradually up from Suvla Point. (April 1998)

LALA BABA

KIRETCH TEPE SIRT

CHESHIRE RIDGE

The New Zealand Memorial on Chunuk Bair recording on engraved panels overlooking the nearby cemetery the names of the large number of New Zealanders who died in the Sari Bair area from the beginning of the August offensive to the end of the campaign. Other New Zealanders who have no known grave are commemorated on the Lone Pine Memorial and the smaller memorials in the Twelve Tree Copse and Hill 60 cemeteries which record respectively the names of those who died at Helles in May and in taking Hill 60 in August. The crowd gathered round the base of the Memorial and the firing party to its left are preparing for the service of remembrance that took place there on 25 April 1998. To the right can be seen the recently erected statue of Mustafa Kemal.

there is a buttress and of the three Commonwealth War Memorials in Gallipoli this is perhaps the most impressive. The simple inscription on its base emphasizes that it commemorates one group of men in particular. On all their memorials, in Gallipoli, France and Belgium, the New Zealanders proudly proclaim that they came: FROM THE UTTERMOST ENDS OF THE EARTH.

When standing on Chunuk Bair it is important for visitors to be aware that it was they who took the summit and they who, with the support of a few British battalions, held it for two days. It was here, on the slopes of Rhododendron Ridge that the first New Zealander of the war, Corporal Cyril Bassett, a bank clerk from Auckland, won his VC for keeping open communications between the forward party on the summit and the support line on the Apex. It is important because the powerful legend of Anzac is usually told as if of Australians only. Part of the reason why this has occurred is that the 'Anzacs' have since been treated as a homogeneous unit, when quite obviously they were not. The different cultures of their homelands produced two distinctive styles of fighting. 'The Australian fighter was an individualist. He

Chunuk Bair Cemetery on the eastern slopes of the hill looking across to Mal Tepe (the rounded peak to the left of centre), the original Anzac objective on 25 April, and beyond it the Narrows north of Çanakkale. The original photograph shows the human remains laid out for re-burial after the war. In the most recent shot the three trees in the distance on the right are held to mark the spot where Mustafa Kemal spent the night before leading the decisive counter-attack against the Farm plateau on 10 August. **(1919/1998)** (Q14338)

would go off and fight his own battle in his own way. And he didn't take very kindly to discipline.'[24] The New Zealanders developed a more sophisticated style of their own. They were 'equally brave, equally tough soldiers. But you could talk to a New Zealander almost as you would to English people. ... You didn't have the same rapport with the Australians who were a rougher diamond.'[25]

It is right to remember this on the slopes of Chunuk Bair. Standing almost at the furthest end of the long ridge that starts at Gaba Tepe, the New Zealand Memorial is the opposite pole to the Australian Memorial at Lone Pine. Most of Anzac lies between them. But unlike the stolid power of Lone Pine, both the Chunuk Bair Memorial and the quiet cemetery that stands on the eastern slopes looking out towards Çanakkale and the Narrows seem very reserved, more sensitive. The obelisk is strong, but it inspires respect not awe, and the reason for this lies in the difference between the two nations. Herbert observed the way the handful of survivors from his Maori detachment would collect together in Old No.3 Outpost after the assault had failed.

> When the day's work was over, and the sunset swept the sea, we used to lean upon the parapet and look up to where Chunuk Bair flamed and talk. The great distance from their own country created an atmosphere of loneliness. This loneliness was emphasized by the fact that the New Zealanders rarely received the same recognition as the Australians in the Press and many of their gallant deeds went unrecorded or were attributed to their greater neighbours. But they had a silent pride that put these things into proper perspective. The spirit of these men was unconquered and uncontrollable.[26] (Major Aubrey Herbert)

It is an atmosphere that still lingers round the summit today. Whether it derives from those men who took the hill or from the tragedy of its recapture, both here and at Hill Q despite the number of bustling Turks who come to visit the scene of Kemal's triumph, an air of sadness hangs, like the heat mist over the bewildering foothills, on the summit of Chunuk Bair.

Reserve Gully to the Aghyl Dere

Down on the coast road which runs north from Ari Burnu, looking back up to the crestline, everything appears much clearer. The broad, open spaces around the mouths of the deres and the singular shapes of the features which cluster closely above them produce a series of more easily understood perspectives. By studying each of these in turn the

The outposts along the coast viewed from Walker's Ridge, with the Suvla Plain and Kiretch Tepe Sirt in the distance. In the immediate foreground is the ridge running down from Turks Point which divides Happy Valley from Malone's Gully. Beyond this, in the centre, is No.1 Outpost and, across the mouth of the Sazli Beit Dere, the larger No.2 Outpost. Note the Great Sap which connects them. Along this strip of shoreline North Beach merged into Ocean Beach. **(1915/1988)** (Q13429)

woven strands of the foothills can gradually be disentangled and what appears unfathomable from the summit finally clarified. Along the complete length of the coast a strange phenomenon slowly becomes apparent which helps to explain why this should be so. The north and south faces of the spurs and hills are opposites. Those facing south are bare and sandy; but those facing north are thickly covered in scrub. Consequently when searching over the foothills from Anzac the shapes of the individual hills can be easily picked out. But when looking back down in the opposite direction from Chunuk Bair the hills are smooth and indistinct, blending seamlessly into each other.

At Ari Burnu the road bends round briefly before beginning its long northern haul up towards Suvla. As it straightens up, the scrub reaches out from its inland edge into the side of Reserve Gully. High up, a faint path appears to wind slowly back and forth across the central stream-bed beneath the shadow of the Sphinx; but its starting point cannot be reached. The entrance to the gully is barred by a dense area of low scrub which, despite its open appearance, is in fact very thick and covered with a crisp carpet of small, brown flowers formed from the desiccated seed heads of wild cistus. Five hundred yards along from the bend the road reaches Canterbury Cemetery, the first of five cemeteries which line the route between here and Suvla. From behind the cemetery there is a panoramic view into the various gullies and features that surround Walker's Ridge. To the right the bleak sides of Mule Gully cut into Russell's Top along the northern side of the Sphinx's outcrop. Directly opposite, across the deep parabola of the gully, the path which runs along the crest of Walker's Ridge levels out in a small plateau before the crest continues down towards sea-level, splitting just before the end around the two pronged foot of the ridge.

To the left, beyond Walker's Ridge, a strip of rock formed by the flat, seaward shoulder of land which runs down from the Nek ends abruptly in Turks Point. Between the two lies Happy Valley. Further round to the north of the cemetery, three hundred yards in from the coast, is the site of No.1 Outpost, shaped like an upturned bowl, with the western edge climbing up gradually from the level of the coast on to a small flat plateau. A short distance across to the east it dips down again, with a rough scrubby patch rolling down from the dip, before a narrow neck climbs back up on to the slopes which form the rear wall of Malone's Gully. It is a clear outline that features prominently in the foreground of all the views over this lower end of the foothills. Between the edge of the post and the sea stands the workshop and maintenance depot of the Commonwealth War Graves Commission still positioned near the original site of the first Graves Registration Unit camp on Ocean Beach.

Beyond No.1 Outpost, across the mouth of the Sazli Beit Dere, are the sites of No.2 and No.3 Outposts positioned on the rear of the hill to the west of Old No.3 Outpost. From these two northernmost points of the old Anzac line, through No.1 Outpost as far south as Reserve Gully, the route along the coast ran through the Great Sap, a deep communication trench which offered a certain degree of protection from Turkish observation to the east.

> *This Sap was a wonderful piece of work sunk to a depth of about ten feet and wide enough for mules to pass, winding up hill and down dale all the way to the Pier. The labour expended upon it in the fierce heat of April and June must have been stupendous: it remains a monument of the unflagging energies of the Australian and New Zealand troops in the great days of the first landing. I well remember that here and there along the Sap were wooden crosses with the name and date of death of soldiers killed by shell or shrapnel bursting directly overhead. We knew how we were progressing by the familiar names which became like guide posts along our journey. I remember too how at the end of this sap there was a fat stumpy howitzer which had an annoying way of going off just as one was thinking pleasant thoughts of a journey nearly ended and giving one an unexpected shock.*[27] (Private Harold Thomas)

As might be expected there remain few apparent signs of even this, the longest and probably deepest trench at Anzac; but twenty-five yards inland from the back wall of Canterbury Cemetery there is a scrubby ditch running parallel to the coast which suggests its likely remains. From the height of No.2 Outpost the shadow of the ditch can be seen clearly trailing through the scrub along the Sap's old course like the chalk scars running down the rolling fields above the River Ancre on the old Somme battlefields.

Following the road north from Canterbury Cemetery, a small track leads off to the right immediately past a stone hut, positioned near the site of Fisherman's Hut, to No.2 Outpost Cemetery. The cemetery, quite separate from New Zealand No.2 Outpost Cemetery which is set directly on the edge of the road a short distance further on, is positioned at the foot of the hill on which both No.2 and No.3 Outposts were built. It is a steep and arduous climb up the hill which is shaped like a small Plugge's Plateau. A third of the way up a small break in the ankle-high scrub forms a rough path that climbs haphazardly up the face to the summit. There the level ground of No.2 Outpost is cut up by a series of three foot deep communication trenches and dugouts. It was to this post that Major General Godley moved his headquarters at the start of the assault on the hills beyond, having a strong set of dug-outs built by Turkish prisoners nearby. The scrub on the top of the hill is thin, with many paths twisting across the beds of the trenches. From here there is a clear view south along the side of Sari Bair showing the difference between the two faces of the hills. Across the foreground the Sazli Beit Dere trails faintly to its wide mouth through the thick scrub like the trace of a finger drawn against the grain of velvet. Looking inland the Farm Cemetery stands out just below Chunuk Bair, clearly indicated by the glinting white tips of the two Memorials and Mustafa Kemal's statue clustered on the summit. Leading off from No.2 Outpost in this direction the land dips across a narrow neck before extending out around the flat plateau of Old No.3 Outpost.

Crossing the neck, one reaches a series of very deep trenches running round the edge of the plateau from all of which there is a direct view down to the sea. Turning round to look again towards Chunuk Bair, Old No.3 Outpost leads away towards the tall sided, flat topped hill of Table Top with Rhododendron Ridge leading up in turn from its far edge towards the distant summit. The northern boundary of the protected Anzac area, in which only scrub and pine trees have been

New Zealand No.2 Outpost Cemetery to Russell's Top (the long, central summit running along the horizon). Moving from right to left the view encompasses the edge of Plugge's Plateau (extreme right), Razor Edge surrounding Reserve Gully, the faint outline of the Sphinx at the end of the bare cliffs of Mule Gully, Walker's Ridge (the scrub covered mass leading down to sea level), Happy Valley, the cluster of trees surrounding the Turkish memorial to Mehmet Çavus at the Nek leading down to Turk's Point and the bare sides of Malone's Gully. Beneath this is the bowl shaped outcrop of No.1 Outpost and rising out of shot to the left is the seaward edge of No.2 Outpost. (April 1998)

No.2 Outpost to Chunuk Bair, with Old No.3 Outpost (left foreground) leading onto the large, rugged mass of Table Top in the centre. Beyond the summit of this a thin firebreak leads up Rhododendron Ridge through the Apex to the Pinnacle in the direction of Chunuk Bair (highlighted on the horizon by the two white memorials on its summit). This view, contrasted to the reverse view shown earlier, clearly shows the difference between the north and south faces of the Sari Bair hills. (August 1988)

allowed to grow, runs through this ridge. A concrete marker post, like those which delineate the boundaries of the cemeteries at Helles and Suvla, stakes out the line along the neck between No.2 and Old No.3 Outposts; it is counter-balanced by another which stands at the southern end of Brighton Beach where the Anzac area begins. Beyond the northern face of this ridge the land once again becomes free of restrictions and is transformed by its sudden liberation. The mouth of the Chailak Dere is the antithesis of the thick and tightly meshed Sazli Beit Dere to the south. Wide and undulating, the green and yellow crops roll softly across it like the shadows of the clouds passing overhead. Set off slightly to the edge of the mouth, four hundred yards inland from the coast, the tip of the opposite ridge is marked by Wilson's Knob, a small, richly cultivated hill set on the end of the long, flat plateau of Bauchop's Hill.

The slopes of Wilson's Knob lie directly inland from Embarkation Pier Cemetery, named after a pier that was built nearby to evacuate the August casualties but which was abandoned after two days because it was so heavily shelled. The wounded suffered terribly during the five days of the battle and the medical arrangements were quickly overwhelmed. Herbert recorded in great detail the tortuous situation of those men who lay 'in the sand in rows upon rows, their faces caked with sand and blood ... many of them in saps, with men passing all the

173

time scattering more dust on them'.[28] He encapsulated the scene in one powerful metaphor when he wrote from No.2 Outpost, 'we have a terrible view here: lines of wounded creeping up from the hospital to the cemetery like a tide, and the cemetery is going like a live thing to meet the wounded.'[29] Today most of these small cemeteries, including two from the Chailak Dere, are concentrated into Embarkation Pier.

Beyond the cemetery the sea can easily be reached. From the beach, to the north, the coast begins to reach out westwards towards Nibrunesi Point at the southern tip of Suvla Bay; but to the south it runs long and smooth almost straight to Ari Burnu. Out to sea, across the limpid, azure water the sunlight twinkles like a mirage on the horizon. In the distance to the right is the faint outline of Samothrace, from where 'the Greek god Poseidon was supposed to have watched the Trojan War', and to the left the darker shadow of Imbros which Lieutenant Baxter described from Gully Beach at Helles.[30] The sunsets across this sea were, and still are, astonishingly beautiful, 'the sea a lake of gold and the sky a lake of fire'.[31] For Lieutenant Powell, like so many others, it was one of the things which made Gallipoli bearable.

Five hundred yards further up the Suvla road a rough track leads off to the right towards 7th Field Ambulance Cemetery, the last of the Sari Bair cemeteries. It is perched at the foot of Walden's Point, the complementary point to Wilson's Knob on the western edge of Bauchop's Hill. Behind the cemetery the ground rises steeply up the side of Walden's Point, but to the right it curves round above a wide bowl called Taylor's Hollow set between the two raised peaks of Wilson's Knob and Walden's Point. The summit of Walden's Point can be reached along the northern edge of the hollow by a sandy path and from there the rounded sides of the bowl can be more clearly seen embracing the fields which reach out to the road near Embarkation Pier Cemetery.

Crossing the back of Taylor's Hollow to the top of Wilson's Knob more broken-down trenches run parallel to the sea; in them there is the familiar smell of wild thyme. From this raised point there is another of the panoramas across the foothills beginning with the long wide sweep of Bauchop's Hill climbing up directly inland towards Little Table Top. Over to the right, across the bed of the Chailak Dere, known at this end as Overton Gully, is the peak of the larger Table Top rising gently inland to the foot of Rhododendron Ridge. Following Table Top back towards the coast the ground starts to fall, crossing first over Old No.3 Outpost, then the new No.3 Outpost and finally No.2 lodged on the rear of the hill as it falls down to the nearby cemetery.

To the north-east of Walden's Point, on the smooth flat plateau between it and Bauchop's Hill, there is a large olive grove. The fields beneath it are ploughed and fall down to the north into the wide bed of the Aghyl Dere. At its head this dere is steep and tortuous, splitting into fragmentary tributaries around the peak of Hill Q. But along these lower reaches it is broad and open, its sides covered with fields and fruit trees. The stream itself, beyond the tip of Walden's Point, is only about five to six feet deep with an area of plain running off it to the north leading out from the two villages lodged further over to the east between the foothills of Koja Chemen Tepe and the Tekke Tepe Ridge.

At this point Anzac ends and Suvla begins, the symbolic junction of the two now being marked by a Turkish memorial set on the tip of the Damakjelik Spur shortly before the track to the Hill 60 Cemetery branches off the Suvla road. Sense can be made of Sari Bair only if the coast is followed from Ari Burnu to this point. The misty, uneven views from the crestline help to reinforce the complexity of the landscape and fail completely to offer any degree of clarification. Driving slowly along the coast, stopping at the cemeteries and carefully placing again the same features of the hills into each new perspective, is the only way to develop any degree of comprehension about where the assault in August took place and how great was the ambition of Birdwood's plan.

7th Field Ambulance Cemetery, beside the road leading north from Anzac to Suvla. Behind the cemetery, Walden's Point can be seen climbing up onto Bauchop's Hill. (April 1998)

Chapter Seven

THE LANDING AT SULVA BAY

Suvla is perhaps the loveliest part of Gallipoli. From Chunuk Bair when the mist is thin there is a sparkling view north across the whole area with the Salt Lake, when it is dry, shimmering diamond white in the sun. Around it yellow fields and green trees are scattered loosely across the lush plain, while, beyond, a harsh black line of hills scours the horizon. To the west the violet blue waters of the bay are kept deathly still, without a tremor of movement passing across them, by an embracing ring of land that reaches out into the Aegean Sea. Along the margin of the bay a long, hot beach of powdery sand runs for several miles without a person on it. It is hard to imagine a more beautiful place.

The hills which run here along the northern shore of the peninsula, facing out over the Gulf of Saros, are called the Kiretch Tepe Sirt. For approximately six miles they climb up from Suvla Point to Ejelmer Bay, passing first behind the area known as Ghazi Baba, where the IX Corps headquarters were finally established, and then through a small peak (541 feet) known as Karakol Dagh, which translates as Coastguard Mountain. Beyond there the summit dips slightly through the Karakol Gap before moving on a short distance through Jephson's Post, which stood at the end of the British line, to the highest point of 650 feet. Midway between there and Ejelmer Bay, a second, higher ridge, branches off at right angles, running inland for just less than four miles. The summit of this second ridge, known as the Tekke Tepe Ridge, also passes through two peaks, first Kavak Tepe (900 feet) and then Tekke Tepe itself (882 feet). At its southern end sits the village of Anafarta Sagir, or Little Anafarta, and directly opposite it that of Biyuk, or Greater, Anafarta at the northern end of the Sari Bair Ridge.

Out of the broad valley which joins these two villages a raised spur of land, called the Anafarta Spur, runs for nearly two miles into the Suvla Plain. Its northern edge is formed by the straight smooth hill called Scimitar Hill and its southern by the rugged slopes of Ismail Oglu Tepe. Directly to the west is another, separate twin-peaked hill known as Yilghin Burnu or to the British as the Chocolate Hills. Two miles further over towards the sea, across the Salt Lake and the flat fields surrounding it, stands the final Suvla hill called Lala Baba (150 feet) which tapers west from its central peak towards Nibrunesi Point, the complementary tip to Suvla Point across the mile wide mouth of Suvla Bay, and north to a narrow spit of land which reaches down to the Cut, the shallow ditch where the waters of Suvla Bay enter the Salt Lake. Beyond this the ground broadens out again around the barely discernible Hill 10, named after its height in metres. Spreading round from there, within the arc of the Kiretch Tepe Sirt and the Tekke Tepe Ridge, is the Suvla Plain. No deep deres run across it as at Helles; no craggy hills grow up as they do at Anzac. It is flat and easy, and leads straight across to the high ground at the back. It is the plain that gives Suvla its unique quality of openness and which first attracted the attention of Hamilton and his General Staff.

If the plan as they conceived it, with its quick, dynamic movement across the plain on to the surrounding ring of dominating hills, had been carried out it would have resulted in great moral and strategic advantages for relatively few casualties and for this reason alone of all the new initiatives begun on the peninsula after the landings in April Suvla offered the most bountiful opportunity. The plain was correctly believed to be empty and the beaches around it largely undefended. There appeared to be little to stop the disembarking troops from overwhelming what few defences did exist before storming resolutely on to the crests of the high hills to establish a strong defensive line down into the Anafarta valley within the three days it was estimated it would take the Turks to march their reinforcements west from Bulair where they were stationed.

The idea of speed lay at the heart of the plan. Both Hamilton and his Staff were aware of the absolute importance of beating the Turkish reinforcements on to the high ground within this short time. It was seen in terms of a race and through surprise the British forces were judged to have a significant head-start over their Turkish opponents. The basic objectives of the landing were outlined in the first written instructions issued to Sir Frederick Stopford at Helles on 22 July. In support of the assault on Sari Bair, Stopford was to land and seize Lala Baba and Ghazi Baba, the two eastern tips of the bay, before advancing inland to take Yilghin Burnu and Ismail Oglu Tepe. In order to secure the area around them Stopford was told that he would also need 'to send a small force to secure a footing on the hills due east of Suvla Bay', that is the unnamed Tekke Tepe Ridge.[1] Once this had been achieved his next objective would be to move across the Anafarta valley towards the northern face of Koja Chemen Tepe to assist Birdwood in his assault on the lower peaks of Sari Bair to the south.

The instructions clearly stressed that it was 'of first importance that Yilghin Burnu and Ismail Oglu Tepe should be captured by a *coup de main* before daylight' and had they been issued to a temperamentally different Corps Commander, like Birdwood or even Hunter-Weston, this brief reference may well have been sufficient to convey a sense of urgency.[2] But Stopford was not of this type. Over the following two weeks he and the IX Corps Staff managed gradually to scale down the plan from a major operation to the limited securing of a beach-head for future operations. Remarkably, GHQ failed to object to this and instead issued a new set of instructions on 29 July that incorporated this revised emphasis. These new instructions no longer included the hills at the back of the plain as an objective and down-graded the primary task of the Corps to the simple securing of 'Suvla Bay as a base for all the forces operating in the northern zone'.[3]

Consequently in the IX Corps orders the idea of urgency had disappeared. They contained no reference to speed and only the ultimate hope that the seizure of the bay would allow 'the heights which connect Anafarta Sagir and Ejelmer Bay' to be denied to the enemy.[4] It was obvious that Hamilton and the General Staff had failed to convey the very essence of their plan, and in this lies the crux of who should bear the blame for the subsequent failure. It had been incumbent on them to insist that their plan be carried out. Yet from the moment Stopford presented his first written reaction it was apparent that a gulf of perception existed between his staff and GHQ. Stopford did not believe in the possibility of success and so did not drive his men to fulfil it. He allowed the failure he feared to come about. In this

New Beach with C Beach sweeping right to left through B Beach and the old A Beach towards Ocean Beach, at the foot of the Sari Bair hills, then North Beach, Anzac Cove and Brighton Beach. In the distance the crest of the Anzac hills climbs (right to left) from Gaba Tepe (right background, at the far end of the beach) over 400 Plateau (first peak) to Baby 700 (second peak), with the rocky faces of Walker's Ridge and Russell's Top beneath them, before continuing through Battleship Hill (third peak) to Chunuk Bair (highlighted by the white memorials on its summit), Hill Q (the twin peaks to its left) and finally Koja Chemen Tepe (extreme left) where the crest begins to fall down to Biyuk Anafarta. (August 1988)

KOJA CHEMEN TEPE

much it was he who was responsible for squandering the bountiful promise of Suvla. Yet the ultimate burden of failure must lie once again with Hamilton. For he failed from the first in his arguments with Kitchener for the Corps Commander he wanted. Subsequently, having accepted Stopford, he failed to keep a sufficiently close watch on him when his character and inexperience should have prompted an even greater vigilance. It is tempting to overlook this and see Hamilton himself as the victim who did everything he could to ensure success. But to do so is to ignore the fact that it was his job to make sure that the apparent lack of nerve and enterprise did not interfere with the successful execution of the plan.

The landing was set for the night of 6-7 August and the 11th Division was to land first. Originally it had been intended that all three brigades of the Division would land along different sections of the same beach. This beach, known in its entirety as New Beach, ran south from Nibrunesi Point to the mouth of the Aghyl Dere; but Stopford had requested that the southernmost of these beaches, A Beach, be moved to a position actually inside Suvla Bay itself. Reluctantly the naval authorities agreed, despite their fears of the uncharted waters inside the bay, and the logical order of the beaches was disrupted. A Beach was relocated to the north, but the letters B and C remained the designated names for the other two beaches. As a result 'from south to north the beaches were lettered B, C, A'.[5]

The first troops were landed on B Beach to begin a long circuitous trek to Yilghin Burnu via the Cut and Hill 10, skirting right round the circumference of the Salt Lake. The decision to follow this route had

HUNUR BAIR   BABY 700   400 PLATEAU   GABA TEPE

BEACH

C BEACH

been based upon the belief that the southern slopes of Yilghin Burnu were more heavily fortified than the northern and that for the inexperienced troops of the 11th Division the greatly increased journey would be balanced by the easier task of attacking the hills from their more vulnerable flank. The first Turkish positions encountered were on Lala Baba. The troops had been ordered to assault the hill using only their bayonets so as not to arouse the garrisons inland; but the consequences of this order were by then familiar. Heavy and disorientating casualties were suffered, including many officers, and even when the hill had been taken the fact that the British were unable to fire at the retreating Turks meant that most were allowed to escape to take up new positions further inland. The 6th Battalion, Yorkshire Regiment, who led the attack, were left too exhausted to press on towards the rendezvous with the troops landing on A Beach and it was not until after midnight that the 9th Battalion, West Yorkshire Regiment arrived to continue the northerly advance down on to the Cut.

During this time the landing inside the bay was being attempted. As a result of two naval errors the troops were taken ashore a thousand yards too far to the south of the chosen beach and in the wrong order with the result that, as the boats set out towards the shore, most of them ran aground on sand-banks hidden in the water. Inevitably these problems considerably added to the confusion surrounding the other parts of the landings. Hesitation and delay gradually began to appear among all the troops on land as battalions from different brigades became intermixed and the brigades of the 10th Division which should have followed up the first troops on A Beach were diverted round to B Beach to avoid further trouble in the bay. Hill 10, the second objective after Lala Baba, where the attacking troops were meant to turn inland towards Yilghin Burnu and Ismail Oglu Tepe, was not finally taken until well after dawn at around 8.00 am on 7 August. But its capture was not followed up by an immediate advance inland as the orders issued from both Corps and Divisional Headquarters produced contradictory instructions among the commanders of the confused units. It was not to be until 3.00 pm that the advance inland finally got under way and even then the orders were for an attack on Yilghin Burnu only. These hills were reached at 5.00 pm and after a short struggle were taken just after 7.00, a little after sunset and over twelve hours later than intended. The first of the available three days had not been used to the full.

The second, 8 August, was completely wasted. Throughout it the IX Corps did nothing. The men rested, swimming in the sea and strolling around the empty plain, while the Turks who had retreated over the Anafarta Spur waited for them to advance. Arriving there in the late morning Colonel Cecil Aspinall, who as Brigadier-General Aspinall-Oglander later wrote the Official History, found a 'holiday appearance' in the behaviour of the men.[6] H W Nevinson, landing later in the day, found that 'in Suvla bay itself a Sabbath peace appeared to reign' and by 6.00 pm when Hamilton himself eventually arrived, having been prevented from landing earlier by another naval error at Imbros, the chances of restoring the situation had passed.[7] He desperately tried to initiate an immediate assault on Tekke Tepe, but his efforts only produced further confusion. By the time his attack began, at dawn on 9 August, it was too late. The race was lost, and as the British troops finally began to climb up the lower slopes of the hills, they encountered the Turks from Bulair streaming down to meet them, driven on by Mustafa Kemal. The advantages of speed and surprise had been thrown away and, once relinquished, Suvla would be no different from all the other areas of Gallipoli, with the Turks positioned on the higher ground and the allied troops dug-in below. With its failure, along with that on Sari Bair, the last possible strategic manoeuvre at Gallipoli had been exhausted.

Lala Baba to Ghazi Baba

Immediately beyond the northern wall of Embarkation Pier Cemetery a small side road branches left off the main route to Suvla towards Lala Baba which is located two and a half miles to the north-west in the middle of the rough triangle of land formed by the Aegean, Suvla Bay and the Salt Lake. For the first half-mile the Lala Baba road winds through a group of new and expensive looking houses, with green lawns and barbecues but soon after they end the surface quickly deteriorates. Between the road and the beach a low earth wall runs erratically, obscuring the view of the sea; but occasional breaks give tantalising glimpses of the calm, azure water reaching south along the coast beyond Gaba Tepe almost to the edge of Helles and rust-stained, concrete pillboxes, lying dotted along the beach, confirm the continued military importance of this long strip of beach where the 11th Division landed.

A mile and a half beyond the last new house the track forks. To the right it leads up on to the small plateau where Lala Baba Cemetery is situated and to the left it carries on towards the end of C Beach, stopping just short of Nibrunesi Point. The beach is shingle and falls away steeply into the sea; above it a small earth cliff rises up to offer a fine southwards view of C and B Beaches. In comparison with other Gallipoli heights the actual peak of Lala Baba is very small, less than 150 feet; but it acquires an enhanced significance through being the only major hill on the seaward edge of the Salt Lake and the Suvla Plain. In addition its capture by the Yorkshire Regiment on 6 August was more important in the history of the war than through simply being the first action of the Suvla Bay landing. For, as the Official History points out, 'it was the first attack made by any unit of the New Army in the Great War, and it was carried out in circumstances that would

The enclosed beach beyond C Beach in the lee of Lala Baba crowded with men awaiting orders on 21 August. (1915/1988) (DOC601)

have tried the mettle of highly experienced troops'.[8] In tribute to the success of the Yorkshire Regiment the other men of the 11th Division named it York Hill.

From the cemetery, positioned on the slightly lower summit of Little Lala Baba, a short distance to the south of the main hill, there are fine views forward on all sides encompassing the bay, the plain and the long sweep down to Sari Bair, with Anzac in the distance beyond. From there, and also from the earth cliff above C Beach, the attractions of the coastline as a point of disembarkation are clear. Off the coast there is ample room for transports to manoeuvre and anchor whilst awaiting their turn to disembark troops. The beaches are sheltered, both from observation and from direct fire, by the earth wall that runs along its length and the land which runs off them appears flat and easy to cross, free of ravines and scrub. There is nothing to compare with it at either Anzac or Helles.

At the very tip of C Beach there is a small, enclosed beach about sixty five yards long, which was often used in the days following the landing to collect together the remnants of units scattered in the first week of the fighting. On the night of 10 August Private Ernest Lye was directed there with the remaining men of his company from the 8th Battalion, Duke of Wellington's Regiment, sleeping fitfully on the

stones as the water lapped over his feet. He had rejoined his regiment earlier that day, having been kept back on Imbros as part of a reinforcement draft. Throughout the morning he had waited on Lala Baba for the return of the Regiment from the front line. He knew nothing about what had happened to them during the past four days and when they finally began to arrive after their long march beside the Salt Lake he was completely unprepared for what he saw.

> *What terrible thing had put that indescribable look of horror in their eyes? They looked haunted with a memory of the sight of hell! With their faces dirty and unkempt, and with their clothes torn and ragged, I thought of them four days ago as they passed me as I stood by the doctor's tent, with their laughing faces and tin triangles. ... There were twenty left of our platoon of sixty-one. Only two Officers left in the whole Battalion: the adjutant, Captain Kidd, and Lieutenant Edwards, our own platoon Commander. We had a roll-call on the slope of York Hill and the sight will be pictured forever in my mind. I thought of a picture I had once seen, giving a similar incident in the Crimean War. The picture was good, but the artist couldn't put into the picture the wild haunted look that I saw in the eyes of my comrades as they answered their names, nor could he put on canvas the heart-broken sobs as some man's name was called and not answered. 'Corporal Scott.' No answer. 'Anyone seen him?' 'Yes, Sergeant.' (This from a man, half-sitting and half-lying on his pack, utterly weary). 'The devils got him before we got off the barge; he never had a chance.' A sob shook him as he put his head into his hands. 'Private Cooney?' 'Present, Sergeant.' 'Private Whitehouse?' 'He's here, allright, Sergeant; I think he's gone to sleep,' and so on, through the sixty-one names the platoon started with.*[9]
> (Private Ernest Lye)

During the subsequent four months at Suvla, Lala Baba became an important divisional headquarters centre. A network of roads was built around the central peak, connecting it with the surrounding beaches as well as the more distant parts of the front line. On the rear slopes of the main hill was the headquarters of the 2nd Mounted Division who arrived at Suvla, dismounted, on 18 August in time for the battle which took place on 21 August. On that day the division was commanded by Brigadier-General P A Kenna VC, who died of wounds received during the battle and is now buried in the Lala Baba Cemetery. Along the shore of the bay there were two more headquarters. In the south, near the inland end of Nibrunesi Point, was that of the 13th Division who held the line around Yilghin Burnu, and a thousand yards to the north at the foot of the spit which ran on to the Cut was that of the 53rd Division. Connecting these two was Main Road and, cutting off this, between Little Lala Baba and the main peak, Cross Road. From the cemetery it can be seen that in its later stages the present road follows the approximate course of the wartime New Chocolate Hill Road and that the Old Chocolate Hill Road wound around the southern edge of the Salt Lake.

On the northern side of Lala Baba the spit of ground, about three hundred yards wide, that leads away from the hill down towards the Cut is rough and uneven. Covered with spiky scrub-grass, although it runs forward along a flat, straight course, it is not easy to follow. Like much of the ground around Lala Baba the covering of loose sand, blown off the beaches by the wind, makes walking slow and journeys take much longer than expected. During the later stages of the campaign the spit was traversed by Cut Road, which led north to the bridge which crossed over the marshy, twenty-five-yard-wide bed of the Cut itself.

The northern bank of the Cut is higher than the level of the spit and spreads out inland over a wide plateau. From this desolate, scrubby ground there is a clear view of the Salt Lake, or Tuzla Geul. Raised up just enough by the height of the plateau to see right across to Yilghin Burnu, the true nature of the surface becomes obvious. The magnificent illusion seen from Anzac and Sari Bair is dispelled by the dirty, brown earth scattered with faint wisps of dried salt. Stripped of its false magnificence, the Salt Lake assumes its real colours. No longer magic or alive, it pales into 'a great, vast, sandy beach' which offers no protection to anyone crossing over it.[10] On the afternoon of 21 August the Commanding Officer of the 88th Field Ambulance, who had arrived at Suvla from Helles the evening before, ordered his men, including Private Denis Buxton, to cross the Salt Lake to collect casualties from Yilghin Burnu on the far side.

We reached the Salt Lake safely. This is a most extraordinary place, absolutely flat and absolutely bare of vegetation, though now dry. It must be well over a mile across. We halted in the middle, and the Colonel went on to a Field Ambulance near the foot of Chocolate Hill, to which our bearers had gone. He soon returned, with a small red cross flag, and led us on, a bit to the left. The Turks patience now apparently gave out, and they sent shrapnel over, which fortunately burst some way behind us. There was absolutely no cover from this, but we came to a little

ridge about 6 inches high which gave us some moral support; and the Colonel stuck up the flag and we lay down. The shrapnel got closer and closer, and one shell burst a few yards off ... I dug a little hole in the soft earth with my pocket knife, and the rampart was soon nearly a foot high. Here I went to sleep, and so did many others as it was hot and we were very tired.[11] (Private Denis Buxton)

By August, 1915, both the Cut and the Salt Lake had sufficiently dried out to allow troops to march across them in this way. This is not always the case. In a footnote Robert Rhodes James states that its complete hardening by August 'gives a good indication of how exceptionally hot the summer of 1915 was. In 1962, regarded as a

Troops disembarking at West Beach Harbour on the northern arm of Suvla Bay soon after the start of the campaign there. (1915/1987) (DOC599)

particularly hot summer, no rain fell between the end of April and the beginning of October, but the Salt Lake did not fully dry out.'[12] In August, 1985, the Salt Lake itself looked dry from the edge; but the Cut, whilst also looking solid, was still wet and sulphurous, brown water, barely hidden beneath the thin, dry surface of matted weeds, bubbled out under the slightest pressure. In July, 1988, a thin puddle of water still covered the south-eastern half of the Salt Lake and ran clearly out into the sea through the Cut.

To the north and south of the Cut are the two beaches involved in the landing inside Suvla Bay. Looking at the two beaches today, a quite significant difference between them is apparent. To the south of the Cut, the beach where the boats actually grounded has an inconsistent, indented shoreline with small ripples of white water passing over the barely hidden reefs for some distance out into the bay and the sand is littered with dried weed. But to the north, the site of the correct A Beach is a steady length of clean sand running out into unencumbered water. No more suitable place to make a landing could be imagined. It is a beautiful, isolated beach, with open, flat ground running off

behind. Only the slight rise of Hill 10, distinguished today by the trees that surround the cemetery there, stands between the water's edge and the Tekke Tepe Ridge beyond the plain. But from the beach where the troops actually came ashore the only perceptible feature is the bleak, inhospitable desert of the Salt Lake.

To go from the Cut to Hill 10, where the landing troops were to turn inland en route for the high ground, there is a choice of two ways - along A Beach, past the skeleton of a barge buried in the sand, before turning directly inland to force a path through the thick, clogging undergrowth, or by following round the edge of the Salt Lake to the seemingly endless fields of sunflowers which run off it into the plain. Sunflowers are the predominant crop at Suvla. Line on line, row on row of six-foot sunflowers, heads so heavy with seed that they twist round beseechingly and clutch at one's shoulder, so exhausted by the sultry heat that they bend their necks and hang down their heads in shame.

The Hill 10 Cemetery stands just off the road that crosses through the middle of the Suvla Plain. Continuing on at Embarkation Pier Cemetery it passes by the last hills of Sari Bair before sweeping left across towards Yilghin Burnu. Passing between the two peaks of that hill the road then drops down into the Suvla Plain until, after about two miles, the small offshoot to Hill 10 is passed on the left. The main road continues on towards Ghazi Baba and Suvla Point. The latter, reached after another two miles, is marked today by one of the concrete Turkish memorials and stands at the head of a rocky shoreline that climbs out of the sand at the northern end of A Beach. In the days following the first landings the area between here and A Beach became the favoured landing point for all troops and supplies arriving at Suvla. Among the tall, craggy rocks a series of small coves were all slowly investigated and, where suitable, turned into landing beaches. Eight hundred yards north of A Beach the first became known as Kangaroo Beach; following the curve of the shore north-west there then followed Little West Beach and the main West Beach Harbour.

Between there and Suvla Point itself there were no more suitable inlets, but around the point on the northern coastline was Suvla Cove. Together the area was known as Ghazi Baba.

From the first few days the ground inland became fortified and covered in dugouts. Over the

West Beach shortly before the evacuation. Although no signs of the harbour remain, the distinctive rocks around the water's edge and the hills in the back-ground provide useful landmarks for judging where it used to be. (1915/1988) (Q13660)

next two months, as the Lancashire Landing camp had grown up at Helles around W Beach, so the headquarters of the IX Corps now began to develop. On the higher ground inland from West Beach a range of ordnance depots and magazines were built. Offices for other auxiliary services were cut out of the rock, with a post office and parcel depot at Little West Beach and an RE Park at Kangaroo. Returning to the area on 3 October after a long spell in the line on the top of the Kiretch Tepe Sirt, Sergeant Ernest Miles, also of the 8th Battalion, Duke of Wellington's Regiment, remarked in his diary on the changes that had taken place there. 'My word! but there's been some work done here since we landed. Little wooden huts in plenty have been erected, and quite a little "town" has sprung up!'[13] Three weeks later, in describing the shellfire at Suvla in a letter to his father, Buxton also drew a picture of the clutter around the beaches much like that he described at Helles in April.

The beaches of course come in for a great deal of attention, but it is really most extraordinary what little damage is done. And yet it is a wonderful target: a few steam pinnaces and lighters by the piers, and stores coming off in quantities and piles of biscuits and bully-beef, boxes 20 feet high and haystacks and piles of sacks of oats and flour; and bags of mails, and on the roads a few motor bikes and ambulance cars, and horses being

IX Corps headquarters at Ghazi Baba looking across Suvla Bay to the distant Sari Bair. (1915/1988) (Q50474)

watered and stray men getting water from the Tanks, and the inevitable and entirely admirable Indian sitting in silence on his mule cart.[14] (Private Denis Buxton)

In order to ease the problems of disembarking stores experienced at Helles and Anzac, a lot of work was done on the building of breakwaters. The *Feremosco* was driven into the shoulder of land separating West Beach Harbour from Little West Beach to extend it further and Lye recalled how this ship, along with a second, was filled with ballast and sunk to form the harbour. 'All our food was landed there and most of the water.'[15] In addition to this a third ship, the *Pina*, was moored parallel to the shore as a condensing plant to manufacture fresh water. The water was then taken to the men in petrol tins and Lye remembered that 'the first time we got these tins we made a grab for the nice new, green-painted ones, but we found there was quite a lot of petrol as well as water in, and when we had one drink - well, ugh!'.[16]

Today the signs of these encampments are still faintly visible in the rough ground. Unnatural depressions in the ground cluster in groups

on top of the high ground above West Beach Harbour on the site of the dugouts that were still there in 1919. Between them and the Turkish plaque on Suvla Point there is a well covered with an old board. Wide gullies climb up on to the hills from the beaches and, as final proof that here they lived, among the loose stones in the grass lie pieces of rum bottle. But in reality, like Helles, Suvla has returned to the life it led before the war and from the coves of Ghazi Baba brightly painted fishing boats sail out again into the blue Aegean Sea.

The Kiretch Tepe Sirt to Yilghin Burnu

The whale-back ridge of the Kiretch Tepe Sirt rises up from the small inlets of Ghazi Baba running exactly parallel to the northern shoreline as the broad, open fields roll away to the south into the expanding area of the Suvla Plain. The distinctive tail of the ridge can be clearly seen from the ground above Suvla Point made up of a series of thick, level shelves of rock embedded at an acute angle into the ground like slates that have fallen off a roof into soft earth; the rough edges of the cliffs beneath the shelves fall away almost sheer into the northern waters. Gradually from there the ridge begins to climb up, with its base broadening slightly and reaches the first peak of Karakol Dagh after about two miles.

The Kiretch Tepe Sirt was the objective of the Manchester Regiment at the landing and it was near Karakol Dagh that their successful advance along the ridge drew to a halt on the morning of 7 August. Later, during the afternoon, Lieutenant General Sir Bryan Mahon and several battalions of his 10th Division who had managed to land on A Beach during the morning advanced in support of the Manchesters and gradually assumed the predominant role in the fighting along the ridge. Dipping slightly through Karakol Gap, where eventually a small cemetery was established 'with its lines of wooden

The remains of the dugouts near Suvla Point looking inland across the distant plain to the 'high ground' at the back, with Kavak Tepe the highest peak (900 feet) in the centre and Tekke Tepe, only 6 yards smaller, beside it to the right. Cutting into the right of the modern picture is West Beach Harbour and beyond the white house the dark ring of trees which surround Hill 10 Cemetery. In the distance behind this can be seen the outline of the Anafarta Spur. (1919/1987) (Q13893)

crosses facing over the Gulf of Saros', the ridge resumes its climb towards Jephson's Post, named after Major J. N. Jephson of the 6th Battalion, Royal Munster Fusiliers, who commanded the attack which captured the post on 9 August.[17] Immediately to the east along the inland side of the ridge is Kidney Hill, 200 feet shorter than the summit, and, although contested fiercely on 9 and 15 August, never actually taken.

The inland edge of the ridge was formed by rough, rocky foothills covered by unusually tall and thick scrub. It was completely different from that found on the banks of Shrapnel Valley or Gully Ravine and made progress difficult and any movements very wearing. To overcome it, a series of definite routes were established running along the side of the ridge. At the end of August the 11th Division crossed the bay and took up positions there. During their first period in the line they watched as, behind them, communication trenches were dug and paths established back to the rear at Ghazi Baba.

> *Roads appeared where only paths had been and these were named after famous streets in London, the main one being Oxford Street which, starting on 'A' Beach, wound its way upwards and forwards to Oxford Circus. This was an open space just on the inland side of the top of the mountain. Here supplies were dumped for the trenches around Jephson's Post, as only a path and communication trenches went there from the Circus. On the left there was an opening in the rock formation and this was called* [Karakol] *Gap. A road starting from this gap was named Hyde Park Road and ... went down the hillside facing the Gulf until it terminated at Hyde Park Corner at the end of another communication trench ... Another road led into Hyde Park Corner, known as Cannon Street; this ran parallel with the cliff-top, but halfway down the mountainside.*[18] (Private Ernest Lye)

The trenches along the top of the ridge could not be dug as easily as they could down in the plain. Instead, the solid rock had to be slowly quarried, with the Royal Engineers blasting the way to speed up the process. Their average depth was about four feet with the remaining height added by ineffectual parapets of sandbags and even then the Turks on the slightly higher ground beyond Jephson's Post were often able to see directly into the line. The post itself was 'overlooked by Johnny Turk from a point known to us as the "Bench Mark" '.[19]

Despite this difficulty, normal sapping was carried out. On the seaward slopes Green Lane was constructed by slowly pinching out a section of no-man's-land and advancing the line across it towards the Turkish line. At the bottom of these slopes, where the line met the sea, there was a little beach known as Silver Beach. It was protected from direct Turkish observation by an overhanging cliff and this allowed the men to swim out a little way into the sea. On the beach, Lye remembered that 'there was a little hillock with a wooden cross facing out to sea. On the cross, burned into the wood, were the words "In memory of an unknown British sailor, washed up by the sea." Just another of us marked "missing" '.[20] Many of the men stayed down on the level of the beach during the day, only climbing back up to the summit near the post at night to boost the scanty numbers left holding the line when rations parties were sent back down Oxford Street to Ghazi Baba. Of those men who remained on the top of the ridge the supporting troops had their dugouts in positions near Oxford Circus which had to be hacked out of the surrounding rock faces.

Following the modern road back from Ghazi Baba into the centre of the plain a fork runs off to the left into the foothills of Kiretch Tepe. Winding up the side of the ridge far below the site of Jephson's Post the rough, rocky track cuts through the edge of overhanging boulders and across the hard, dry beds of streams, alongside strips of land still covered in the same thick scrub the soldiers saw. Along the highest slopes a coarse grass grows and on it flocks of goats feed, their dull bells ringing in the thin air. The scene is almost Alpine and quite different from the hot, still atmosphere of A Beach less than three miles to the west. A short distance along the track before it really begins to climb is Azmak Cemetery, the northernmost cemetery on the battlefields, and among the headstones there are twelve for soldiers of the Newfoundland Regiment who joined the 29th Division at Suvla on 20 September as part of the 88th Brigade. With the arrival of the Newfoundlanders at Gallipoli the campaign finally reached out to the last British Dominion and touched the only remaining continent of the Globe.

From the ground just above the cemetery, looking down along the rolling slopes of the ridge, the beauty of the plain stretches out unbroken for three miles to Yilghin Burnu. Open, cultivated and with a faded mixture of yellow and green fields, it embraces the whole area

around the Salt Lake and behind the idyllic sands of A Beach. Occasional trees and small shelters evoke a scene almost exactly as it appeared in 1915.

The country here is very pretty; a combination of Devonshire and Upper Burma. In places it is exactly like the scrub jungle round Mandalay or Thayetmyo. We are in a little nullah, thick gorse growing all over it, and big grey stones coming up in all directions. There is the dry bed of a stream at the bottom and a few willows to one side. All

Captain Guy Nightingale outside his dug-out at Suvla in September 1915. (HU63642)

round the country are patches of wheat and oats, some still growing, some cut, and some standing in sheaves exactly as it was left by the peasants when the landing took place.[21] (Captain Guy Nightingale)

In addition to the stream beds across the plain there were also a large number of trees. In both, Sir Ian Hamilton noted, 'a very considerable number of Turkish snipers are concealed, sometimes up in the trees, sometimes down in hollows amongst the grass. Quite close to the beach and a mile behind our troops, I am told there are still some undiscovered.'[22]

The free and roomy feel of the plain is protected by a blanket of peace laid across the air, creating a sense of tranquillity like that felt on awakening from sleep on a summer's afternoon. There is no discernible wind, no burbling sea surf; just the soporific swaying of the sunflowers that goes mostly unheard like the singing of the birds overhead. But both are there, trapped in by the solid walls of the distant hills. Looking out across this scene to the distant sparkling water, it is not hard to realize why, when given no specific orders, the essentially civilian soldiers of the New Army divisions, flushed with success and excitement, sat down on the beach, made tea and swam in the sea.

However, although extremely difficult, when standing on the slopes above Azmak Cemetery in the height of summer it must also be remembered that it was over this same ground that the worst ravages of the great storm of November, 1915, swept. From September onwards the weather at Gallipoli slowly deteriorated. Prolonged rain, such as had not fallen since the early days in April, began to reappear. Sudden strong winds would blow up, devastating the fragile piers and driving lighters up on to the shore. But nothing prepared the soldiers in the front lines for the storm that began during the night of 26-27 November. Lieutenant Thomas Watson, holding the line down in the plain when it began, wrote home to his mother a week later with a graphic description in his letter:

We've had another fiend of Hell vouchsafed us lately and one infinitely worse than shot and shell. We had been digging hard on a new trench and just made it fit to occupy by Friday night last when down came the most glorious thunderstorm I've ever seen and I never want to see another like it. Lightning and thunder absolutely incessant for 2 hours and rain indescribable since the Flood. It simply dropped in lumps, whole solid chunks of it which washed everything before it and at the end of those two hours our trenches in the worst places were knee deep in

*water and mud. It was in some parts all you could do to bale out
and people who stood still for a short space literally had to be
dragged out. ... And yet we were not by any means badly off
compared with some and more especially the Turks, whose
trenches were more in the valley. Some of them were drowned by
the deluge, their bodies washed down the valley next day. Also on
our left our own troops suffered much more than we. In one place
they had to climb into trees to avoid drowning. In another several
were actually suffocated in 8 foot of impassable mud.*[23]
(Lieutenant Thomas Watson)

Up on the top of the Kiretch Tepe Sirt the trenches, hewn out of the
rock, did not wash away as they did down in the plain but contained the
falling water within their walls. 'The men in the front line at each side
of Jephson's Post were in a terrible plight. The trench acted as a sewer
for the mountain side and a roaring torrent swept them off their feet.'[24]
The streams of water washed away the precarious walls which
supported the bivouacs in Oxford Circus and drenched every man in
the !ine along with his spare kit. But were they downhearted?

*By rights I suppose we should have all been miserable, for we
were wet through and very cold. The younger ones talked of the
feeds they were going to have (I had a craving for hot muffins
with piles of steaming butter), while those older ones talked of
the pints they would drink when they got back to their favourite
'pub'. Someone started a song which was taken up by all of us,
until you would have thought we hadn't a care in the world. In
my four years in the Army I always found that the worse the
conditions the more cheerful was the British Tommy!*[25] (Private
Ernest Lye)

During the second night conditions worsened. By the morning of 28
November, although the rain had stopped, the temperature had fallen
and everything - the ground, the men and their wet clothes - had all
frozen. Once again, on Kiretch Tepe this presented unexpected
problems.

*In the morning light the whole mountain-top glistened with
ice. One couldn't walk; you just slid to where you wanted to be.
Broken arms and legs were not uncommon and were looked upon
with something like envy by those who hadn't them, for they
meant a trip to Imbros, Lemnos, Malta or even 'Blighty' itself.
Greatcoats were so frozen that to bend them was like bending a
board. Some of the fellows with soaked blankets threw them over*

the bushes, with the remark that 'they would dry sometime'. In less than an hour these blankets could be reared on end, much in the same way as a large sheet of three-ply wood. All work was, of course, suspended and so were hostilities, not a shot being fired. It was said that the ships and artillery were afraid of their guns bursting, it was so cold. I picked up my rifle only once during this time and touching the steel part, I was surprised to find that it 'burned' my fingers. We made a raid on the R.E.'s dump and 'won' as much wood as we could carry, with which we made a huge bonfire in the centre of the Circus and danced round it. Looking over towards Anafarta village, we saw that the Turks had hit upon the same idea for keeping warm, for from our vantage point we could make out three fires from behind their line and could see tiny figures moving round them.[26] (Private Ernest Lye)

However, still it was not finished; for the weather had one more final development in store. During the following night the slight rise in temperature did not bring with it relief from the difficulties. Instead, when the men awoke they opened their 'eyes to a white world, for snow had fallen during the night until it lay two inches thick.'[27] Travelling back from the summit of the hill to Ghazi Baba, they 'had to go right along the edge of the cliffs and the snow was thick underfoot, while there was a very high wind blowing, making the journey both difficult and dangerous.'[28]

The snow remained on the ground for three days. Then, as suddenly as the storm had appeared, this winter weather vanished and it became once again bright and sunny like an English spring. But the effect of the storm had been terrible. On 12 December Birdwood wrote to Hamilton in London, following the latter's replacement as Commander-in-Chief by General Sir Charles Monro, and described the losses they had suffered as a result of the storm. The IX Corps at Suvla had fared worst of all having 204 killed and needing to evacuate 6500 more. 'As bad as a real big fight, while it left men really more prostrate and downhearted than a big fight possibly could do.'[29] Yet for the men their concerns were more fundamental. Remembering it 70 years later Sergeant Joe Guthrie concluded more simply: 'Yes, that blizzard was a swine, that was. We managed it; managed to survive somehow. But how? God only knows.'[30]

Heading due south again across the centre of the plain, the main road from Ghazi Baba follows the approximate course of the final front lines. Passing one by one the smaller areas along its inland edge, such as Kuchuk Anafarta Ova, Sulajik and Ali Bey Chesme, as well as the vanished sites of its redoubts like Dublin Castle, Gloster Post and the Blockhouse, it runs almost parallel to the high ground directly opposite the bay. In the centre of the ridge is Kavak Tepe, the tallest peak, as tall as Hill Q in the Sari Bair range, and to its right the shorter Tekke Tepe with its broad flat summit. These were the two peaks that for Hamilton constituted the high ground; and, however irrelevant it was by then for him to complain in his published diary entry of 8 August that 'viewed from the sea or studied in a map there might be some question of this hill, or that hill, but on the ground it was clear to half an eye that Tekke Tepe was the key to the whole Suvla area', it was nevertheless true.[31] For more so even than Achi Baba or Chunuk Bair did this hill eventually come to overlook all the British activity on the plain and it remains incredible to wonder how any invading commander could fail to realize that this would be so.

In the end this ridge played little part in the fighting. Instead, what occupied centre stage of this northern theatre was the Anafarta Spur, running out south-east from the village of Anafarta Sagir into the southern edge of the plain. On the northern edge of the spur the ground rolls down to the plain over a smooth, gentle slope that curves round from in front of Yilghin Burnu to the inner edge of Abrikja where the men ordered forward by Hamilton's intervention on 8 August started to climb up towards Tekke Tepe. This hill, referred to officially as Hill 70 after its height in metres, was more commonly known as Scimitar Hill because along its seaward edge there ran a long curving blaze of sandstone which appeared 'from the sea to be shaped like a Gurkha's "kukri" or an old-fashioned Turkish scimitar'.[32] In the south, beyond a deep amphitheatre, was the spur's complementary but antithetical head. Ismail Oglu Tepe, officially known as Hill 112 (again after its height in metres), was also given a more easily remembered nickname. Its face was, and remains, scarred by a series of bare, perpendicular gullies. To the men, as a result of this 'waving outline', they became known as the W Hills.[33] This outline can be seen most clearly from the road between Yilghin Burnu and Hill 60 and the relationship of the hills to one another from across the Salt Lake on Lala Baba.

Having taken and secured Yilghin Burnu on 7 August but failed to advance onto Tekke Tepe by 9 August, the troops on the southern end of the Suvla line were then prevented from any further advance by the barrier of these two hills. Before any new attempt on the high ground to the left could be attempted, they would have to be taken. In an attempt to do this a large scale attack was planned for 21 August and to bolster the inexperienced New Army troops the 29th Division was finally transferred from Helles to lead it. The plan was for the 11th Division to attack the W Hills on the right, while the 29th Division attacked Scimitar Hill on the left from the Suvla Plain.

From the first events went awry. The 11th Division wheeled across the edge of the ground to the south in the wrong direction and failed to reach the W Hills. On the opposite side the 29th Division at first appeared to succeed, with the 87th Brigade taking the top of Scimitar Hill. But those troops who crossed over it were immediately cut down by hidden Turkish positions on the reverse slopes. On Yilghin Burnu the 86th Brigade watched as these leading battalions disappeared. Later in the day the dismounted yeomanry of the 2nd Mounted Division crossed over the Salt Lake to renew the attack, but merely added to the confusion.

One particular feature of the fight for Scimitar Hill came to distinguish it from all other battles at Gallipoli. Taking place at the end of a long, hot summer, the scrub over which the attack took place was tinder-dry and slowly, as the shrapnel burst over it in ever increasing intensity, it was set alight until a great blaze burnt. Nightingale, on Yilghin Burnu, watched as the flames spread across towards him.

> *Many of our wounded were burnt alive and it was as nasty a sight as I ever want to see. ... Our Head Quarters was very heavily shelled and then the fire surrounded the place and we all thought we were going to be burnt alive. Where the telephone was, the heat was appalling. The roar of the flames drowned the noise of the shrapnel, and we had to lie flat at the bottom of the trench while the flames swept over the top. Luckily both sides didn't catch simultaneously, or I don't know what would have happened. After the gorse was all burnt, the smoke nearly asphyxiated us! All this time our battalion was being cut up in the open and it really was very unpleasant trying to send down calm messages to the Brigade Headquarters, while you were lying at the bottom of the trench like an oven, expecting to be burnt every minute, and knowing that your battalion was getting hell a hundred yards away! The telephone wires finally fused from the heat. The whole attack was a ghastly failure. They generally are now.*[34] (Captain Guy Nightingale)

After the attack many renamed Scimitar Hill '"Burnt Hill," which was no distinction'.[35]

To the west of the amphitheatre between Scimitar Hill and the W Hills a slight dip leads across to Yilghin Burnu. The two hills which form this were also confusingly known in Turkish as Mastan Tepe, but together were referred to in English as the Chocolate Hills. This name also led to a certain degree of confusion because the smaller of the two peaks, set off to the west, was similarly called Chocolate Hill in the singular. It was named after the burnt earth which distinguished it from the taller mound beside it to the east which remaining covered in vegetation and was called Green Hill. At times this hill was also officially known by its height in metres as Hill 50. The distinctive double-humped shape of the two hills can be clearly seen from the Suvla Plain immediately before the road starts its slight climb up towards the level ground between them and the original difference between them, which inspired their names, is ironically still obvious from their appearance today. The thick ring of trees which surrounds the Green Hill Cemetery has ensured that it is still green, while the rich crops on Chocolate Hill, though no longer brown, do maintain the distinction. Modest and unobtrusive, these two hills are actually the most distinctive Suvla feature, seeming to slip quietly into the background of all its views.

The billets of the 53rd (Welsh) Division on the rear slopes of Chocolate Hill looking inland from the edge of the Salt Lake. The scrub which now runs across the summit of the hill covers the still extant remains of these trenches and dug-outs. (1915/1988) (Q13445)

Around the top of Chocolate Hill, like a green tonsure, a ring of thick scrub protrudes from the fields which surround it. Climbing up the side of the hill from the road, when the scrub is finally reached it is much thicker than it looks from a distance. Beneath it the old trenches which used to skirt around the hill are completely covered. Although still on average four feet deep the scrub which hides them is very sharp and hard. Because of this they cannot be followed from inside, but they can be traced along their edge, twisting round from west to east in the direction of Sniper's Corner where they entered the front line on the forward slopes of Green Hill. They stood at the inland end of the Old Chocolate Hill Road which skirted the southern edge of the Salt Lake en route from Lala Baba.

Descending again to the dusty gap between the two peaks, by the cemetery's gate there is a brilliant view southwards to Sari Bair and Anzac. Turning round to face north, an equally resplendent view unfolds across the Suvla Plain along the new road and the old front line to Jephson's Post on the Kiretch Tepe Sirt. In shape and in practice Yilghin Burnu is the gateway into Suvla. Gazing down from near here in September, 1915, 2nd Lieutenant Baxter described the country of the plain in a letter home and in his description used a metaphor that went some way to explaining why Suvla should appear so attractive to British eyes. 'We are still in the same place, our little bit of English countryside, with its oaks and evergreen oaks and its olives and its hedgerows and cornfields and wagtails and rats and flocks of migrating geese.'[36] It was a countryside that he knew well and recognized, that reminded him and many others of home. Today this feeling is still present. Suvla is homely and welcoming, gently drawing in visitors. Its warmth overwhelms the memories of the fires and the storms, remaining wholesome and free in a nostalgic vision of England that those buried here might once have known and loved themselves.

Chapter Eight

HILL 60

Running south from the gateway into the Suvla Plain the road drops down from Yilghin Burnu and twists its way back towards the foothills of Sari Bair across a second area of plain to the south that surrounds the broad valley of the Azmak Dere. As at Helles, files of trees, casting long shadows over the grass, trace out the stream beds as they trickle down towards the sea, but nothing higher breaks out of the flatness except for a small rise set off to the east of the road. Known to the Turks as Bomba Tepe or Bomb Hill, this unobtrusive hillock

The view from the seaward edge of Hill 60 across the Azmak Dere Valley to Suvla Bay. To the left of centre is Lala Baba, beyond the Salt Lake, and opposite this on the right the rear slopes of Chocolate Hill. In the distance on the right is the outline of the Kiretch Tepe Sirt. (1919/1988) (Q14386)

overshadowed by the massive hills behind was better known to the British and Anzacs as Hill 60. To the north-east of the Damakjelik Spur, it stood at the head of Flat Hill at the point where Anzac once merged into Suvla and it came to symbolise the junction of the two Corps' lines. Despite its meagre height of just sixty metres its position as the only hill within the valley allowed it to dominate the surrounding area with an influence disproportionate to its size and the need to take it produced one of the fiercest battles of the whole campaign.

As soon as it was clear that the attacks at Sari Bair and Suvla had failed, the importance of linking the two theatres became obvious. It was decided that on 21 August, with this primary aim in mind, Sir William Birdwood would co-operate with the 11th Division's attack on the W Hills by launching a minor assault against Hill 60. The lowness of the hill's summit and the scrub, a full three feet thick, which grew right across it had prevented any detailed observation of the area, either by air or from the ground; but despite this the planners of the attack believed that the summit was encircled by a complete ring of deep trenches. If this ring could be captured the new position would look down on to the inland slopes of the hill and give a clear view across to the north-west and Biyuk Anafarta.

The attack was initially set for 3.00 pm, but later postponed and the preceding bombardment cut to thirty minutes. When the Australians, on the right, emerged from their trenches on the Damakjelik Spur, the Turkish positions which enfiladed the Kaiajik Dere from Flat Hill had been little damaged and were able to cut most of them down before they could cross the dere. Next to them in the centre the New Zealanders fared a little better, a small party managing to reach trenches on the western edge of Hill 60 before the Turkish guns isolated them by moving their fire down the valley from the Australians. On the left, after successfully capturing the wells at Kabak Kuyu, the Connaught Rangers failed to capture the east of the hill in a frontal charge and by early evening little real success had been achieved along any of the line.

During the night two communication trenches were dug across the dere to establish a link with the New Zealanders on the hill. It was decided that this small success should be exploited. On the following day a new attack was launched across the front of this position towards the upper half of the ring by the 18th Australian Battalion. Barely understanding the object of their attack, at first light on 22 August they charged the hill from the east. The initial assault was successful and a long length of the Turkish trench running along the upper half of the ring was seized. Yet, slowly, the Turks returned and with machine guns and bombing started to force the Australians back towards the edge of the New Zealanders' original position and by the end of the second day the position was little altered. Like the attack at Suvla the assault on Hill 60 had failed to seize its objective. However, it had at least established a grip on the Turkish line; but still the vital Anzac-Suvla link remained unsecured.

Birdwood sanctioned another attempt for 27 August and the new attack began at 5.00 pm. A fierce fight, like those for Lone Pine and the Vineyard, developed on the southern slopes around the positions held. Moving out of their trench the New Zealanders forced their way into a new Turkish trench, subsequently called No.2 Trench, that had been dug parallel to their own starting line. Although not yet connected, this trench led in the direction of the upper ring along which the Connaught Rangers were again moving slowly. As they began to consolidate their gains the New Zealanders moved men further on towards another trench exactly like No.2 but shallower and shorter still, named in succession No.3 Trench. Within an hour it appeared the whole ring had been taken. But then, as before, the Turks began to counter-attack. Despite fierce pressure, the New Zealanders in Nos.2 and 3 Trenches retained their delicate hold; but beyond them the Rangers, exhausted by the day's fighting, were soon being relentlessly driven back along the same path as the 18th Battalion.

At 9.00 pm one final effort was made to link the upper ring to the New Zealanders position in the centre. The 9th Regiment, Australian Light Horse, from the brigade that had attacked the Nek, were initially successful, but again failed to consolidate before the Turkish counter-attack. For the second time within the space of twelve hours this same trench was taken and for the second time lost. By dawn on 28 August the overall position had changed only in the centre and throughout the day both sides tried to consolidate. That night one more assault was attempted. The 10th ALH again pushed their way along the upper ring; but this time a fresh, second line followed in their wake, ready to clamber over the first once they had reached the head. Led by Lieutenant Hugo Throssell, in the early hours of the morning of 29 August this second wave threw down their first barricade, then retired thirty yards and built a second. Throughout the night the Turks attempted to move them, but Throssell, who won the VC, and his men remained. At dawn the barricade still held. The ring had finally been taken.

On Hill 60 itself daylight brought with it a depressing realization.

The ring did not, as had been expected, command the summit. Instead it was positioned just beneath it on the seaward slopes. The new position did not overlook the ground beyond. On reaching their objective, the attacking force found itself confronted by a new line as formidable as the one it had just taken and which still looked down on it from higher ground. Although the new position did provide a focal point for the security of the Azmak Dere valley it was little better than the one from which they had started. It was another chapter in a familiar story. Like the landings, the battles for Krithia, and the assault on Sari Bair, the hoped for success had not been achieved. It had remained elusive like the succulent fruit before Tantalus.

The fight for Hill 60 was to prove the last concerted offensive to be mounted at Gallipoli. After this there was only the winter and the evacuations to follow. Yet, as in the first efforts on 25 April, in this final act the campaign seemed to throw up another symbol of its whole effort. Side by side the troops of many different divisions had fought together. Australians, New Zealanders, Gurkhas, Irish and British, all sustaining a bitter effort towards one single goal that despite its partial capture had failed to produce victory. In describing the failure of the first attack on the hill on 21 August the Official British Historian concluded with a statement that could be applied with equal truth to the whole campaign itself: 'Despite magnificent gallantry on the part of the assaulting troops the day's plan had failed.'[1]

In the week between the two efforts to take the ring, the 54th (East Anglian) Division had been moved across from the Kiretch Tepe Sirt to the area around Chocolate Hill and at the beginning of September the Division's front was extended to include Hill 60. The 4th Battalion, Northamptonshire Regiment was selected to relieve the remnants of the regiments who had survived and Captain Dudley Pendered, the Commander of A Company, was led up in advance of the Battalion to familiarize himself with the trenches they were to take over.

> *First impressions are generally the most accurate, and I shall never forget the horrible smells, the dust, the constant ping of bullets overhead, the thud of bullets in the parapet of the trenches, and the effect of weeks and weeks of hard work and excitement on the Australians and New Zealanders who were manning the trenches.... The sight of a dead hand sticking out from the wall of a trench with fingers and great long nails, as if in the act of scratching, was most revolting; as was that of a half decomposed scalp hanging over the parados.* [2] (Captain Dudley Pendered)

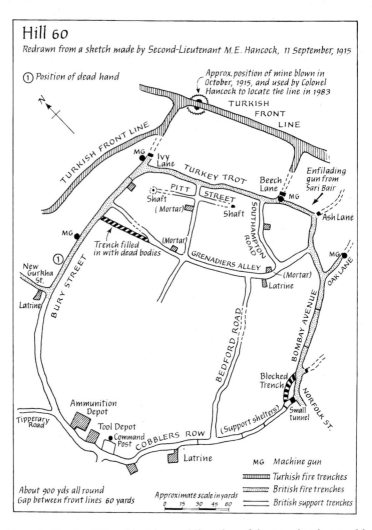

Hill 60

Redrawn from a sketch made by Second-Lieutenant M.E. Hancock, 11 September, 1915

① *Position of dead hand*

Approx. position of mine blown in October, 1915, and used by Colonel Hancock to locate the line in 1983

TURKISH FRONT LINE

N

TURKISH FRONT LINE

MG — Ivy Lane

TURKEY TROT

Beech Lane — MG

Enfilading gun from Sari Bair

PITT STREET
Shaft (Mortar)

Shaft

SOUTHAMPTON ROAD

Ash Lane

MG

Trench filled in with dead bodies

(Mortar)

GRENADIERS ALLEY

MG

①

New Gurkha St.

BURY STREET

OAK LANE

(Mortar)
Latrine

Latrine

BEDFORD ROAD

BOMBAY AVENUE

Blocked Trench

NORFOLK ST.

Small Tunnel

Ammunition Depot

Tipperary Road

Tool Depot

Command Post

COBBLERS ROW

(Support shelters)

Latrine

MG — *Machine gun*

▭▭▭ *Turkish fire trenches*

▨▨▨ *British fire trenches*

═══ *British support trenches*

About 900 yds all round
Gap between front lines 60 yards

Approximate scale in yards
0   15   30   45   60

Many bodies lay littered just beyond the edge of the trenches but could not be brought in. Those that had been retrieved were piled together in a section of the line between No.2 Trench and the upper ring, filling it completely, until it could be covered with a shallow layer of earth. It was a foul, unwelcoming place.

Following his initial visit Pendered led the rest of his company into the line, moving left through the New Zealanders' first position into the upper ring. Behind Pendered came 2nd Lieutenant Malcolm Hancock, a subaltern in the same battalion.

> *The scene when we got there was almost indescribable. Many, many of the bodies were still there. They'd been in the scorching*

sun a week or ten days and I don't know whether you can imagine what sort of state of putrefaction they were [in] but they were, in places, part of the trenches.[3] (2nd Lieutenant Malcolm Hancock)

Naturally, in filing up towards the firing line, Hancock also passed the beseeching hand.

And it was all dried, completely dried, probably been there a fortnight, three weeks. And I think I'm right in saying it was a New Zealander who said as we went up there, he said, 'Well, that chap I've known him for some time. He must have been a dry old stick.' It's awful to joke about it. But from that moment on I think every man as he went past shook hands.[4] (2nd Lieutenant Malcolm Hancock)

Without callousness but reacting instinctively in a bid to reduce the repulsion of the features with which they daily had to live, the soldiers absorbed and accepted the grotesque nature of their environment. It was to be their home, on and off, until the evacuation and they quickly developed a routine.

Roughly the trenches were in the shape of an O of which half were fire trenches and the remainder communication trenches. The Centre Sector fire trench was, as you may imagine, the nearest to the Turk, and was within bombing distance nearly all the way along. It was known as Turkey Trot. The other sectors soon got named and some of them, Bury Street, Bombay Avenue, Southampton Row, Cobblers' Row, soon became familiar. These names were always used for descriptive purposes. My dug-out with telephone and R.E. signaller, was about five yards from the Centre Sector in Southampton Row, and a most unhealthy spot it was too. Firstly it was just within bombing distance, and a well-directed and well-thrown bomb might easily have landed at the front of my Headquarters and finished one or two of us off; especially if the occupants had happened to be oblivious of the arrival of a live bomb. Happily this did not occur. Secondly the roof of the dug-out was covered with sand over boards, and on top and rather far back there were one or two bodies but half buried, which gave a most unhealthy and unpleasant odour that seemed to take away one's appetite. One corpse up there went by the name of 'Old Joe,' and (it is a gruesome thing to look back on) many a jest had to be made at 'Old Joe's' expense to kill the hump he would have created. 'Old Joe' asserted himself daily,

207

and he was never properly subdued, not even when disinfectants could be obtained.[5] (Captain Dudley Pendered)

While Pendered took up residence in the side of Southampton Row (or Road), Hancock chose a more reliable spot in the parados of Bury Street. It was no further from the Turkish line and neither was it out of bombing range, but at least it faced west, away from the guns that enfiladed the top-right corner of the trenches near the junction of Turkey Trot and Bombay Avenue - the same guns that had devastated the Anzacs in the Kaiajik Dere on 21 August - and their shrapnel became a regular feature of life on Hill 60. Like the whole position, this part of the line was overlooked from the heights of Sari Bair. But the geography of the ground did give the British at least one advantage of their own. In the morning when they stood-to an hour before sunrise the lightening sky behind the high ground picked out the Turks as silhouettes, outlining any still working above the parapet. 'They couldn't see us, we were in the shadow ... and we used to do a bit of execution there sometimes. Highly satisfactory.'[6]

Having taken over the position from the Anzacs, the East Anglians set-to to invest it with an English flavour, giving the different positions descriptive names that recalled familiar places and associations. Norfolk Street, Bury (St Edmunds) Street and Bedford Road reminded them where their real homes were, and Cobbler's Row harked back to the civilian trade of the Northampton territorials' home town. Yet, most characteristic of all, was the name they gave to the front line trench, Turkey Trot, a popular pre-war dance like the Bunny Hug and the Kangaroo Hop; but now this light-hearted reference to more frivolous days also kept their enemy ironically in mind.

The firing line itself ran round the inland half of the ring. Starting at the point where New Gurkha Street cut into Bury Street from Susak Kuyu, it ran north-west past the desiccated hand and the trench filled with dead to Ivy Lane. This was the upper ring that had cost so many lives and at its head, beyond the barricade in Ivy Lane, was where Throssell had won his VC. There the line turned abruptly to the right to form Turkey Trot, based on an enlarged extension of No.3 Trench. Leading westwards two communication trenches branched off this to the right. The first led down to Grenadier's Alley or the old No.2 Trench; the second was Southampton Row itself. Beyond this Turkey Trot pushed on past Beech Lane to end in Ash Lane, where a right turn led down into Bombay Avenue, past Oak Lane and finally into Norfolk Street, where the firing line dropped down into the Kaiajik Dere. The ring itself carried on into Cobbler's Row, the support line, past the

Commanding Officer's post to a fork and it was this length of trench that the New Zealanders' first rush had seized and into which the communication trench had been built. At the fork this latter trench led left down to Tipperary Road and the Rest Pits, while the line itself curved right up towards the upper ring and the western end of Bury Street, thus completing the circle.

It was a close and tightly packed position. At night officers patrolling along the fire trenches could not avoid treading on the faces of their sleeping men. The British lines were almost as near to the Turks as were the Anzac posts that ran along Second Ridge, so close in fact that when the British artillery needed to register their guns Turkey Trot had to be evacuated to minimize the danger of short-falling shells. The distance from Bury Street and Turkey Trot to the Turkish front varied from twenty five to thirty yards and at Ivy Lane and Beech Lane they even shared the same trench where the two original communication trenches that had led out of the ring towards the rear of the Turkish lines had been quickly sealed by sandbag barricades at both ends by Turks and British alike. Machine gun positions were then established alongside them and the intervening trenches had become almost literally dead ground.

Once this had been done the positions were relatively stable. As a result, the work of the Hill 60 garrison was limited and epitomized the frustrating futility of the trench warfare system. There was little constructive work to be done, instead the troops were reduced to 'just being a damned nuisance as far as we could'.[7] The sandbag barricades of the shared trenches provided an ideal target for this kind of mischievous irritation and Hancock proved adept at gradually using his periscope rifle to weaken the Turkish barricade.

> *By systematically aiming at the top of the sandbag it made a little jag in the sandbag. You then went down two or three inches lower and you gradually split that sandbag down.... And you could see the part that had been built up to hold a machine gun begin to slip. And we were rather pleased with it. Of course they built it up again at night. And next day it was back again.[8]* (2nd Lieutenant Malcolm Hancock)

However, the main work was bombing. On the right of Turkey Trot, in the parados of the trench that ran between Beech and Ash Lanes, there was a small bay just large enough to hold one man. There, fed with bombs by a colleague from outside, the bomber could stand and reach his throwing arm right down behind his back to get the maximum power behind his throw. According to Hancock, his Battalion's

Bombing Officer, it was 'exactly like overarm bowling'.[9] There were three kinds of bombs.

> *One was the jam tin. The other was a cricket ball which looked exactly like a cricket ball made of cast iron. And the other was what we called a hair brush and that was a flat piece of wood with a handle. On that flat piece was wired on a slab of dynamite. It had a bit of fuse wire and a detonator stuck in. You lit the end. You waited about five or six seconds possibly, and you chucked it. The detonation was the thing; there was no metal attached to it at all. But the detonation, anywhere near, was very, very upsetting.... The only bomb we identified, at least I did, was the Turkish jam tin and that was practically the same as ours only slightly smaller and very thin tin. Now I should think 20%, one in five, failed to go off, which was really very satisfactory. You heard it drop, this was at night, you heard it drop just in front of the line and you knew there was a bomb out there which had not exploded. So one or two of us used to go out, crawl over the parapet at night, crawl over into no-man's land and bring these back. I then re-fused and re-detonated them and then chucked them back and every time they went off! Most satisfactory![10]* (2nd Lieutenant Malcolm Hancock)

And so life went on. Bombs were thrown routinely along the line and the shrapnel from Flat Hill struck back. Machine gun posts were enlarged and new ones built from scratch; in October the Welsh Horse engineers blew up a mine beneath the Turkish line and in November it was repeated all over again. But it led to nothing, as had been expected. It simply helped to pass the time and maintain the offensive spirit.

Field Marshal Lord Kitchener (second from left) and General Birdwood (left) looking across to Lala Baba and Sulva Bay from the heights of Anzac, November 1915. (Q13594)

On 11 October Lord Kitchener asked Sir Ian Hamilton to state the possible casualties he felt might result from an evacuation of the peninsula. Hamilton was incensed and replied three days later with a severe estimate of 50%. The following day he was replaced in command by General Sir Charles Monro who was charged by Kitchener to report on the situation in Gallipoli and to determine whether the deadlock could be broken or whether the moment had passed and 'from a purely military point of view' it would be better to evacuate.[11] Arriving at Imbros on 28 October, Monro had inspected all three areas of the peninsula and talked to the three corps commanders within two days. His conclusion was clear and on 31 October he recommended to Kitchener a complete evacuation. However, in London doubts still remained and at its first meeting the newly formed War Committee decided to despatch Kitchener himself to investigate further. Leaving London on 4 November he arrived at Mudros within five days and had carried out an inspection of the positions within a week. His conclusion was the same as Monro's, except that he believed Helles should be retained after the evacuation of Anzac and Suvla both to mitigate the admission of failure which this would signal and in deference to the wishes of the Royal Navy.

On 23 November he sent this decision to the Prime Minister who indicated that he would prefer a complete evacuation but that the ultimate decision would have to be taken by the complete cabinet. It was not until 7 December that the cabinet agreed to the evacuation of Anzac and Suvla and the retention of Helles, by which stage events at Gallipoli, most notably the great storm at the end of November, had shown how much conditions had changed since Monro first submitted his report thirty seven days beforehand. However, following Kitchener's departure preparations had been started in anticipation of the decision and a Joint Naval and Military Committee had decided on the basic outline that the evacuation would follow. It would be conducted in three separate stages: preliminary, intermediate and final. The first would remove all troops, stores and animals not needed for prolonged defence throughout the winter; the second would reduce these levels, over ten nights, to a level capable of holding out against Turkish attacks for one week should the weather disrupt the evacuation and the third stage would then remove this remaining number. Monro insisted that this stage must not last more than two nights.

Within these parameters the plans were drawn up and immediately after the orders were received from the cabinet on 8 December the Intermediate Stage at Anzac and Suvla began. By 18 December all was

Hill 60 Cemetery under construction by the Greek labourers of the Graves Registration Directorate and in its finished state today. Note the outline of Lala Baba in the distance of both pictures. The cemetery was built inside the ring of British front-line trenches. (1919/1998)

ready for the Final Stage and that night the first half of the garrison was removed. The next day all was quiet and in the early hours of 20 December the last men of the two corps were removed safely. The operation had been a remarkable success, incurring no casualties at all. A week later, on 28 December, the evacuation of the remaining position at Helles was also finally ordered. The same outline plan was followed again, except that this time it was decided to reduce the duration of the Final Stage to one night only in view of the increasingly unpredictable weather. The first two stages proceeded steadily and on the night of 8/9 January, 1916, the last member of the MEF was taken off the peninsula. For the men who had lived through the battles, the squalid trenches and the extremes of the weather it was a strange sensation to be lifted off silently in the middle of the night. There was a sense of dishonour and furtiveness; but for most this was outweighed by the relief of having survived.

Looking down from Cobblers' Row in the early autumn of 1915, with the sea to the left and the Salt Lake to the right, the mouth of the Azmak Dere valley seemed to Hancock to form a second open space, similar to that at Suvla, which he called the Anafarta plain and where the land 'was rough, uninviting, scrubby-looking, [with] thorn bushes growing up to four and five feet high ... And it wasn't very green. It was terribly hot and very, very dry. There'd been no water or rain for months. And it was dreary-looking country really.'[12] It was an enervating view that through its 'dull misty grey' sapped all energy and zest for life.[13] There was no colour, no living form not covered by a film of achromatic dust, and it reflected exactly the sense of death and torpor that had settled on Hill 60. Today, into this stifling scene colour has rushed like air into a void. Strips of glinting yellow crops flash between the deep green of the leaves. Hedgerows and bushes dance together, twisting and leaning among the outstretched shadows of the trees as they trail away as if from English church spires. Across it, ubiquitous, the fine mist rolls. Only now it eddies in swirling patches, like a sea spray, blowing in off the Salt Lake. It spreads a placid calm across the ground, like that felt inside the confines of Suvla's hills, but wilder, slightly less refined. Gone is the mouldering emptiness, replaced instead by new vitality within the Anafarta plain.

In April 1983, almost 68 years after he had been taken off on a hospital ship and having served his country again during the Second World War, the now Lieutenant Colonel Hancock returned to Gallipoli. With his son he visited his old battle grounds. At Hill 60, he found it very different. Inside the ring of trenches a clean cemetery had been carefully laid out over the ground where so many men had been hastily buried in September 1915 and the trees which ran around the white stone wall had changed the scene entirely - 'there were no trees before'.[14] But underfoot the ground was still the same. There was one particular feature, beyond the cemetery wall in the field that now covered the summit and the old Turkish lines, that Hancock felt he might still find. In October 1915 he had watched the Welsh miners detonate their mine. A terrific explosion had ripped open the Turkish front, throwing a great section up into the air and creating a deep, dark crater, over thirty feet wide. This scar might still be there, just under the summit of the hill. If he could find this he knew he would be able to use it to locate the position of his own trenches. Drawing on the hidden instincts seared into his memory all those years ago, he sought it out.

> By means of searching outside the cemetery, amongst the still very rough and scrubby ground, I found the crater.... By retracing my steps some twenty-five yards back, I was then able to find the faint, but quite clear, indentations of our own front line and of a machine gun post. That was an exciting, but at the same time,

sobering thought to be at the scene once more of a stern struggle for existence. The memory came back to me of leading those parties of men, night after night, down the dry river bed of the Aghyl Dere to the beach to bring back the precious water ration on which we had to exist. The allowance for a great deal of that time was 1 pint per man and this had to do for everything including cooking.[15] (Lieutenant Colonel Malcolm Hancock)

Outside the cemetery's wall the shallow trench that circles round towards the bank of trees and which in places is less then two feet deep can be seen as all that remains of the old British line and from its twisting course it can be deduced that the cemetery has actually been built inside the ring. Placing the plan of the cemetery over that of the trenches it appears that the Stone of Remembrance stands near the crossroads in Grenadiers Alley and the burial ground so hastily filled with dead at its western end is now submerged beneath the simple rows of headstones near the entrance. The cemetery is small and round, looking west to Lala Baba and east to Sari Bair, and sits like a cap pushed back on the head of the hill.

However, the names of many of the men who were buried there have since been lost. The missing Australian and British soldiers are now commemorated on the great memorials at Lone Pine and Helles; but, as at Helles in Twelve Tree Copse, the New Zealanders here have a memorial to their missing dead around the base of the Great Cross. Yet there are few East Anglian graves in the cemetery, except for a cluster of men from the Suffolk Regiment killed on 8 and 9 October. The men from the other battalions of the 54th Division who were killed or wounded were usually carried down the line beyond the Rest Pits. Nearby the battalions had small burial grounds of their own and after the war these were moved not into Hill 60 but south to become part of 7th Field Ambulance Cemetery. It is there that the wartime cemeteries of the Bedford, Essex, Suffolk and Norfolk regiments have all been concentrated together, around the small cemetery that was established during the war by the Australian ambulance unit encamped nearby. And it is there, also, that the dead of the 4th Northants now lie. Out of the 59 headstones in the first two rows, 31 are from this one battalion, and of these, four are from Hancock's own platoon.

A few hundred yards north, beneath the surface of Hill 60 Cemetery, the communication trenches once populated by these long-gone Englishmen still seem to cut across the ring. Southampton Row twists back beneath the hedgerow, passing Pendered's dugout buried beside the graves in Grenadiers Alley. Outside the gate, from a space cleared of scrub, the rough dirt track trails back down the hill to the Suvla road. It follows a course parallel to the old Bedford Road down to the sea where the barges of water acted as the hill's reservoir. In the evening calm as the soft breeze blows through the setting shadows of the trees all becomes clear. There is a strange familiarity in these flickering shapes and in them life on Hill 60 is discernible again.

Although to the north of the cemetery the British trenches still run in the thick scrub, they are confused and unclear. No clues remain to the events that took place in them or the people who lived there. Their appearance has been irrevocably changed. The wind and rain of eighty years have washed away the wartime landscape, a process that began before the campaign was even over during the great storm in November. Holes, ditches, drains to guide away the melting snows, features that are found in any landscape are all the trenches would seem without a guide to tell one otherwise. Returning from the crater to his own line Hancock 'knew where it was. And there it jolly well was', just where it had been since he left it.[16] It was like the re-discovery of a long-lost toy from childhood. Immediately everything came flooding back, all the sensations and pain of years before. But in the discovery there was also confirmation. 'After all those years it was rather a relief to actually see it again. It was almost like laying a ghost, if you know what I mean. And I felt it was very satisfying to have done that.'[17]

Across the whole peninsula other men's ghosts have not been laid to rest like this. Even at Hill 60 it is simply one among many hundred and this one minor position is but a small part of a much greater area. Over it all one feels these spirits moving, motivated by a sense of haunting restlessness. They cannot sleep, like the murdered King Hamlet; instead they pace endlessly over the hidden places where once they were alive. They drift, hopeless, seeking out their former lives; but life has vanished with the battlefields. As the trenches fall away into ditches and the once familiar names slip into obscurity, they are divorced from them. Each year the signs of the struggle continue to disappear beneath the ever-crumbling sands and matted fronds of scrub; slowly the scars on the beautiful face are healing. Yet as they do so the spirits feel forgotten, betrayed, and sense the vital tragedy of their life dissolving into loneliness. It is only through the visitors who come that there is hope. Through them their lives can be renewed. For in the memories of today we keep alive the spirits of the dead.

AFTERWORD

In September 1914, George Horridge, a subaltern in the 1/5th Battalion, Lancashire Fusiliers, left England on board the SS *Neuralia* for Egypt. As part of the territorial East Lancashire Division, his regiment was directed there shortly after the outbreak of war to relieve the garrison of regular troops. At the beginning of May 1915 the Division was sent to Gallipoli as the campaign's first reinforcements. They arrived just in time for the Second Battle of Krithia and from then until the evacuation they suffered steady and heavy casualties. Horridge himself returned twice to hospital in Egypt, the first time wounded and the second sick. On each occasion when he rejoined his battalion he could see it gradually dwindling away with more and more familiar faces gone. Almost seventy years later, looking back at the campaign, he recalled one particular aspect of the voyage out to the Mediterranean, with all these losses yet to come and his men looking forward to their adventure with a mixture of excitement and trepidation, that seemed to capture the air of pathos and tragedy that still hangs over much of the battlefields today.

As the time went on and we got into nice weather, at night the fellows used to have sing-songs on the deck. And I always remember one thing we sang which even today I think terribly sad. It was a song that went like this:

> *Homeland, homeland, when shall I see you again?*
> *Land of my birth, dearest land on earth.*
> *Homeland, homeland, when shall I see you again?*
> *It may be for years or it may be forever,*
> *Dear homeland...*

Making me cry now.[1] *(2nd Lieutenant George Horridge)*

INTRODUCTION

1. Moorehead, Alan, *Gallipoli*, (1956), pp.368-9.
2. Steel, Nigel and Peter Hart, *Defeat at Gallipoli*, (1994), published as a paperback by Papermac in 1995.
3. Oglander, Brigadier-General C. F. Aspinall-, *History of the Great War. Military Operations: Gallipoli*, Vol.II, (1932), p.479.

THE LANDINGS, 25 APRIL

1. Oglander, *Op.Cit.*, Vol.I (1929), p.52.
2. Hamilton, General Sir Ian, *Sir Ian Hamilton's Despatches from the Dardanelles*, ([1915-16]), p.21.
3. Nightingale, Captain G. W., MC, letter to his mother, 1 May 1915, (Department of Documents, IWM). Extracts from these letters are included in Moynihan, Michael, *A Place Called Armageddon, Letters from the Great War*, (1975).
4. The 'modern story' is best seen in the version of Gallipoli presented for a wide audience on television in *1915* and *Anzacs* and in Peter Weir's film *Gallipoli*. All of them present very good pictures of the conditions of life at Anzac but introduce this incorrect idea of British failure being solely responsible for Anzac suffering.
5. Hamilton, General Sir Ian, *Gallipoli Diary*, (1920), Vol.I, p.61.

Helles

1. Oglander, *Op.Cit.*, I, (1929), p.135.
2. Tizard, Lieutenant-Colonel H. E., unpublished typescript, 'The Landing at 'V' Beach, Gallipoli' (19pp),p.5, (held in the collection of Stoney, Lieutenant Colonel G B, DSO, in the Department of Documents IWM).
3. For these details, as for so many other insights into the campaign from the Turkish perspective, I am grateful to my friend and guide, Izzet Yildirim. The statistics and a myriad of other facts are also recorded in *Adim Adim Çanakkale Savas Alanari*, (Çanakkale, 1997) by Ekrem Boz whose wise counsel I would also like to acknowledge here.
4. Oglander, Op.Cit., II, p.484.
5. *History of the Great War Based on Official Documents: Statistics of the Military Effort of the British Empire*, (1922), pp.284-287, and the French statement at the entrance to their Gallipoli cemetery.
6. Cooke, A. E., unpublished typescript, 'Account of Time in Gallipoli (April 1923 - July 1924) as an Engineer in Charge of Building Cemeteries and Memorials', p.5, (Department of Documents, IWM).
7. Buxton, 2nd Lieutenant D. A. J., ms diary, 25 April 1915 (Department of Documents, IWM).
8. Oglander, *Op.Cit.*, Vol.I, p.232.
9. Rickard, E. E., ms letter to his sister, 7 May 1915 (Department of Documents, IWM).
10. Tizard, *Op.Cit.*, pp.6-7.
11. Oglander, *Op.Cit.*, I, p.232.
12. Stoney, *Op.Cit.*, letter to his brother, 10 May, 1915.
13. Oglander, *Op.Cit.*,I, p.232.
14. Oglander, *Op.Cit.*,I, pp.230-1.
15. Moorehead, *Op.Cit.*, p.367.
16. Stewart, A. T., and Revd C.J.E. Peshall, *The Immortal Gamble and the part played in it by H.M.S. 'Cornwallis'*, (1917), pp.133-4.
17. Mackenzie, Compton, *Gallipoli Memories*, (1929), p.76.
18. Mahmut, Colonel, commander of the 3rd Battalion, 26th Regiment, ts report on the landings translated from the Turkish, p.6, (Department of Printed Books, IWM).
19. Hamilton, *Despatches*, Op.Cit., p.14
20. Blunden, Len, letter to his mother, 28 May, 1915, (held in the collection of 2nd Lieutenant E. H. Bennett in the Department of Documents, IWM).
21. Williams, Colonel W. de L., copy of a letter, 22 May, 1915, (held in the collection of Doughty-Wylie, Mrs L. O., in the Department of Documents, IWM).
22. The Imperial War Museum VC and GC Collection held in the Department of Documents contains a series of files on all holders of the VC and much of the information included here has been taken from the appropriate file in this series. Further information can be found in Snelling, Stephen, *VCs of the First World War: Gallipoli*, (1995).
23. Nightingale, *Op.Cit.*, letter to his mother, 4 June, 1915.
24. Cooke, *Op.Cit.*, p.8.
25. Hamilton, *Despatches*, *Op.Cit.*, p.14.
26. Longworth, Philip, *The Unending Vigil*, (1985), p.112.
27. *Ibid.*
28. Hamilton, *Despatches*, *Op.Cit.*, pp.20-1.
29. *Ibid.*, p.20.
30. Talbot, Captain A. D., letter to Captain T. Slingsby, 2 May, 1915, (Department of Documents, IWM).
31. Clayton, Captain H. R., quotation from a letter included in Creighton, Revd O., CF, *With the Twenty-Ninth Division in Gallipoli: A Chaplain's Experiences*, (1916), pp.59-60.
32. Shaw, Major H., *Ibid.*, pp.60-3.
33. Adams, Major G., *Ibid.*, pp.57-8.
34. Talbot, *Op.Cit.*, letter to Dorothy Turle, 27 May, 1915. Extracts from these letters are included in Moynihan, Michael, *Greater Love: Letters Home 1914-1918*, (1980).
35. Nightingale, *Op.Cit.*, letter to his mother, 25-26 August, 1915.
36. Citations included in the relevant files in the IWM VC and GC Collection.
37. Hare, Major General Sir Steuart, 'Special Brigade Order issued to the 86th Infantry Brigade', quoted in full in Creighton, *Op.Cit.*, p.46.
38. Buxton, *Op.Cit.*, 26 April, 1915.
39. Buxton, 2nd Lieutenant D. A. J., ms letters, letter to his sister, 8 May, 1915 (Department of Documents, IWM).
40. Bartlett, E. Ashmead, *Some of my Experiences in the Great War*, (1918), p.86.
41. *Ibid.*, p.87.
42. *Ibid.*, p.89.
43. Creighton, *Op.Cit.*, p.89.
44. Talbot, *Op.Cit.*, letter to his mother from Major Holberton, another officer of the Lancashire Fusiliers transferred to the Manchester Regiment, 30 July, 1915, included after his own letters.
45. *Ibid.*, printed extract from the British Roll of Honour including a quotation from a letter from Major Pearson, Talbot's former company commander.
46. *Ibid.*
47. Newenham, Lieutenant Colonel H. G. B., account of the landing at X Beach included in Creighton, *Op.Cit.*, pp.55-6.
48. *Ibid.*
49. Tizard, *Op.Cit.*, p.13.
50. Hare, *Op.Cit.*.

The Northern Limits

1. Samson, Commodore C. R., *Fights and Flights*, (1930), pp.246-7.
2. Oglander, *Op.Cit.*, II, p.177.
3. Samson, *Ibid.*.

4. Hamilton, *Despatches, Op.Cit.*, p.19.

5. Oglander, *Op.Cit.*, I, p.327. C.E.W. Bean, *Official History of Australia in the War: The Story of Anzac*, Vol. II, (1981) uses a similar arrangement, but gives the four spurs different names. As this book refers mainly to the British History it is the British names which have been used here.

6. Bartlett, E. Ashmead, *Despatches from the Dardanelles*, (1915), p. 110.

7. *Ibid.*, pp.111-12, also quoted in nearly the same form in Bartlett, E. Ashmead, *The Uncensored Dardanelles*, (1928), p.35.

8. Buxton, letters, *Op.Cit.*, letter to his sister, 8 May, 1915.

9. Nevinson, H. W., *The Dardanelles Campaign*, (1918), p.202-3.

10. Cooke, *Op.Cit.*, p.5.

11. I am indebted to Mike Hibberd at the IWM for this suggestion.

12. Jerrold, Douglas, *Georgian Adventure*, (1938), p.142.

13. Peters, A. R., photocopy of a manuscript pocket-book, (Department of Documents, IWM).

14. Buxton, diary, *Op.Cit.*, 2 May, 1915.

15. Mackenzie, *Op.Cit.*, p.68.

16. Nevinson, *Op.Cit.*, p.92.

17. Nevinson, *Op.Cit.*, pp.203-4.

18. Baxter, Captain C. W., MC, letter to his mother, 18 July 1915, (Department of Documents, IWM).

19. Buxton, diary, *Op.Cit.*, 4 August, 1915.

20. The words 'Supply Reserve Depot' are imprinted into the wax seal of a re-sealed rum jar marked SRD held in the Department of Exhibits and Firearms at the IWM and, although the most mundane explanation of the meaning of SRD, they would appear to be the most reliable. Once again I am grateful to Mike Hibberd for his help in locating the rum jar.

21. Buxton, diary, *Op.Cit.*, 23 May, 1915.

22. Bartlett, *Despatches, Op.Cit.*, pp.146-7.

23. Creighton, *Op.Cit.*, pp.136-7.

24. Oglander, *Op.Cit.*, I, pp.201-2.

25. Quoted by Moorehead, *Op.Cit.*, p.145.

26. Stoney, *Op.Cit.*, letter to his brother, 5 July, 1915.

27. *Ibid.*, letter to Stoney's brother Tom from Brigadier-General C. H. Tindall Lucas, 20 October, 1915.

28 *Ibid.*, letter to Stoney's brother Tom from Captain C S Stirling-Cookson, 16 October, 1915.

29. In addition to being included in his file in the IWM VC and GC Collection, the citation is also quoted in his entry in the Twelve Tree Copse cemetery register.

30. Nightingale, *Op.Cit.*, letter to his mother, 13 June, 1915.

31. Oglander, *Op.Cit.*, II, p.170.

ANZAC COVE, APRIL TO AUGUST

1. Rhodes James, Robert, *Gallipoli*, (1984), p.105.

2. The quotations were first published in Bush, Captain E W RN, *Gallipoli*, (1975), pp111-114.

3. Metcalf, Captain J S RNR, ts account of the landing attached to a chart showing the course which he believed was followed by the tows (Department of Documents, IWM).

4. Waterlow, Commander J. B. RN, microfilm copy of ms journal, 25 April 1915 (Department of Documents, IWM).

5. Bush, Captain E W RN, copy of an ms account of the landings at Anzac and Suvla (21pp.), (Department of Documents, IWM), pp. 6-7. His papers also contain his Midshipman's Journal, which gives an almost identical account, together with the research notes for his book *Gallipoli.Op.Cit.*

6. Miscellaneous 262, anonymous typescript account, pp.1-2, (Department of Documents, IWM).

7. Hearder, Captain D., unpublished typescript memoir, pp.11-12 (Department of Documents, IWM).

8. Miscellaneous 262, *Op.Cit.*, p.2.

9. Hearder, *Op.Cit.*, pp.12-13.

10. Oglander, *Op.Cit.*, I, p.299.

11. [Herbert, Hon. A. N.,] *Mons, Anzac and Kut by an M.P.*, (1919), p.109.

12. Longworth, Op.Cit., p.112.

13. Headstones of: Cannan, 351 Trooper F. W., 7/ALH, Killed 31 July, 1915; Fawcett, 1519, Pte W. C., 23/Battalion AIF, Killed 20 September, 1915; Owens, 559 Pte J., 3/Battalion AIF, Killed 7/12 August, 1915.

14. Bartlett, *Experiences,* Op.Cit., p.81.

15. Hamilton, General Sir Ian, unpublished letters to Lord Kitchener contained in file 5/1 of the Hamilton Papers held in the Liddell Hart Centre for Military Archives, King's College London, letter dated 3 June, 1915.

16. Powell, Captain I., unpublished typescript 'Gallipoli Anti-climax', (Department of Documents, IWM).

17. Oglander, *Op.Cit.*, II, p.23.

18. Herbert, *Op.Cit.*, p.122.

19. Thomas, Reverend H. A., unpublished typescript, 'A Parson-Private with an Aspect of Gallipoli by Augustine', p.40 (Department of Documents, IWM).

20. Oglander, *Op.Cit.*, I, p.185.

21. Herbert, *Op.Cit.*, p.97.

22. *Ibid.*, p.120.

23. *Ibid.*, p.134.

24. Bartlett, *Experiences, Op.Cit.*, p.83.

25. McGrigor, Captain A. M., typescript diary, 12 October, 1915, (Department of Documents, IWM).

26. *Ibid.*

27. Hamilton, *Diary, Op.Cit.*,II, pp.254-5.

28. Bean, *Op.Cit.*, pp.617-8.

29. Rhodes James, *Op.Cit.*, p.276.

30. McGrigor, *Op.Cit.*, 22 November, 1915.

31. Hamilton, General Sir Ian, unpublished correspondence with Field Marshal Lord Birdwood, contained in file 5/10 of the Hamilton Papers held in the Liddell Hart Centre for Military Archives, Kings College London, typescript letter to Hamilton from Birdwood, 14 June, 1915.

32. Nevinson, *Op.Cit.*, pp.161-2.

33. Bartlett, Despatches, *Op.Cit.*, p.134.

34. Herbert, *Op.Cit.*, pp.115-6. The full unexpurgated text of Herbert's diary for this day is given in Chapter 9 of his biography, FitzHerbert, Margaret, *The Man Who Was Greenmantle*, (1985), pp.161-2.

35. The rumour about the Turkish staff officers is given in Herbert, *Op.Cit.*, p.136; those concerning Kemal in Moorehead, *Op.Cit.*, p.189 and Sanders in Nevinson, *Op.Cit.*, p.163; and the name of the trench *Ibid.*, p.190.

36. Herbert, *Op.Cit.*, p.118-9.

37. Nevinson, *Op.Cit.*, p.126.

38. *Ibid.*, p.207.

39. Hamilton, *Diary*, I, *Op.Cit.*, p.257.

40. Bartlett, *Experiences*, *Op.Cit.*, p.84.

41. Nevinson, *Op.Cit.*, p.233.

42. Ibid., p.232.

43. Oglander, *Op.Cit.*, II, p.180.

44. Hamilton, General Sir Ian, *Ian Hamilton's Final Despatch,* (1916), p.43.

45. Longworth, *Op.Cit.*, p.113.

46. Oglander, *Op.Cit.*, II, pp.181-2.
47. Moorehead, *Op.Cit.*,p.241.

The August Offensive

1. Oglander, *Op.Cit.*, II, p.26.
2. Moorehead, *Op.Cit.*, pp.138-9.
3. Oglander, *Op.Cit.*, II, p.74.
4. Moorehead, *Op.Cit.*, p.242.

The Assault on Sari Bair

1. See also Bean, *Op.Cit.*, II, pp.567-8, who uses a similar model only using the left hand.
2. Hamilton, Diary, *Op.Cit.*, vol.I, p.331.
3. Nevinson, *Op.Cit.*, pp.273.
4. Phipson, Colonel E. S., unpublished typescript Thoughts at a Royal Review', p.2, (Department of Documents, IWM).
5. Hamilton, correspondence with Birdwood, *Op.Cit.*, letter to Hamilton from Birdwood, 10 August, 1915.
6. For further details on this point see Nevinson, *Op.Cit.*, pp.274-5, and Rhodes James, *Op.Cit.*, p.286.
7. Hamilton, correspondence with Birdwood, *Op.Cit.*, letter to Hamilton from Birdwood, 10 August, 1915.
8. Oglander, *Op.Cit.*, II, p.307.
9. Herbert, *Op.Cit.*, p.170.
10. Oglander, *Op.Cit.*, II, p.182.
11. Nevinson, *Op.Cit.*, p.252.
12. Oglander, *Op.Cit.*, I, p.167.
13. *Ibid.*, II, p.485.
14. *Ibid.*, II, pp.485-6.
15. Uluaslan, Huseyin, *Gallipoli Campaign*, (1986).
16. Nevinson, Op.Cit., p.260.
17. *Ibid.*, p.253.
18. Rhodes James, *Op.Cit.*, p.219.
19. Nevinson, *Op.Cit.*, p.261.
20. Hamilton, letters to Kitchener, *Op.Cit.*, letter dated 21 September, 1915.
21. Herbert, *Op.Cit.*, p.179.
22. Hamilton, letters to Kitchener, *Op.Cit.*, letter dated 21 September, 1915.
23. Hamilton, correspondence with Birdwood, *Op.Cit.*, letter to Hamilton from Birdwood, 21 August, 1915.
24. Hancock, Lieutenant Colonel M. E., MC, Recorded Interview, 7396/14/7,(Sound Archive, IWM).
25. *Ibid.*
26. Herbert, *Op.Cit.*, p.163.
27. Thomas, *Op.Cit.*, p.23.
28. Herbert, *Op.cit.*, p.159.
29. *Ibid.*, p.160.
30. Powell, Captain Ivor, private interview with the author, 10 May, 1985, (copy held in the Sound Archive, IWM).
31. Herbert, *Op.Cit.*, p.181.

The Landing at Suvla Bay

1. Oglander, *Op.Cit.*, II: Maps and Appendices, p.16.
2. *Ibid.*, p.16.
3. *Ibid.*, p.19.
4. *Ibid.*, p.27.
5. Oglander, *Op.Cit.*, II, p.151.
6. *Ibid.*, p.276.
7. Nevinson, *Op.Cit.*, p.312.
8. Oglander, *Op.Cit.*, p.236.
9. Lye, E., unpublished typescript, 'A Worm's Eye View of Suvla Bay', p.12, (Department of Documents, IWM).
10. Wright, William, private interview with the author, 2 April 1986, (copy held in the Sound Archive, IWM).

11. Buxton, diary, *Op.Cit.*, 21 August, 1915.
12. Rhodes James, *Op.Cit.*, p.239.
13. Miles, E., unpublished typescript, 'A Brief Diary', p.56, (Department of Documents, IWM).
14. Buxton, letters, *Op.Cit.*, letter to his father, 21 October, 1915.
15. Lye, *Op.Cit.*, p.28.
16. *Ibid.*, p.28.
17. *Ibid.*, p.34.
18. Lye, *Op.Cit.*, p.28.
19. *Ibid.*, p.24.
20. *Ibid.*, p.26.
21. Nightingale, *Op.Cit.*, letter to his mother, 25 August, 1915.
22. Hamilton, letters to Kitchener, *Op.Cit.*, note added to letter dated 11 August 1915.
23. Watson, Captain T.P., letter to his mother, 2 December 1915, (Department of Documents, IWM).
24. Lye, *Op.Cit.*, p.31.
25. *Ibid.*, p.31.
26. *Ibid.*, pp.31-2.
27. *Ibid.*, p.32.
28. Miles, *Op.Cit.*, p.60.
29. Hamilton, correspondence with Birdwood, *Op.Cit.*, letter to Hamilton from Birdwood, 12 December, 1915.
30. Guthrie, Joe, private interview with the author, 29 April, 1986, (copy held in the Sound Archive, IWM).
31. Hamilton, Diary, *Op.Cit.*, II, p.68.
32. Nevinson, *Op.Cit.*, p.288.
33. *Ibid.*, p.287.
34. Nightingale, *Op.Cit.*, letter to his mother, 25 August, 1915.
35. Nevinson, *Op.Cit.*, p.288.
36. Baxter, *Op.Cit.*, letter to his mother, 19 October, 1915.

Hill 60

1. Oglander, Op.Cit., II, p.358.
2. [Pendered, Captain R. Dudley,] *The Tale of a Territorial*, (ND), p.132.
3. Hancock, Lieutenant Colonel M. E., MC, recording of a talk given in Oxford, 17 November 1987, (copy held in the Sound Archive, IWM).
4. Hancock, interview, *Op.Cit.*, 7396/14/8.
5. Pendered, Op.Cit., pp.138-9. In this quotation Pendered uses fictionalized names for the officers of his company, as he does throughout his book. For example throughout Hancock is referred to as Horrock and Pendered himself as Pemberton.
6. Hancock, talk, *Op.Cit.*
7. Hancock, interview *Op.Cit.*, 7396/14/4.
8. Ibid.
9. Hancock, talk, *Op.Cit.*
10. *Ibid.*
11. Oglander, *Op.Cit.*, vol.II, p.399.
12. Hancock, interview, *Op.Cit,* 7396/14/4.
13. *Ibid.*
14. Hancock, Lieutenant Colonel M. E., MC, unpublished typescript, 'Gallipoli 68 Years Later', (Department of Documents, IWM).
15. *Ibid.*
16. Hancock, interview Op.Cit, 7396/14/14.
17. *Ibid.*

Afterword

1. Horridge, Major G. B., Recorded Interview, 7498/9/1,(Sound Archive, IWM).

BIBLIOGRAPHY

For reasons of space only those sources quoted in the text are given below.

1. Published Sources

Bartlett, E. Ashmead, *Despatches from the Dardanelles,* (London: George Newnes Ltd, 1915).
          Some of My Experiences in the Great War, (London: George Newnes Ltd, 1918).
Bean, C. E. W., *Official History of Australia in the War: The Story of Anzac,* 2 volumes, (Brisbane: University of Queensland Press, 1981).
Boz, Ekrem, *Adim Adim Çanakkale Savas Alanari,*(Çanakkale: Düzeneleme & Baski, 1997)
Bush, Captain E. W., RN, *Gallipoli,* (London: George Allen & Unwin, 1975).
Creighton, Revd O., CF, *With the Twenty Ninth Division in Gallipoli: A Chaplain's Experiences,* (London: Longmans, Green & Co., 1916).
Hamilton, *General Sir Ian, Sir Ian Hamilton's Despatches from the Dardanelles,* (London: George Newnes Ltd, [1915-16]).
          Ian Hamilton's Final Despatch, (London: George Newnes Ltd, 1916).
          Gallipoli Diary, (London: Edward Arnold, 1920).
[Herbert, Hon. A. N.,] *Mons, Anzac and Kut by an M.P.,* (London: Edward Arnold, 1919).
History of the Great War Based on Official Documents: Statistics of the Military Effort of the British Empire, (London: HMSO, 1922)
James, Robert Rhodes, *Gallipoli,* (London: Pan Books Ltd, 1984).
Jerrold, Douglas, *Georgian Adventure,* (London: The 'Right' Book Club, 1938).
Longworth, Philip, *The Unending Vigil,* (London: Leo Cooper Ltd/Secker & Warburg Ltd, 1985).
Moorehead, Alan, *Gallipoli,* (London: Hamish Hamilton Ltd, 1956).
Mackenzie, Compton, *Gallipoli Memories,* (London: Cassell and Company Ltd, 1929)
Nevinson, H. W., *The Dardanelles Campaign,* (London: Nisbet & Co. Ltd, 1918).
Oglander, Brigadier-General C. F. Aspinall-, *History of the Great War. Military Operations: Gallipoli,* 2 volumes, (London: William Heinemann Ltd, 1929-32).
[Pendred, Captain R. Dudley,] *The Tale of a Territorial,* (Wellingborough: Perkins & Co., No Date).
Samson, Commodore C. R., *Fights and Flights,* (London: Ernest Benn Ltd, 1930).
Snelling, Stephen, *VCs of the First World War: Gallipoli,* (Stroud: Alan Sutton, 1995)
Steel, Nigel and Peter Hart, *Defeat at Gallipoli,* (London: Macmillan, 1994)
Stewart, A. T., and Revd C. J. E. Peshall, *The Immortal Gamble and the part played in it by H.M.S. 'Cornwallis',* (London: A. & C. Black Ltd, 1917).
Uluaslan, Husseyin, *Gallipoli Campaign,* (Çanakkale: privately published, 1986)

2. Unpublished Written Sources

I. The Department of Documents, Imperial War Museum, the collections of: Captain C. W. Baxter, MC
2nd Lieutenant E. H. Bennett for the letter written by Len Blunden
2nd Lieutenant D. A. J. Buxton
Captain E. W. Bush RN
A E. Cooke
Mrs L. O. Doughty-Wylie for the letter written by Colonel W. de L. Williams
Lieutenant Colonel M. E. Hancock, MC
Captain D. Hearder
E. Lye
Captain A. M. McGrigor
Captain J. S. Metcalf RNR
E. Miles
Captain G. W. Nightingale, MC
A. R. Peters
Colonel E. S. Phipson
Captain I. Powell
E. E. Rickards
Lieutenant Colonel G. B. Stoney, DSO including the account written by Lieutenant Colonel H. E. Tizard
Captain A. D. Talbot
The Reverend H. A. Thomas
Commander J. B. Waterlow RN
Captain T. P. Watson
Miscellaneous 262

II. The Department of Printed Books, IWM:
Mahmut, Colonel, commander of the 3rd Battalion of the 26th Regiment, ts report on the landings translated from the Turkish, 316.706 K34980

III. The Liddell Hart Centre for Military Archives, King's College, London
The Papers of General Sir Ian Hamilton, files 5/01 (letters to Lord Kitchener) and 5/10 (correspondence with Lord Birdwood).

3. Oral Sources

I. Recordings made by the author, copies of which are now held in the Sound Archive, IWM:
Joe Guthrie (interview, 29 April, 1986)
Lieutenant Colonel M. E. Hancock (talk in Oxford, 17 November, 1987)
Ivor Powell (interview, 10 May, 1985)
William Wright (interview, 2 April, 1986)

II. Interviews carried out by the Sound Archive, IWM:
Lieutenant Colonel M. E. Hancock, MC, (007396/14)
Major G B Horridge, (007498/9)

Index